The
Long-Awaited
Stork

THE
LONG-AWAITED
STORK

A Guide to Parenting after Infertility

ELLEN SARASOHN GLAZER

Lexington Books
An Imprint of Macmillan, Inc.
NEW YORK

Maxwell Macmillan Canada
TORONTO

Maxwell Macmillan International
NEW YORK   OXFORD   SINGAPORE   SYDNEY

Lexington Books
An Imprint of Macmillan, Inc.
866 Third Avenue, New York, N. Y. 10022

Maxwell Macmillan Canada, Inc.
1200 Eglinton Avenue East
Suite 200
Don Mills, Ontario M3C 3N1

Macmillan, Inc. is part of the Maxwell Communication
Group of Companies.

First Lexington Books Paperback Edition 1993

Printed in the United States of America

printing number
1 2 3 4 5 6 7 8 9 10

Library of Congress Cataloging-in-Publication Data

Glazer, Ellen Sarasohn
    The long-awaited stork: A guide to parenting after infertility /
Ellen S. Glazer.
            p.   cm.
    ISBN 0-02-911814-X
    1. Parenting.   2. Infertility—Psychological aspects.
    I. Title.
    HQ755.8.G56   1990
    306.874—dc20
                                                    90-32720
                                                    CIP

For my parents,
IRA SARASOHN AND SHIRLEE SARASOHN,
and for my children,
ELIZABETH AND MOLLIE GLAZER.

Contents

Introduction

I am concerned that the pain of infertility will always be with me. I worry that even if I am able to have a baby, I will continue to feel damaged by the experience. I am wondering if I will always feel infertile?

THESE were the words of my first infertility patient, a woman whom I met shortly after the adoption of my daughter, Elizabeth. At the time, I thought that I had answers to her questions. My recent burst into motherhood had convinced me that the arrival of a child, whether it be by birth or adoption, was an instantaneous and total cure for the pain of infertility. I was tempted to advise her to look forward to a time when her infertility would vanish.

Fortunately, I said nothing. Instead, I listened to her concerns and thought about them in the weeks and months that followed. As Elizabeth grew and as I became more comfortable with my new identity as her mother, I began to realize that the pain of infertility had not vanished on her arrival. It remained with me, in ways that I was just beginning to discover.

My infertility made several cameo appearances during those early months of motherhood. I noticed it first when I was around other mothers. I felt like them, but I also felt different. One big difference was that they were all enjoying their firstborn and I was already thinking about how we might manage to have a second child. Would I conceive? Would we be able to adopt a second? Why were my reservations about adoption returning when I was so delighted with Elizabeth? While I was asking myself these questions, my fertile friends were reminiscing about labor and delivery. They were talking centimeters and epidurals and I was thinking about pergonal and p.k.'s. I realized then that although adoption had "cured" my childlessness, it had done little for my infertility.

As luck would have it, I conceived shortly after Elizabeth's first birthday. That pregnancy, which ended in miscarriage, proved to be an affirming experience. Even after it ended, I felt better about myself. I no longer felt infertile! For a few brief weeks, life had grown inside me.

As more luck would have it, I became pregnant again a few months later, and this time I went on to have a successful pregnancy, resulting in the birth of our second daughter, Mollie. Part of the ecstasy that I felt at Mollie's birth had to do with my sense that I was now a real mother: to both girls. Being pregnant and delivering a baby had authenticated me. Now I felt certain that infertility was behind me.

To my surprise, it was not. When Mollie was a few months old, my infertility returned for another visit when I took Elizabeth for her first haircut. She was three and Mollie was a few months old. With absence of forethought, I had scheduled Elizabeth's haircut at a crowded and glitzy suburban hair salon on a particularly busy afternoon.

Enter our threesome: me, Mollie on my back, and Elizabeth, screeching. She was terrified of the place and the process and she let everyone know it. Then Mollie joined in the commotion and flung the bottle she was holding out of the back carrier and straight into a basket of curlers. By this time everyone in the salon was staring at us.

Most of those who looked at us seemed to have expressions of annoyance or pity. I imagined that they saw the episode as a parental nightmare, as well as a public nuisance. I remember looking back at them and realizing that they had no idea how lucky I was, how much I cherished this moment. They had no idea how long I had waited and wanted and worked to be a mother. I realized then that Barbara Menning was right when she referred to infertility as "an old friend."

A few months later my "old friend" dropped by for another visit. This time I was picking Mollie up at her family day care and saw that there was a new baby there. I asked Chris, Mollie's day-care "mother," about the baby and she told me that the little girl's father had been treated several years earlier for Hodgkin's disease. Single at the time, he had had the presence of mind to insist on banking some sperm. Years later, he married and he and his wife decided to try to have a baby. This meant flying to Paris to retrieve his frozen semen, shepherding it safely home, and using it for what proved to be a successful insemination. The new baby at Chris's home was, indeed, a miracle child.

When Chris told me this story I reacted with intense emotion: I cried all the way home. Each day that I saw the baby I held the tears in just long enough to get to my car. Then I sobbed. I wondered if any of my fertile friends would have reacted this way? Would they have been so moved by this story and could they appreciate the wonder of this baby's birth?

Nine years have passed. During this time I have had lots of opportunity to think about the ways in which infertility lives on — and revisits us — long after we become parents. As my own children have grown and as I have had more time to spend with infertile clients, both before and after they become parents, I have been able to further explore the ways in which a history of infertility affects parenting.

This book is the outgrowth of my personal and professional experiences with parenting after infertility. I wrote it because I believe that there are many people who expected, as I once did, that their infertility would vanish with the arrival of a child. Now parents, they are puzzled by the fact that they continue to feel the impact of infertility. Many are surprised and puzzled to find that they still feel different from their fertile friends.

I hope that *The Long-Awaited Stork* will help to diminish their isolation. To my knowledge, no book has been published on the subject of parenting after infertility. When I placed a notice in the national newsletter RESOLVE (the national organization that offers education, support, and advocacy to infertile couples and the medical community) announcing my intention to write this book and asking for help from members, I was amazed and moved by the hundreds of people who contacted me, eager to share their observations and experiences. Several wrote to me and said that they wished there had been a book on this subject when they were pregnant or in the process of adopting. Many noted the fact that they were still RESOLVE members, long after the arrival of their children. One woman wrote,

> I am now the mother of four children under the age of six. I am usually too busy to read a newspaper or a magazine but when my RESOLVE newsletter arrives, I drop everything and read it from cover to cover. I still cry as I read it. I am convinced that infertility has changed my life.

Although *The Long-Awaited Stork* is addressed primarily to people who are themselves long-awaited parents, I hope that professionals working in the field of infertility will also read the book and find it useful. I hope that it will help them see that infertility is not a problem that is "resolved" with a successful pregnancy or adoption. Professionals do their patients a disservice when they assume that there is a discreet end point to the experience of infertility. In fact, many of those who have experienced long term infertility say that it reverberates in their lives for years to come.

I hope that couples who are still in the midst of infertility treatment will also read this book. I know that it is difficult for many of them to imagine that they will ever succeed in becoming parents, and so it may be painful for them to approach this book. Nonetheless, I do feel that it would be of value, both in helping them to prepare for parenthood (there is a chapter devoted to this subject) and in introducing them to some of the situations that they may find themselves in.

The Long-Awaited Stork is divided into two parts. The first half of the book takes a developmental approach, looking at some of the feelings and questions that arise for infertile couples at the time they become parents and in the years that follow. The emphasis is on the early years of parenting. Rather than try to examine the ways in which infertility may remain with people throughout the entire life cycle, I chose to stop at adolescence. Although I have a sense that infertility lives on in some ways beyond that time, I feel that there are so many intervening life circumstances that it becomes increasingly difficult to separate out the role of infertility.

The first half of the book ends with a vignette, one family's story of infertility. The story was told to me by a close friend, someone who has conceived and carried three babies with relative ease, but who is the daughter of an infertile couple. Her family's experience says something, I feel, about the way that infertility can cast a shadow from one generation to the next.

The second half of the book is about the special circumstances that couples find themselves in as a result of infertility. Each chapter focuses on some form of parenting after infertility and identifies some of its unique features.

I have used a number of comments and personal anecdotes throughout the text, and end each chapter with one or more brief family stories. Nearly all stories, as well as all quotes, have been carefully disguised to protect people's privacy, something that I regard as of great importance for all parents after infertility. However, in a few situations, families preferred to be identifiable; in those cases I did not attempt to disguise material, but rather sought to present it as accurately as possible.

There are several people without whose help this book would not be possible. First, there are my daughters, Elizabeth and Mollie, who have taught me, in countless ways, how to be a mother. I am grateful to them for their patience, for their good humor, for their affection, and for their ability to forgive and forget. I am grateful to them, also, for allowing me to hog the computer and the telephone in my efforts to prepare this manuscript. I hope that they will always know how much it means to me to be their mother.

I would also like to give special thanks to Susan Cooper, my friend, colleague, and co-author (*Without Child: Experiencing and Resolving Infertility,* Lexington Books). Without Susan's support, companionship, good humor, advice, criticism, and abundant energy I never would have had the courage to undertake this project. More than anyone else I have known, Susan knows how to work and how to play. I enjoy doing both with her and try my best to figure out how she manages to do so much so well.

A special thanks, also, to my editor, Margaret Zusky. Without her enthusiasm and perseverance this book might never have been published.

I very much appreciate the major contribution of Linda Hammer Burns, Ph.D., of the University of Minnesota Medical School. Dr. Burns read my request for contact in the RESOLVE newsletter and graciously shared her doctoral dissertation on parenting after infertility with me. This ground-breaking work informed me in a number of ways. I am particularly grateful to Dr. Burns for introducing me to the concept of boundary ambiguity and for identifying the role that it plays in many infertile families.

I would like to thank several of my colleagues in the field of infertility, some of whom are also parents after infertility. They include Sally Brandon, Karen Berkeley, Carol Frost Vercellone, Diane Clapp, Merle Bombardieri, Julie Ramsey, Helen Greven, Joyce Pavao, Liz Fragola, Jeanne Springer, Roz Blogier, Jean Souci, Becky Pike, Pat Johnston, Vicki Moss, Bob Raphael, Ann Soper, and Kathy Fulton. A special thanks to Barbara Eck Menning, the founder of RESOLVE, to Shirley Pratten of the New Reproductive Alternatives Society in Canada, and to Kathe Linden of the Organization of Parents through Surrogacy.

I would also like to thank Joan Jack of Serono Symposia, USA, for her ongoing support and encouragement. With warmth and vitality she brings help to countless infertile couples and their caretakers.

Hundreds of men and women responded to my inquiries in the RESOLVE and Stars of David newsletters and by word of mouth. I cannot list all of them here, and many have asked to remain anonymous, but the following is a partial list of the people who contributed to this book: Terry Cummings, Susan Byers, Janet and Ray Caputo, Sharon Salveter, Nina Morse, Elaine Jacoby, Cetta Bellomo, Cheryl Herman, Susanne Sullivan, Penny Linde, Stephanie McLaren, Jim and Naomi Shand, Dinah Steel Bourdon, Barbara and Peter Welanetz, Ronnie Nichamin, Holly and Doug Miner, David Johnson, Kate Moody, Laurel Hoffman, Gail Scott, Darlene and Rick Faherty, Ann Cope Mueller, Donna Erickson, Deborah McKnight, Minda Szejnwald, Carolyn Marshall, Sybil Morrison, Mary and Jeffrey Peart, Judith Bradshaw, Diane Ripstein, Nancy Kuehler, Daphne Webbe, Jill Powell, Linda Corsun, Lynn Villagran, Nancy Lewis Hagerty, Cindy Aron, Karen Drucker-Stern, Ann Derderian, Judi Kloper, Kevin and Karin Austin, Jeannie Williams, Susan Kroll, Barbara Burns, Joanne Dennis, Rhonda Srubar, Beth Warren, Donna Thompson, Carol Jones, Michele Quinn, Linda and David Kay, Joel Cohen, Linda Brownlee, Diane Koczot, Dan and Lynn Clements. A special thanks to

Shirley Zager, Helene Satz, and Sybil Morrison for reviewing parts of the manuscript. Special thanks also to Dr. Daniel Gott-segen for his ongoing support, and to Ann Woodfork, LICSW, who was, and will remain, my long-awaited stork.

There are also some friends who have been especially helpful in getting this book to press. Howard Weiss patiently helped me work through my computer phobia and introduced me to the wonders of word processing. Without his help, this book would probably remain in longhand. Karen Levine and Julie Arnow read and commented on sections of this book and offered me helpful advice as well as enthusiastic support. And when the book was nearly complete, and I began to worry that my computer would be stolen or go up in flames, Lillian Sober-Ain offered to give the manuscript a safe home away from home.

Finally, on a sad note, I say a posthumous thank you to my friend, colleague, and mentor, Connie Dineen. With wise words and a twinkle in her eyes, she taught me some of my first lessons in parenting after infertility. I was, and will remain, deeply sad-dened by her death.

There are a few things about the style, format, and content of this book that readers should be aware of before beginning it. First, you will notice that I frequently use the words *some, may,* and *possibly.* This tentative tone is intentional. While I believe that what I am talking about applies to many parents after infertility, I am aware through my research that there are some infertile parents who do not agree with me. It is out of respect for their feelings and experiences that I have adopted this tentative voice.

Second, I need to say something about gender. While this book attempts to be for and about both mothers and fathers, the major-ity of people that I spoke with were women. This was because most of those that responded to my requests for contact through RESOLVE were women. One area that I was surprised and pleased to find men eager to participate in was the discussion of donor insemination (D.I.). Although most of my D.I. respondents were women, several men phoned and wrote expressing their willing-ness to share their experiences.

Third, I want to mention that this book focuses on normative experiences and minimizes pathology. That is not to suggest that some parents after infertility do not get into serious trouble, but their difficulties are beyond the scope of this book. My intent, again, is to look at the thoughts, feelings, and questions that arise for many parents after infertility.

Fourth, I want to acknowledge that I had a problem with numbers. As will be discussed at different times throughout the book, a history of infertility almost always has an effect on how many children a couple has. However, the result varies: some couples end up with fewer children than they wanted and others may end up with more than they are prepared to raise. In writing the first part of the book, it was often difficult to account for differences in family size and composition. For example, I am aware that it feels different sending a child off to school if he is your only child than if you have four other little ones at home.

Fifth, I would like to say something about terminology. Readers will notice that I say *second-child infertility* rather than *secondary infertility*. This is intentional. I do it because I want to include efforts and decisions around second-child adoptions as well as efforts to conceive.

Readers will also notice that I mention a number of books and organizations in the text of the book without giving further information about them. For the addresses of all organizations listed and for the full references for books, please turn to the Resources and Readings section at the back of the book.

Finally, readers may wonder why I wrote three chapters on adoption, rather than one long and inclusive one. I decided to discuss adoption in this way because I feel that although there are certain experiences and feelings that apply to nearly all adoptive parents, whether their adoption be foreign or domestic (and by *domestic* I refer to the adoption of a child that is of the same race as the adoptive parents), there are some substantial differences between these two forms of adoption. Similarly, I feel that families that include both biological and adopted children are different from families in which the children are all adopted. Consequently, I have included special chapters on foreign adoption and on families that combine biological and adopted children, knowing that much of what is in the chapter on domestic adoption also applies to these families.

Readers may also wonder why I have not included a chapter on raising children born from donor eggs or donor embryos. The reason for this is that although I am aware that these are among the brave new frontiers of parenting after infertility, I was unable to locate couples who became parents through these assisted technologies. I hope that in the future, books on this subject will be able to address the special needs and special circumstances of these parents.

Writing this book has been a challenge, an adventure, and an opportunity. It has introduced me to a number of interesting, creative, and courageous people. It has offered me an insider's look at the new frontiers in reproduction and adoption. Finally, it has allowed me to revisit "my old friend" infertility in yet a new and different way. I hope that my readers will enjoy it and find it helpful.

PART
I

1

Preparation for Parenthood

When I was trying to conceive, I idealized parenthood. When I encountered the realities of it on a day-to-day basis, I landed with a big thud.

I N some ways, a history of infertility is good preparation for parenthood. Going through infertility teaches people to be patient, to cope with uncertainty, and to prepare for and accept the fact that there are times in life when things go wrong. When infertile couples finally become parents, they often feel well prepared to roll with the punches. At the same time, however, they may also feel disappointed. The experience they looked forward to for so long is rarely what they imagined it would be.

This chapter identifies some of the tasks that infertile couples face as they approach parenthood:

1. giving up the fantasized child
2. developing a realistic approach to bonding
3. accepting ambivalence
4. redefining and realigning the family

Giving up the Fantasized Child

When anticipating parenthood, most couples form a mental image of the child they will have. Many imagine what the child will look like, identify its gender, note its interests and personality, and even choose a name. Then most go on to have real children who are different from the offspring of their dreams.

For fertile parents, the transition from fantasy to reality is unlikely to be dramatic. Certainly, there are situations in which an individual or couple has a strong preference for a son or a daughter, perhaps following a loss such as the death of a parent or a child. However, most fertile parents do not have much time to think about their fantasy child—and to cultivate these fantasies—before their real child arrives. They may experience some disappointment, particularly relating to gender, but generally there is an acceptance that their child will be who he will be.

Couples undergoing prolonged infertility have much more time and energy to create a dream child. Often this child is experienced as a missing member of the family. His childless mom and dad think about him often. He becomes larger than life, their perfect child. As they wait for him, they become his perfect parents, always patient, tolerant, caring, and appreciative. Then comes "the big thud": their child arrives and he is no more a perfect child than they are perfect parents.

The big thud can be especially troubling for adoptive parents, who may worry that they aren't bonding properly with their child. However, difficulties reconciling reality and fantasy hit biological parents as well. They, too, prepare for the arrival of a real child, someone who may bear little resemblance to the child they imagined for themselves.

> When I was going through IVF [in vitro fertilization], I dealt with the stress of it all by fantasizing about the little girl that would be the reward for all my efforts. She had blond curly hair and blue eyes and a rather placid disposition. She was, I'll admit, the replica of me as a child.
>
> After five failed IVF attempts and my forty-first birthday, I began to realize that I was never going to have my dream child. At that point, she took on a name, Emily. I wrote a poem to her—to my child never born—and I cried a lot. The grief I felt at losing Emily was intense. I was saying good-bye to someone I had loved and cherished but never really known.

Then Jeffrey bounded into our lives. To our surprise, the adoption took only three months and there we were with a son. He has dark hair and a playful impish way about him. He bears little resemblance to Emily.

When Jeffrey was three weeks old; I had a strange and wondrous realization. This little boy, so different from the child I had imagined, was truly the child that I wanted. No one, I decided, could be more perfect for us. I thought of Emily with a detached curiosity, as I cradled Jeffrey in my arms.

Not all infertile parents say good-bye to their dream child with a name and a poem, but most do find that some form of grieving enables them to move on. One couple, who later had an IVF baby, chose to plant trees for each of their unborn children. They describe a very sad and very personal ceremony in which they cried and held each other. It was a painful occasion, but it was also healing. When their "miracle" baby did arrive, they were able to truly rejoice, feeling that much of their sorrow had been laid to rest.

Infertile couples planning to adopt develop fantasies about their adopted children, just as they did about the biological children that they had hoped to have. If an adoption falls through, or is otherwise interrupted, it is essential that the couple grieve the child they had expected.

We tried for four years to have a baby and were told by several doctors that there was little chance that I could conceive. We accepted that news and decided to adopt a child from Chile. We entered into the adoption process enthusiastically and looked forward to having a little girl (the program we were in allowed us to state a sex preference) with dark skin and dark eyes.

Shortly after a child was assigned to us I learned that I was pregnant. To my complete amazement, I had a healthy pregnancy and an uncomplicated delivery. Around the time that we had expected to go to Chile, I delivered my son, Alex.

Alex is eight now, and I have two younger daughters as well. Our family is, by all appearances, complete. Still, even eight years later, someone is missing. She is a dark-skinned girl born in Chile. She was to be part of our family and there are moments when I long for her.

Developing a
Realistic Approach to Bonding

We hear a lot these days about "bonding." It has the aura of a cosmic event, a magical, mystical moment in time when parent and child form a lasting and sacred bond. Understandably, many parents-to-be approach bonding with unrealistic expectations. Parents after infertility, with their history of loss, are particularly vulnerable to feeling that they have failed at bonding.

In preparing for parenthood, it is important for infertile couples to understand that bonding is not necessarily immediate. Countless satisfied parents will admit that it took them days or weeks, even months, to feel connected to their child. Many describe it as an ongoing process, one that begins when the child is quite young and continues over time.

Infertile parents need to give themselves — and their children — permission to bond in their own ways, at their own pace. Remember that your experience has conditioned you to expect loss. This conditioning may make you more cautious when you finally have a child. If you adopt your baby, the adoption experience, especially the wait for finalization in court, may make bonding a more gradual process. Finally, there is the simple fact that you are two people getting to know each other. For all the power of bonding, it is not always love at first sight.

> Eliza is three months old now and I adore her! However, that was not how I felt when we first met . . . .
>
> Mark and I decided to do a private adoption after years of unexplained infertility and six failed IVF attempts. Because both of our families live in Kansas City and have many contacts in the medical and legal communities there, we decided to focus our efforts to find a baby there and not in New York City where we are living. As we had hoped, Mark's uncle, a physician, quickly came across a pregnant young woman and we set the adoption process in motion.
>
> What we hadn't anticipated was how difficult it can be to have your baby born in one state and adopted in another. The social-service legal process turned out to be quite complicated. We spent

the last several weeks of our birthmother's pregnancy not worrying about whether she would keep the baby but focusing, instead, on the logistics of the adoption. We wanted to bring our baby home as soon as possible.

Despite all our anxiety ahead of time, things went very smoothly once Eliza was born. We received the call on a Saturday and flew to Kansas City that afternoon. The surrender had been signed and our lawyer had worked things out so that we were permitted to take Eliza to New York as soon as she was discharged. When we met with him, he took out a bottle of champagne and said, "Let's go to the hospital and meet your daughter."

We were totally unprepared! We'd spent so much time thinking about how we'd coordinate things that we never paused to imagine what the meeting would be like. Suddenly, there we were, in a hospital elevator, on our way to meet the little stranger who would be ours for life.

I could see, through the window of the nursery, that there were ten or twelve babies there. I couldn't see them well, but most looked cute. Both Mark and I are fair with blue eyes, and the infants I spotted looked, indeed, like they would match us well. That is all but one—a round-faced, dark-eyed baby with black hair matted to her scalp. She was not a pretty baby. She was not familiar. She was Eliza!

My heart sunk when we met. This was not the baby I had been waiting for, hoping for, longing to have and to hold. What's more, when I looked at Mark, I could see that he shared my disappointment. We left Eliza (as planned), went to our car, and burst into tears. All the way back to Mark's brother's house we discussed whether we were making a mistake.

Then something strange began to happen. I began to really care about Eliza. I began to miss her. I began to think about the nurses holding and changing her and to wish I was there. The doubts that I'd had moments before began to vanish. By the time we returned to see Eliza the next afternoon, I couldn't understand why I'd felt so let down the day before.

Love grows. When Eliza came home with us that Tuesday, three months ago, I cared deeply about her, but I could not say that I was madly in love. I would say that I was tired, confused, happy, and beginning to feel like a Mommy. It was over the days and weeks that followed, especially in the quiet of the night when she lay in bed with Mark and me, that I began to fall in love. Is this what they mean by bonding? I guess so. Love starting small and growing.

Accepting Ambivalence

The parent-child relationship, like all other intimate relationships, is an ambivalent one. Mothers and fathers find, usually
early on in their parenting experience, that the same little person
who causes their hearts to dance with delight can easily frustrate
and infuriate them. While many parents are somewhat hesitant to
acknowledge this ambivalence, their little cherubs demonstrate
no such reluctance.

> When my son was four, he taught me about ambivalence. We had
> had a very rough day, during which he told me that he hated me.
> Then, as I was tucking him into bed, he told me that he loved me.
> I was puzzled by this and said, "Tell me, Paul, if you love me then
> why did you tell me that you hated me?" Paul replied, without hesi-
> tating, "Because I did hate you." Now even more perplexed, I said,
> "How can you love me and hate me?" Paul said matter-of-factly,
> "Sometimes I love you, other times I hate you." "Well, how do you
> know when you love me and when you hate me?" "That's easy," said
> Paul, "when I hate you there is a cold breeze in my tummy. When
> I love you, it's not there."

In approaching parenting after years of infertility, it is important to remember that there are times when we all have cool
breezes in our tummies. There are times when all of us dislike or
resent those whom we love most. This can frighten couples who
longed for a child and who promised to be ever grateful if they
succeeded in becoming parents. If you adopted your child, or
took an alternative route to parenthood, the ambivalence can be
especially threatening. You may feel guilty for having negative
feelings toward your child. You may even fear that you will be
punished and that your child will be taken from you.

> One thing that infertility robs us of is the opportunity to be ambiv-
> alent about parenthood. I cannot imagine not having my child, but
> there is a certain freedom that I miss.

It helps infertile parents to acknowledge ambivalence openly
when their baby is very young. Fertile parents don't hesitate to

grumble that they are tired, that the baby is fussy, that they have no time for themselves. Why should you be any different?

> I'm one of the lucky ones. I have a two-year-old son whom we adopted as a newborn and a daughter who was born to us one year later. I went from being childless to having my hands full. Most of the time, I really enjoy my busy life, but there are times when it gets to be overwhelming. What has been hardest for me is that I get the message—from fertile and infertile friends alike—that I have no right to complain. After all, I got what I wanted. Their attitudes really make me feel bad. They play into all my fears of being undeserving. They also make me feel angry and alone.

Redefining and Realigning the Family

For most people, marriage and parenthood alter their definition of family. Until they marry—at whatever age—men and women regard their families of origin as their family unit. When they marry this shifts, as spouses become part of each other's families and as the couple itself forms a fledgling family. However, the real transition from a family of origin to a family of one's own usually occurs with the birth of a first child.

The arrival of a child brings about many changes in the family. Names change. The couple becomes Mom and Dad. Their parents become Grandma and Grandpa, or Nana and Papa. Siblings get the titles Aunt and Uncle added to their names. These new titles are concrete means of acknowledging the multiple shifts that occur in a family across generations.

With an infertile couple, the shift to familyhood is more complex. For one thing, would-be grandparents have been waiting a long time. Infertile couples may be surprised by their parents' reactions to the arrival of a grandchild, either by birth or adoption. It may have been hard for them to think about, or acknowledge, how much their parents wanted to be grandparents.

> We had very little notice before we adopted Jessica. Because my parents live far away, they were not able to come to meet her for several weeks after she arrived. Still, they immediately sent us a letter that I will always cherish. It included the following:

To Our New Granddaughter, Jessica,

Welcome home, Jessica! We have waited for you for a very long time! We are so happy to have you in our family and we can't wait to meet you. We're enclosing a check for you and hope that your Mom and Dad will start a bank account for you.

Love,

Grandma Ruth and Grandpa Joe

I remember being touched and surprised by their letter. I was touched that our newly adopted daughter—to them a stranger—was immediately welcomed into the family. I was amazed by the seeming ease with which they became Grandma and Grandpa. I was moved that they were willing to send what was for them a sizable amount of money to a child that they had never met. I realized that while I was still feeling very tentative as a parent and toward Jessica, they were able to take a giant leap of faith. I realized, also, that while we had been suffering with infertility, they too had suffered a loss.

With grandparents, there is another issue of loss: the years that a couple has spent in pursuit of pregnancy may have included major changes in their parents' lives. Parents have aged, some have become sick, some have died. The arrival of a child may bring a sad reminder of grandparenting that has been lost.

When we first set out to be parents, I had two healthy parents, eager to have a grandchild. My father is now in his late seventies and suffers from lung disease. My mother, in her mid-seventies, remains active but she has lost a lot of the spirit that she had even a few years ago. They are very excited about Deborah's arrival but it is clear to me that they will never have the kind of times with her that I so enjoyed and treasured with my grandparents, their parents.

The boundaries of the family are sometimes unclear in an infertile family. Couples who experienced severe marital stress during their infertility may feel less comfortable defining themselves as a new family unit, because that unit can feel so vulnerable. Couples who adopt or use D.I. or surrogacy may have some lingering concerns about lineage. Even those who give birth after prolonged infertility sometimes feel hesitant to celebrate their new family unit because they have been conditioned to expect loss.

As you near parenthood, bear in mind that among the many changes you will experience is an alteration in your definition of family. As with bonding, this is likely to be an ongoing process. Understand that you may feel somewhat conflicted about this and that the process may seem simpler for your fertile friends. For them, "first comes love, then comes marriage, then comes . . . wheeling the baby carriage." For you, that natural order has been disrupted.

When we were married eighteen years ago my husband said to me, "We'll have a baby by our first anniversary." Thirteen years later, our daughter Sandra arrived. As much as we wanted her, it was a *big* adjustment.

2

Pregnancy after Infertility

D URING the time they are trying to conceive, most infertile couples come to idealize pregnancy. Many endure unpleasant diagnostic procedures and stressful treatments by fantasizing about the pot of gold at the end of the rainbow. They imagine that a positive pregnancy test will usher in nine months of celebration. Most are ill-prepared for how stressful pregnancy after infertility can be.

Prolonged infertility causes people to anticipate loss. It convinces them that their bodies do not work right and it heightens their awareness of what miracles conception, pregnancy, and childbirth really are. Those who do become pregnant after infertility are likely to expect—or at least to worry—that the pregnancy will go the way of all their failed conceptions. For them, a positive pregnancy test brings nine months of fear and anxiety.

The following are concerns that frequently arise for couples who have achieved a pregnancy after long-term infertility:

1. fear of pregnancy loss
2. fear of birth defects
3. difficulty becoming a regular obstetrical patient
4. "in no-person's land"; feeling neither fertile nor infertile
5. dealing with a high-risk pregnancy

Fear of Pregnancy Loss

If you are pregnant after long-term infertility, you are likely to worry a great deal about pregnancy loss. Many people find their fears are most intense in the first trimester when the risk for pregnancy loss is greatest and when the pregnancy itself seems least real. However, many are surprised to find that concerns linger on, even after such significant milestones as hearing the heart beat, learning good news from an amniocentesis, or passing the point of viability. Indeed, for some people, fears of loss continue right up to delivery.

> When I think back on it, I must have sounded very strange in the delivery room. There I was, with an eight-pound basketball for a belly, in the midst of active labor, and I was telling the nurse that I thought I was having a miscarriage. The truth is that I never, ever believed I would be taking home a healthy baby.

Infertile women often feel bewildered when they first learn that they are pregnant. Even those that say they know the moment they conceived feel a sense of disbelief when the pregnancy test is positive. They spend the first trimester checking for blood, feeling for breast tenderness, and waiting for the first sign of nausea. Many worry they feel "too good" and interpret any twinge or tickle as a sign that something has gone wrong.

If you are pregnant after infertility, don't be surprised to find that the hours crawl by during those first weeks. Infertile women are never a month or two pregnant; they are three weeks and two-and-one-half days along, or six weeks, one day, and one hour pregnant. You may find also that you resent the confidence that your fertile friends seem to have about their pregnancies. They are able to assume that their pregnancies will go well and seem strangely unaware of all that could go wrong.

> When I was eight-weeks pregnant, my sister-in-law phoned. "Guess what?" she said. "We're going to have a baby." My heart fell, since it still hurt to hear that women were pregnant (even though I was supposedly now among them!). When I gathered my composure, I asked her when her baby was due, expecting that it was three or four months away. To my surprise, she named a time that was a full two weeks after my due date. It turned out that she was only six weeks pregnant and she was already making public announcements!
> When I hung up the phone, I thought that she was very fool-

ish—she seemed totally unaware of how often early pregnancies end in miscarriage. Really, I guess that I felt jealous of her—she was able to be so happy and excited and I was a worried mess.

Fears of pregnancy loss are certainly greatest for those who have experienced earlier pregnancy losses, those who are at known risk for ectopic pregnancy, those who are older, and those who have other risk factors such as Diethylstilbesterol (DES) exposure. If you are in one of these categories, you are likely to protect yourself by regarding your pregnancy as tentative. Friends, family, and physicians will probably support you in this stance, recognizing with you that there is a substantial chance that the pregnancy will not go to term.

If you are pregnant after infertility but are not at known risk for pregnancy loss you may find yourself in a more confusing position. Others, perhaps even your husband, expect you to be happy. After all, you have finally achieved what you sought for so long. There is cause for celebration. People seem to have a hard time understanding how frightened and confused you are. They may even become impatient with you, leaving you to feel all the more isolated and alone.

The magical thinking that you developed in the midst of infertility treatment is likely to remain with you as you guard against pregnancy loss. You may find that you are dwelling on past wrongdoings—especially an abortion—fearful that you will now be punished. You may find yourself behaving in a carefully prescribed way in regards to diet, activity, and sex in the hope of protecting yourself from pregnancy loss. You may be disappointed to find that your efforts to ward off danger offer you only temporary relief and that all too often, fears return.

The best ammunition that you have over your fears, especially the irrational ones, is information. Read and ask your doctor or nurse about pregnancy. Learn what the known causes for concern are so that you don't panic over every tingle and twitch. If you are frightened that something is going, or has gone, wrong, don't be afraid to ask for help. Sometimes an extra ultrasound or exam will allay your fears—at least for the moment.

Don't be reluctant to read about pregnancy loss. If you familiarize yourself with what happens in miscarriage and ectopic pregnancy and in premature delivery, you may feel like you have more of a handle on things. Remember that infertility has left you feeling out of control and that reading can help you feel some sense of mastery. It won't prevent these events from occurring, but it might make them slightly less scary should they happen. And in a strange way, reading about pregnancy loss may be easier for you than reading about normal pregnancy.

Your fears of pregnancy loss may prevent you from "bonding" with your unborn child. You may hear other pregnant friends talking about their fetus as they would a child, perhaps even referring to it by name. By contrast, you find that you are much more tentative: you hesitate to think about your baby, to imagine what he or she will look like. You may worry that you will jinx yourself if you take too much pleasure from your pregnancy.

> I was very hesitant to enjoy my pregnancy. When the baby kicked I'd feel a moment of exhilaration and then great caution would set in. I'd say to myself, "there's a kick" instead of allowing myself to rejoice. When the amnio came back, I was afraid to learn the sex of the baby because I thought that that would make it more real. It felt easier to think, in a very vague way, of some unformed, almost alien being. I remember feeling envy of other pregnant women who seemed so content and confident.

Fears of Birth Defects

Along with fears of pregnancy loss, women pregnant after infertility worry that something will be wrong with their baby. Many undergo ultrasounds, amnios, and other forms of prenatal testing to resolve these fears, but realize in the process that these tests cover only certain fetal problems. There are any number of things that can still go wrong genetically, congenitally, in utero, and during birth. When you are conditioned to expect failure, it is hard to disregard these troublesome possibilities.

An additional concern for many women who become pregnant after infertility has to do with the measures they went through to conceive. If you took medications to assist you in conceiving or maintaining a pregnancy, you may wonder if physicians will someday discover that these medicines are damaging. If you became pregnant with the help of IVF or gamete intrafallopian transfer (GIFT), you may find that you have some feelings, perhaps wholly unexpected, about having tampered with the natural order of things.

> I became pregnant on my second Pergonal cycle. At first, I was ecstatic about the pregnancy, but as time passed and it became more real to me, fears crept in. I began to think about all the women who, in innocence and good faith, took DES. It was the miracle drug of their time. I began to wonder whether Pergonal, too, would come back to haunt us.

Women pregnant by D.I. frequently report fears about their baby. Some worry about how they and their husbands could deal with a child who was conceived in this fashion and then turned out to have some genetic defect. Others worry, in a less rational way, about bearing some alien being. Who will this child be? Will he or she have some strange feature that will inform the world that the parents used donor sperm?

Finally, age is a factor in concerns about birth defects. Even with the benefit of amniocentesis, older women are at somewhat greater risk for delivering a child prematurely, an event that can possibly lead to lifelong problems. For this reason and others many people undergoing infertility treatment set some point beyond which they will not try to conceive. Nonetheless, many do become older "primiparas" and then face the risks involved.

> I am a very young forty. I swim a mile each day, have lots of energy, and many people mistake me for thirty. Hence, it was hard for me to think of my uterus as old, or my eggs as geriatric. During my pregnancy, I kept reminding myself that all my energy and all my smooth skin could not make my reproductive system any younger.

Fears of birth defects are especially difficult to manage after long-term infertility because you may not feel at liberty to use prenatal diagnostic tools. Your fertile friends seem to turn to amniocentesis and other tests with relative ease, aware of but not usually deterred by the risks involved. For you it is far more complicated. This may be your only chance at a pregnancy, and you are unwilling to take any risk, no matter how small.

Just as many infertile couples have a problem turning down high-tech treatment options, so is it also difficult to take the minority position that amniocentesis is not for you. Especially if you are over thirty-eight, you may feel a lot of pressure to undergo it. Remember that the choice is yours and also, that the test is by no means foolproof. Results are sometimes ambiguous, leaving couples with more questions than answers.

Finally, try to maintain the perspective that this is one in a long line of parenting worries. Once you decide to become a parent, you sign on for a lifetime of worry. Birth defects concern you now, but after your child is born you will worry about sudden infant death syndrome (SIDS). When that time passes, you will move on to other age-appropriate anxieties. It will be helpful to you and your child if you begin now to develop a perspective that acknowledges and allows for worry, but does not permit it to become all consuming.

Difficulty Becoming a Regular Obstetrical Patient

Infertility patients get to know their physicians very well. For better or worse, they spend hours in their offices. They get to know the office staff, the nurses, and often the other patients in the waiting room. Much as the treatment is stressful, there is also something comfortable about the familiarity that develops.

If you are pregnant after infertility, it is probably difficult for you to leave your infertility specialist. Not only are you well acquainted with his or her practice, but you are now a success story. Everyone is delighted for you and wants to celebrate your pregnancy. At the same time, however, they will be telling you to leave.

Infertile mothers-to-be can feel abandoned by their physicians. Now that they are finally pregnant, their doctors don't want to see them anymore. Worse still, they are referred to the practice of busy obstetricians, who cannot know all that they have gone through. (For women in some states, this dilemma is compounded by the fact that many obstetricians are closing their practices or even leaving obstetrics altogether due to high malpractice claims. These women, some of whom are even IVF successes, are in the strange predicament of having difficulty finding a physician to care for them now that they are finally pregnant.)

If you are pregnant and have transferred from your infertility specialist to an obstetrician, you may be feeling that she does not appreciate your concerns. Your new doctor may consider your pregnancy uneventful because, by her criteria, all is going well. Little does she know that for you, your pregnancy is punctuated by a series of near catastrophes. A small weight gain between visits or the fact that you are feeling energetic may seem inconsequential to her — or perhaps even matters to be thankful for — but for you they are signals that something has gone terribly wrong.

> My first visit to my obstetrician was really a letdown. After all that I'd been through, I guess I expected to be treated as special. At least a few drum rolls if not a parade! I thought that the nurses would welcome me with excitement. "Hurray! Margie Sutherland is here at last. Look at the miracle pregnancy!" Instead they told me to have a seat in the waiting room! I had no idea what I was doing there!
>
> The doctor was nice, but very matter-of-fact. He told me that everything was normal, gave me a few pamphlets, and told me to come back in a month. A month! What am I supposed to do between now and then??

Obstetricians do not realize the seriousness with which you hear their comments. A simple question about your dates, wondering if your baby is really due a week or two earlier or later than what was thought, is enough to send you into a tailspin. Infertile mothers-to-be know their dates — without error — and questions of this sort suggest to them that there is something wrong with the baby.

During your pregnancy you may need to explain some things to your doctor. Don't be afraid to let him know how frightening and bewildering this experience is for you. Try to let him know that it is hard for you to believe that you are really pregnant, nearly impossible for you to imagine that you are actually having a baby. Tell him that you may need extra explanations, perhaps even some unnecessary tests, in order to feel calmer. The pregnancy is still likely to be stressful for you, but, hopefully, some of that stress will be alleviated if you feel your physician understands that, for you, this really is "high risk."

In "No Person's Land": Feeling Neither Fertile nor Infertile

Many infertile women describe feeling alienated from both the fertile and the infertile worlds. Their infertile friends usually envy them and have a hard time being with them. At the same time, the fertile world remains foreign terrain.

> When I was pregnant, I used to see other pregnant women and still feel angry, resentful, and jealous. Often, I'd have to remind myself that I was actually — believe it or not — one of them. I, too, had a big belly!
>
> After I delivered, it became very difficult. There I'd be, carrying around my newborn daughter in her Snugli, and I'd feel sad seeing a pregnant woman. I knew that my daughter was my flesh and blood, but I still could not believe that I had really been pregnant.

Feelings of being different often become pronounced in a childbirth class. There they are, the pillow-toting couples, worrying about labor pains, wondering whether they should have an epidural or a spinal. How naive they are. They should only know what a long labor really is. Yours, after all, has been three or four, perhaps even seven or ten years. They should know the pains of active labor pale by comparison to the long, dull, chronic ache of childlessness.

Some of the difficulty that you feel being around other pregnant women may be that you envy their ambivalence. Having finally gotten what you wanted for so long, you feel that you have no right to complain. When your pregnancy is uncomfortable or you feel frightened of labor and delivery, you remind yourself of the Pergonal shots or you remember how awkward it was to have to schedule intercourse so that you could get to your doctor's office for a postcoital test. When that twinge of doubt about whether you're really ready for parenthood creeps in your mind, you remind yourself of how you couldn't pass the diaper display in the supermarket without bursting into tears.

Try to believe that your fertile friends have not cornered the market on ambivalence. They have a right to their doubts and their fears, their aches and their pains, but you do, too. If you try to hold yourself to higher standards than they do, you only increase and prolong your isolation. Accept that you may never feel as free as they do to complain, but the fact that you toiled endlessly for this pregnancy does not obligate you to smile your way through it.

> When I was first pregnant I felt sick. As *thrilled* as I was to be pregnant, I felt nauseous, tired, as if a cold was coming on. I don't think that I complained a lot but if people asked me how I felt I answered honestly. Their responses were really upsetting. One friend, pregnant with her third, said, "See I told you it wasn't so great." Another said, "Well, this is what you wanted, you better not complain. Remember how miserable you were when you weren't pregnant." Had I been in a better state myself, I would have tried to educate them — to explain to them that they were perpetuating my sense of being different, of being held to higher standards, and that they were treating me like a second-class citizen. But I was too out of it to do anything more than cry and go to sleep.

Dealing with a High-Risk Pregnancy

Unfortunately, all infertile pregnancies are not medically uneventful. Some couples achieve a pregnancy only to then go on to endure the tragedies of miscarriage, ectopic pregnancy, even stillbirth. Others are more fortunate in that their pregnancies can be managed and brought to term, but this management is, itself, a difficult ordeal.

Many women with high-risk pregnancies are instructed to spend some part of their pregnancy on bedrest. *Bedrest* can mean different things, but it usually involves a severe restriction of activity. Women are instructed to stay at home, some are told to keep their lower body elevated so as to keep pressure off their cervix, and many are advised to rest their minds as well as their bodies.

My daughter was born at twenty-two weeks and she lived for only
six hours. Her birth and death seemed exceptionally cruel punishment to us, coming as they did after five years of infertility.

When we were finally healed enough to consider another
pregnancy, my doctor told me that if I did become pregnant again,
he'd recommend a cerclage, a stitch that would attempt to prevent
my cervix from dilating prematurely. Then he added that he would
advise me to stay on bedrest for much of the pregnancy. When I
asked what that meant (thinking I'd have to lie down for a few
hours each afternoon!), I was stunned to learn that he meant complete inactivity—for four months! When I heard that news, I felt
like I was in for the most fiendish time. It sounded like a medieval
torture chamber.

To my surprise, I conceived after eight more months of trying.
By that time, I was well prepared for my bedrest pregnancy. I left
my high-pressured job in my fourth month and became a lady of
leisure, passing the hours knitting in bed. I kept my spirits up
because I was so thrilled to be pregnant, but I also felt very alone.
My infertile friends who finally got pregnant, were pregnant. They
could work and exercise and go out and have fun and still be pregnant. But me, I was different. I was home and alone, with not even
the supports that I had had during my infertility.

If you have gone from infertility to high-risk pregnancy, don't
feel reluctant to complain. You have been doubly cheated and
you have every reason to feel angry and resentful. You look
around you and even many of your infertile friends seem to have
it easy.

Try not to be alarmed if you find that some of your feelings are
focused on your unborn child. As caring and protective as this
may feel, it is also natural to feel frustrated. This child of yours
isn't even born yet, and she is already disrupting your life. Trust
that your feelings will neither hurt your baby nor will they be
damaging to your future relationship with her. In fact,
acknowledging feelings may help you to feel better during your
pregnancy and may set the foundation for a relationship with
your child that is open and loving and not bound by guilt.

Your high-risk pregnancy is likely to put stress on your marriage, not only because you are both frightened about the outcome, but also because you are being forced to make major shifts

in your relationship at a time when it has already been stressed. Anticipate that you may be impatient with each other and that you may take out some of your frustrations on the very person who is most dear to you. To the extent that you can both see this as but another example of how unfair your situation is, you can pull together rather than feel that you are being torn apart.

Pregnancy after infertility is, indeed, a lonely experience. The joy, so long awaited, is seldom there. In its place can be fear, loneliness, and isolation. While couples manage at some point to relax and to celebrate, there remains a dark side to their experience. Infertility has caused a loss of innocence. Once you have been infertile, you know that bad things don't just happen to other people. You have learned that no matter how good you are and no matter how hard you try, things can go terribly wrong. But for all their fears, the majority of infertile couples who achieve a pregnancy do go on to have healthy babies.

3

The Arrival

T HE arrival of a child, whether it be by birth or adoption or
through some alternative route to parenthood is a time of
celebration for anyone who has experienced long-term infertility.
Finally, your ordeal is over. Fears that something will go wrong
in labor and delivery, or that the adoption will fall through, have
passed. Now you have a shopping cart full of diapers and you
want to stride down the baby-care aisle shouting, "Look at me
folks, look who has rejoined the world of the living."

When you arrive at the checkout line, your baby begins to cry.
You peer into her Snugli and wonder whether she is wet or hungry
or simply uncomfortable. You are trying to figure out whether to
dismantle her Snugli and feed her in the middle of the supermarket or try to make it to the car and hope that she falls back
asleep on the way home. While you are sorting this out, she
begins to cry loudly, and the little old lady ahead of you in line
says that it is because the baby is cold and should have a hat on.
The old lady adds that your daughter will probably catch cold or
worse yet, pneumonia. You want to get angry but instead you
burst into tears and run from the scene with your now screeching
infant.

Welcome to the world of parenthood! All new parents are sleep
deprived, confused, feeling vulnerable, and wondering what they
have gotten themselves into. Your experience with infertility
makes all these feelings more pronounced. Chances are that
while you were trying to conceive, you romanticized parenthood.
You may have imagined that the arrival of a child would usher in
several months, or even years, of boundless joy. Now you are find-

ing that while the joys are there, this is clearly the hardest job you've ever done. And it's "on-the-job training."

As a new parent, you face several tasks, some made more complicated by your infertility experience. Like all parents, you will recognize that from the moment of birth, your child moves away from you. Each developmental milestone is a sign of his independence or her increased ability to function in the world on her own. Because you were without him for so long, this movement toward separateness can be painful. This is often especially true for adoptive parents who are trying to establish a firm sense of oneness within their families.

In addition to the task of separating, which will be lifelong, parents after infertility face a number of other concerns:

1. feeling not quite in the club
2. vulnerability
3. the imprint of childlessness
4. concerns about privacy and secrecy
5. the loss of the role of infertility patient

Feeling Not Quite in the Club

While you were struggling with infertility, you probably felt isolated, alone, different from most everyone else. Perhaps, you knew others who were infertile—possibly you developed a strong support network—but you were still living in a fertile world. Wherever you went and whatever you did, you saw pregnant women and parents with very young children. Often, it felt like there was a giant club of parents and everyone else was a member.

Now you are in the club. Now you are a parent, and as a parent you have all the rights and privileges of club membership. You have a baby to carry around in a Snugli. You get to have a car seat in your car. On trash day, you too can leave empty boxes of diapers out with the bundles of newspapers you no longer have time to read. And, when you are at a cocktail party, you can finally join in on conversations about day care and toilet training, no longer standing on the sidelines and looking on.

You are in the club, but you are not quite there. Something feels different. If you adopted your child, then this feeling of difference comes up when the other mothers start speaking about labor and delivery. You suddenly feel left out as talk turns to centimeters and epidurals. When the other mothers nurse their babies, you may feel inauthentic, fearing that bottle feeding your baby is evidence to all that you are not a real mother.

A sense of being outside of the club exists for those who give birth after long-term infertility as well as for those who adopt. If you eventually had a baby after years of trying, you may find yourself resenting the glib way in which others seem to talk about becoming parents. It may seem like it was easy for them, and you may feel angry that they seem to take it all for granted. You may also feel envious that they can complain about a long labor or a caesarean birth, so apparently oblivious to what it means to spend years pursuing parenthood.

The sense of being both in the club and out of it can be bewildering. Most likely, you will find that these feelings come and go. There will be times when you feel greatly relieved to be like everybody else, and other times when you feel like an outsider.

> When Rachel was four months old, I took her to the tiny tots music "class" at our local community center. I enjoyed doing it with her, and it was an opportunity for us to meet other mothers and babies. We all had fun together during class, but afterwards the others would retreat to the snack bar and I would pull away. I'd found that their conversation often found its way back to pregnancy, to labor and delivery. After feeling so much a part of things, I'd end up feeling different.

If you are feeling outside the club, try to remember that the clubbiness does not last forever. The concerns of mothers change, and in a few years, when your child is in preschool, talk about planning pregnancies and about labor and delivery will diminish if not vanish. There will be moments when you feel like an outsider, but by and large you will not have to feel like you have only one foot in the door of a very important club.

Vulnerability

All new parents feel vulnerable. Even those who have had years of experience with children feel ill at ease when they become parents. They find it bewildering to try to decode the language of a newborn, particularly when they are operating on only a few hours' sleep. It is a small wonder that many new mothers and fathers feel incompetent.

Parents after infertility can feel even more vulnerable than do other new parents. In addition to feeling inexperienced, you may feel like a fake. If you turned to a new reproductive technology in order to become pregnant or if you adopted your child, you may retain some feeling of having tempted fate. Perhaps you were not meant to be a mother or a father after all. Perhaps your baby is telling you something when she cries inconsolably. Perhaps, the little old lady who says that your daughter will catch cold because she doesn't have a hat on knows you are not a "real" parent after all.

> When my daughter was six months old, I went to visit a small private museum which housed a fine art collection. A very proper, genteel, New England lady was our guide. Abigail began the tour asleep in her Snugli but, when she awoke, she let out a loud, piercing cry that lasted for several minutes. Once I'd calmed her down and she began to nurse, my tour guide said to me, "I guess that the good Lord knew what he was doing when he didn't make me a mother." I was amused, but also somewhat troubled by her words. She reminded me of how close I, too, had come to not being a mother.

All new parents worry about their child's health and safety, but again, infertile parents often find that their experience has heightened these feelings. Sometimes this comes as a surprise. When you are going through infertility diagnosis and treatment, you may have imagined that this difficult experience would protect you from further disappointment. Perhaps you felt that you had paid your dues in suffering and that once you had a child, everything would be fine. Now, as a parent, you realize that life holds no guarantees. Earlier losses offer no protection against future pain. You know all too well that things go wrong.

> During Megan's first few months, I was blissfully happy. I had some notion that I had "done my time with infertility" and that I was magically protected from further harm. Then, I heard about some-

one whose baby had died from SIDS. I went into a panic — even to the point of having Meg undergo elaborate testing to determine if she might be at risk for SIDS. I realized then that becoming a parent didn't mean signing off on worries. Rather, it meant signing on to a lifetime of caring and concern.

What you must unfortunately accept now that you are finally a parent, is that your child's safe arrival by no means marks the end of your worries. The vulnerability that you feel because you are new to parenting will probably diminish, but the bond that is growing between you and your child leaves you newly vulnerable. Someone has entered your life who will always lay claim to your heart.

> When my son was quite small, I realized that I did not feel that I could live without him. He was a fussy baby and sometimes I was so frustrated that I felt like throwing him out the window. But all the while, even at my darkest moments, I felt that no one could be more precious to me. I understood then why some parents will sacrifice their lives for their children.

The Imprint of Childlessness

Your fertile friends probably remember their child-free days with pleasure. As delighted as they are to be parents, they can easily recall how nice it was to sleep late on a Sunday morning or to go out to a movie at the last minute without worrying about a baby-sitter. They can also anticipate a time in their lives when they will no longer feel so tied down.

Chances are that it is more difficult for you to remember your prechild days with pleasure. If memories of a time with more freedom do come to mind, you may push them aside, feeling guilty. After all, you wanted a child so much and suffered greatly in your quest. To even briefly imagine any child-free time can make you feel ungrateful, perhaps uncaring.

Long-term infertility may have left you with an indelible imprint of childlessness. This imprint can make it difficult for you to be apart from your child. Separations may remind you of childlessness and threaten you with a return to that painful state. You may exaggerate the risks involved in leaving your child with a sitter or even a family member.

You may also find that you envy and resent your fertile friends. Again, it seems so easy for them. They can leave their children in the care of others and not worry that they will lose them. They can enjoy time away from their child. They seem strangely unaware of how precious children really are.

If you adopted your child, conceived by IVF or GIFT, or went to any other unusual measures to become a parent, the imprint of childlessness may be particularly powerful. After all, you came very close to being childless. Good fortune intervened on your behalf, but it may feel tenuous. You can easily call to mind the feelings of loneliness and isolation — of living your life on hold.

> Our son was born after five years of infertility, including numerous tests and two major abdominal surgeries. During his first two years, I left him with sitters for fifteen hours each week so that I could work part-time. That was somewhat difficult, but not nearly as stressful as the prospect of going out with my husband without him. The few times we tried it, I felt guilty. This was the child that we had wanted for so long. We had spent so many lonely nights planning our fertility strategies. Now here he was and we were finding ways to spend time without him. I felt we were being ungrateful and feared we'd be punished.

Perhaps the most formidable task for a new parent after infertility is to begin to develop a child-free reference point. This may mean pushing yourself to spend some time away from your child, however brief and however conflict laden it may be. During these times, it is important to remember that infertility promotes magical thinking and that some of this magical thinking may enter into your parenting experience. For example, you might feel that if you enjoy time away from your child, even look forward to it, you will somehow be punished. Try to remind yourself that this is not realistic and that separations, though they may be difficult at first, actually promote growth and development.

Concerns about Privacy and Secrecy

No one tells new parents that having a child will make them public people. Where they could once go out in public without having strangers stop them to talk, they now have a little bundle with them who invites commentary. Strangers never hesitate to talk to you about your baby. They ask questions. They give advice. They are friendly, but they intrude on your privacy.

Parents after infertility may find that having their private life made public is especially confusing. For one thing, it is reminiscent of your infertility treatment. You remember what it was like to take the most personal aspects of your life out of the bedroom and into the doctor's office. Those of you who adopted, or looked into adoption, had to take all of this a good deal further. After your bodies were poked and prodded, the adoption agency took over and examined your life-style, values, religious beliefs, and more. Now you are minding your own business in the video store and one woman wants to know how old your baby is, how much she weighs, and where she was born. Another woman who is pregnant asks if you had a difficult labor and delivery, and an older man suggests that you rent a musical "because babies respond well to singing." You begin to wonder whether you will ever again regain your right to privacy.

The desire for privacy is complicated for some infertile parents by the issue of secrecy. Many of you have secrets or potential secrets. Those of you who adopted or used IVF may feel that although your experience is not a secret, it is not something that you want to talk about with strangers on the street. Those of you who used donor insemination or a surrogate may have decided that this is information that you do, indeed, want to keep secret. Either way, the intrusive questions and comments of "busybody passersby" are upsetting. You may find yourself feeling like you are being secretive, when all you are really doing is trying to maintain your privacy.

Remember that strangers really have no right to intrude in your life. People don't stop you on the street and ask you how your mother is feeling, or where you went to school, or what your mortgage payments are. If they feel compelled to talk to you about your baby, then it is because they have some confusion about privacy. At the same time, however, you may find that there are times when it feels good to be a public person. On occasion, you may enjoy people's friendliness, the camaraderie that naturally develops among parents. This, too, is okay. You shouldn't have to fiercely guard your privacy for fear of losing it.

When our daughter was a few months old, we took her out to dinner with us. There was a friendly couple at the next table, people
about our parents' age. They thought Rachel was adorable and told
us so. Then the wife turned to me and said, "I hate to say it, Mom,
but she looks just like her Dad." For a split second, I thought I
should tell them she was adopted, but instead, I smiled and said,
"Yes, I think so, too. But that's okay. I really like the way that he
looks." I left there feeling good. The brief exchange with friendly
people was nice, but it also felt good to maintain some privacy.

Those of you who adopted, used D.I. or IVF, or became parents
via surrogacy will recognize, early on, that you do face serious
decisions regarding privacy and secrecy. For you, the task goes far
beyond maintaining your privacy when you are out in the world.
You need to determine what is in the best interest of your child—
and of your family—and then decide how to act. This is often a
complex and confusing process, but you need not feel that claim-
ing your right to privacy makes you any less open, honest, or
forthright parents.

The Loss of the Role of
Infertility Patient

In entering into the complex maze of infertility diagnosis and
treatment, individuals take on a new identity: that of infertility
patient. This is an identity that initially troubles most people
because it has multiple consequences for their personal, social,
and professional lives. Most find a way of adjusting to this new
identity—even embracing it—and learning to put other identities
on hold.

If you experienced long-term infertility, you probably devoted
a good deal of energy toward being a patient. Chances are that
you read all that you could about infertility and spent time talking with knowledgeable people. Most likely, your relationship with
your physician and his or her office staff became a central focal
point in your life. You worked hard to communicate effectively
with them and enjoyed the familiarity that developed between
you.

Now it is over. Whether or not you will ever return to treatment, you are now involved in parenthood, not patienthood. You may be very surprised to find that you feel a sense of loss. The role of patient had its drawbacks—lots of them—but it also had its rewards. You found that when challenged, you could handle a difficult situation. You found that you could develop new skills, such as giving and getting injections. There was a new language to be learned and you became fluent in it. Much as you looked forward to the end of your ordeal, there were aspects of it that you valued.

IVF and GIFT patients often report a strong sense of loss on leaving treatment, especially if the treatment was not successful. After all, being a "high-tech" patient feels special in many ways. As lonely as the rest of infertility treatment can be, IVF and GIFT offer patients the opportunity to feel part of a collaborative effort. In the course of an IVF or GIFT cycle, patients become intensely involved with each other as well as with their physician and office support staff. While this is not the "club" of parents to which they are actively seeking admission, a sense of community does develop. People feel a connection with others whose conversation centers around "Pergonal amps" and follicular measurement.

To give up on IVF or GIFT means more than the loss of the hope for a miracle baby. Still outside the club of parents, former IVF and GIFT patients are suddenly outside the program as well. Even if an adoption follows in fairly short order, the feeling of loss—and of failure—remains.

> It was very hard for me to say good-bye to the IVF coordinator and the rest of the team, as well as to the other patients. We had all grown close. Even the secretary for the program became an important person in my life. And one nurse, in particular, became very special. It was she who phoned each afternoon and instructed me as to how many amps of Pergonal to take. She also had the dreadful task of telling me that my pregnancy test was negative.
>
> In the months following my fifth and final IVF attempt, I really missed everybody. It felt strange waking up without having to head for the hospital for bloodwork and ultrasounds. Afternoons felt empty with no Pergonal call to wait for. I felt very alone and isolated, as if I came to the end of the line and was standing alone in an empty railroad station.

Then Arianna arrived. She is a little miracle, so loving and so full of life. She was a quick cure for my loneliness. I take her everywhere with me and feel that I have finally joined the world of parents. Still, it is difficult for me to pass the hospital where I tried IVF. It is still hard to visit the staff there, even with Arianna. Everywhere else, she represents the long-awaited and joyous resolution to my infertility. But at the program, it feels like she is a reminder of their failure—and my own.

IVF and GIFT successes also feel a sense of loss, although it is very different than that of those who do not bring home babies. High-tech pregnancies, although on the increase, are still highly prized, particularly in the newer and smaller programs. Many IVF and GIFT successes become minor celebrities, especially within their programs. Even though their pregnancies are usually followed in regular (or high-risk) obstetrical practices, they remain connected to the program. Pregnant patients are greeted with enthusiasm when they come back to visit. They boost staff morale as well as program statistics. In a sense, they remain IVF or GIFT patients throughout their pregnancies.

When a high-tech miracle baby is born, there is cause for celebration. In a new program, this may involve a fair amount of fanfare—an article or picture in the town paper. In a more developed program, it usually means that if the baby is born in the hospital where the program is located, staff will visit and the obstetrical nurses will be tuned in to the fact that this is, indeed, a special delivery. Hence, IVF and GIFT patients experience their loss of patienthood later, after they leave the hospital and return to the real world.

Mark was born at a hospital far from where we did IVF and so I didn't expect much excitement around his arrival. I had an "uneventful" pregnancy (it was a BIG event for me!) and a fairly easy delivery. But then word got out that I had conceived through IVF and several of the nurses came to see us. They were all very enthusiastic, and that was really nice for me. I realized then that, in a strange sort of way, I'd been missing my IVF experience. While I was relieved to be a "normal" obstetrical patient, it had also felt somewhat lonely. Being an IVF patient, for all its stress, had felt special.

The process of saying good-bye to patienthood—whether it be temporary or permanent—may pose almost as big a challenge as becoming a patient once was. For some of you, this means saying good-bye to medical treatment, treatment that may or may not have worked. Even some of those who were successful will not seek further treatment because of age, multiple births, or because you prefer a one-child family. Others who met with failure may have moved on to adoption, deciding not to return to medical interventions. However, many of you will continue to regard yourselves as medical patients, taking a break from active treatment because of the birth or adoption of your child. Again, the task here is not to take a particular course of action, but rather, to recognize that people who have known long-term infertility, often have complex and ambivalent feelings about patienthood.

In the face of all of these challenges—and others that follow—let us not lose sight of the fact that a child who comes after long-term infertility usually brings great joy. Your long-awaited baby fills a space in your home and in your heart that has been empty for too long.

Yesterday, a man stopped me in a restaurant where my daughters and I were having dinner. He said, "I want you to know that you have world-class children—they are truly lovely." I smiled and said, "I know." I did not tell him how long I had waited for them, how much I had wanted them, how grateful I am to be their mother. I did not tell him that my prayers had been answered. But quietly, I thanked him for reminding me.

4

Settling into Parenthood

NEW parents often feel like they are in a daze for the first several weeks of their child's life. The combination of lack of sleep and their infant's total dependency leaves many new mothers and fathers with limited ability to focus on anything other than their little "bundle of joy." But somewhere along the way, things begin to change.

By the time that your child reaches six months, you will probably have remembered that you have a life of your own. While you may not be ready to resume all of your old interests or commitments, most likely you will begin thinking about certain questions. "Should I return to work?" (usually a mother's question, but fathers, also, may find themselves with some work-related questions). "Should we try to have or adopt a second child?" "How have my relationships with family and friends and, particularly, with my spouse, changed as a result of our child's arrival?" The experience of long-term infertility may have an impact on the way that you ask—and answer—these and other questions and issues, including:

1. how and when a second child will arrive
2. career questions, particularly for mothers
3. a renewed—and new—relationship with your spouse
4. developing and renewing friendships
5. the obligation to be superparents

How and When a Second Child Will Arrive

All parents think about how many children they should have and about how they might ideally be spaced. However, fertile parents usually enjoy their first child for several months or more before considering a second. Unless they are older, or have other reasons to anticipate problems, most assume that they can wait until they are ready.

Things are different for infertile parents. Within a few months of your child's arrival, you probably realize that while your life is full, your family is not complete. You cannot simply relax and enjoy your first child because you know that it may be difficult, even impossible, to have or adopt a second. Years of infertility and/or adoption efforts may have made you an older parent. Hence, you face the unpleasant prospect of returning to fertility treatment and/or adoption efforts before you are ready. Better, you think, to be too soon than too late.

Many infertile parents face the puzzling dilemma of not knowing how their next child will come to them. Some may have achieved a miracle pregnancy on the brink of an adoption and may doubt that it can happen again. They wonder if they should initiate simultaneous efforts to conceive and adopt. Others have adopted with still inconclusive fertility and are hopeful that the rapid advances in technology will yet enable them to have a child. One thing is clear: when there is ambiguity about how another child will come to them, couples feel all the more pressure to move rapidly.

We all know infertile parents with two, even three children under the age of three. They represent one possible outcome of the pressure of trying too soon. Although many couples encounter difficulty having or adopting their second child, some do not. Some women become unexpectedly pregnant after finally giving birth or adopting. Other couples find that a second adoption comes along before they are ready. Experience has cautioned them not to let opportunities to parent pass them by, and so they go ahead and adopt a second child while their first is still quite young. Hence, there are a number of infertile parents who find themselves in the unexpected predicament of having more children than they'd planned, sooner than they had ever imagined.

> Everything about Marisa's adoption was terrific. John and I flew to Bogota to get her and it was love at first sight. We spent a wonderful week there meeting other adoptive parents as well as the people who had cared for her in the orphanage. Even the immigration paperwork went smoothly. At last we had reached the end of our long, difficult quest to become parents. When we arrived home, I felt sick to my stomach. For a few days I assumed it was "tourista" and I suffered in silence. After all, it was a small price to pay for our beautiful baby. I was very tired, but that, too, was part of the deal since Marisa was not yet sleeping through the night. Only when my breasts began to swell did it occur to me that I might be pregnant. Our son, Daniel, was born when Marisa was just one year old. They are both delightful children, and there are some real advantages to having them so close together. But I also feel cheated. I never had a chance to enjoy Marisa without being pregnant or having another baby to care for. I couldn't really enjoy my long-sought pregnancy because Marisa needed so much of my time and energy.

An unexpected pregnancy or adoption is obviously a mixed blessing. It robs you of the chance to relax and enjoy a one-to-one relationship with your first child but it does relieve you of the worries of planning for a second. If it happens, you will probably feel both burdened and blessed. If it does not, then you may want to begin a dialogue with your spouse in which the two of you begin to consider when and how you will try to enlarge your family.

Career Questions, Particularly for Mothers

"Every mother is a working mother." This quote has popularly adorned t-shirts, buttons, and bumper stickers because it speaks a truth not always fully acknowledged: being a mother is a full-time job. Nonetheless, for a variety of reasons including finances, personal and professional growth, and emotional well-being, many mothers decide to take on or continue a second job. The decision of when and how to do this is rarely without conflict.

If you are a mother after prolonged infertility, the decision about returning to work is likely to be all the more complex. Now that you have what you wanted for so long, you may find yourself questioning, even feeling guilty over, your interest in the world of work. Unless finances or the specific nature of your job mandate that you return to work full-time, you may feel obliged to at least cut back to part-time work. You may wonder if working more means that you are selfish and ungrateful, unable to appreciate what you have. You may fear that others will be judgmental, questioning why you wanted a child so much if you intended to leave it.

Another possibility is that you will be surprised by how little interest you have in returning to work. You, who were once so focused on your career, may be unexpectedly content to remain at home, enjoying the slower pace that allows you to spend time with your child. You may not know what to make of this change and you may find it unsettling, wondering whether you will ever again have the inclination and ability to return to work.

Remember that fertile mothers also feel confused when they think about returning to work. They, too, have questions about who will take care of their children and about what they will miss when they are at work. They, too, feel guilty and fear that no decision they make will be the right one. What is likely to differ between you and your fertile friends is the matter of choice: they feel that they have choices, difficult as they are to make. You may find yourself bound by certain constraints, real or imagined.

If you adopted your child, the constraints, at least initially, may be quite real. The adoption agency may have made you agree to stay home for a designated period of time, often six months. Because many jobs do not offer a six-month maternity leave and because some jobs do not even grant a leave to adoptive mothers, this could force you to give up your job. This dilemma is a particularly upsetting one after all that you have been through with infertility and with the adoption process, and it certainly serves to perpetuate feelings that you are not in control of your own life.

The finances involved in adoption and in high-tech fertility treatments further complicate the question of when to return to work. Many of you spent enormous amounts of money, perhaps even your entire savings, in your effort to become parents. Now you face the costs of raising a child. It is difficult for you to consider giving up one of your incomes, even for a limited period of time.

Finally, there is an issue of loss. Because many infertile couples are older by the time they become parents, they have often had the opportunity to advance in their careers. As much as you have sought after and longed for a baby, you may also find your job to be immensely satisfying. Staying home with a baby, for all the joy that it brings, may represent the loss of a significant source of gratification.

> Before we adopted Jordan, I worried that people would say cruel things to us—and to him when he was older. Jordan is five now, and I can honestly say that no one has said anything about his "real" parents, nor commented on how lucky he is to have us as parents, nor pronounced us lucky to have gotten a white baby when they are so hard to come by. No one has rubbed our noses in adoption. The only area that I have felt discriminated in has had to do with work. From the start, I have been very sensitive to people's comments about my working.
>
> When Jordan arrived, with less than twenty-four hours notice, I wanted to work part-time for a month or so, so that I could get my life back in order. One of my colleagues, whom I respected a great deal, said, "Why worry about your work—you've waited so long for this baby?" Perhaps she meant well, but her words stung. I may have been overly sensitive, but I had the feeling that she would not have made this comment if our baby had been born to us.

Although women typically face more questions about combining work and motherhood, fathers, too, are trying to figure out how they can be active, involved parents and still maintain their careers. Many men remember their fathers working six days a week and feel they want to do things differently. They don't want to find that they missed the best years of their children's lives because they were too busy earning the money to send them off to college.

Infertile fathers may be especially reluctant to leave all the parenting to their wives. Having spent years on the sidelines as their wives underwent all sorts of procedures (even if the problem was in the husband), they are ready to play a more active role. This may be especially true for adoptive and D.I. fathers, for whom there is the added issue of authenticity, but other fathers after infertility share their heightened appreciation of parenthood.

> When Meg and I married we planned to have a large family. True, we were career-minded "yuppies," both busy advancing in our respective companies, but we came from large families and had an appreciation for how nice a pack of kids can be. Hence, it was a real disappointment for us when Meg's first five pregnancies ended in miscarriage.
>
> Meg is pregnant again and this time it looks like things will be okay. We are talking about trying to work something out where we can both work part-time and spend time with the baby. I imagine that my bosses will be surprised if I ask them for part-time work, to say nothing of paternity leave. They are men whose wives stay home and they each have three children. They know nothing about what it means to try for over four years to become a father. Nor do they know how it feels to stand by helplessly as your wife wrenches in pain and expels your ten-week-old fetus.

A Renewed — and New — Relationship with Your Spouse

When parenthood is long awaited, the transition to Mommy and Daddy can be a complicated process. In addition to the excitement and the sense of wonder felt by most new parents, there may also be questions of authenticity. Certainly these questions are more troubling to adoptive parents and to those who used D.I., but anyone who is finally a parent after years of infertility can feel challenged in making the transition to this new role. While fertile couples playfully try on their new identities as Mommy and Daddy, infertile parents are more apt to fear that their new roles are not quite real. You may question yourself in your new role. Was I really meant to be a mother? Am I bonding with my baby?

Will she know that I'm her Daddy? You may feel awkward and uncomfortable with your spouse and even fear that he or she is judging you.

> I was really a discombobulated mess those first few months. Larry would come home and there I was, still in my bathrobe! A whole day had gone by and I hadn't even figured out how to get dressed! I was embarrassed to have Larry see me this way, as he'd known me as a competent professional. I wondered whether he would think that I was failing motherhood.

Infertile parents may also be reluctant to tell each other that they feel disappointed. After all, this is what you wanted for so long — most likely spent countless hours and dollars on — and now you feel tired, frustrated, perhaps at moments fearful that you made a mistake. It can be very hard to share these feelings with your spouse, but to avoid them is to risk adding to the stress between you.

> I adore my baby but there are moments when I wish she would disappear. Peter works long days and I get to the point, late in the afternoon, when I am counting the minutes until he gets home. When he walks through the door I want to pour out all my frustrations. But I hold back, not only because he is too tired to take them, but also, because I'm afraid he'd resent me. My worst fear is that he will throw it up in my face and remind me that I got what I wanted.

Remember that becoming parents together is an enormous stress on any marital system. The fact that you have been infertile does not exempt you from this stress: most likely it contributes to it. Your decision to become parents had to be a very deliberate one; there was nothing accidental about it. Having made this very conscious choice, and pursued it until it happened, it can be hard to acknowledge the ambivalence that you feel.

Try to work with your spouse to develop and maintain a sense of humor about your situation. You need to be able to laugh together about the absurdity of it all. Here you are, two competent adults, letting a tiny creature rule your lives. Who else could boss you around this way? If you can laugh together as you bumble through it, you will set a good foundation for parenting together in years to come.

> When Johanna was five months old, we took her on an airplane for the first time. We were going to visit my parents in Florida. In the past, Judy and I had viewed air travel as a quiet time, away from the telephone, when we could catch up on popular magazines, perhaps even read a short spy novel. We soon learned that Johanna had different plans for us!
>
> The flight from New York to Ft. Lauderdale is a little over two hours. During that time, Johanna needed—and I do not exaggerate—eleven diaper changes. Every time one of us returned from the lavatory with our newly changed infant, she would deposit another load in her pants. Once when I was in the toilet with her, it took three diapers before we could return to our seat!
>
> Eventually Johanna fell asleep and Judy and I had a few minutes to read. Just as we were settling in to our magazines, the pilot announced that we were landing. Judy turned to me and said she had never been so glad to be on her way to see my parents. We needed some loving, diaper-changing grandparents to the rescue. We laughed together about how our little poop machine had nearly done us in.

In the middle of infertility diagnosis and treatment, most couples feel that their marriages are being severely stressed. This is especially true for couples in which only one partner has an identified problem and the other is presumably fertile. It is also true for couples in which one member is quite openly upset by the infertility while the other does not express much pain regarding the situation. If you had one of these experiences, or if you and your spouse had difficulty deciding on a second choice route to parenthood, you may have wondered if your marriage would survive infertility.

The fact is that most marriages do survive infertility, and many are actually strengthened by it. You and your spouse may have experienced a great deal of tension, but you probably developed some important coping skills as a couple, as well as individuals. You may have turned to humor or found new activities or interests that you could share. Hopefully, you developed effective ways of collaborating. One way or another, you got through the crisis and made your way to parenthood.

As parents after infertility, you need to continue to develop new ways of relating to each other. Not only have you begun to relate as Mom and Dad, but you probably also need to revive the romance in your relationship. Years of scheduled sex, possibly followed by a pregnancy that felt tentative, and certainly followed by several exhausting weeks with an infant have most likely depleted your relationship. Now that you are launched as a family, you can begin to reexperience the pleasure, the passion, and spontaneity that were once essential ingredients in your relationsionship.

> We realized, after all was said and done, that our marriage had not really suffered. Infertility taught us that we can pull together in a crisis, make difficult decisions, that we can deal with disappointments, anger, and grief without dividing. We learned that we could cry together and that when the chips were really down, we could laugh together as well. When Jesse finally arrived, we were proud, confident, prepared.
>
> It wasn't until Jesse was nearly a year old that we realized what was missing. We'd forgotten about romance! We'd been so busy coping and communicating and problem solving that we'd forgotten what it meant to simply have fun together — to enjoy our relationship as a couple.
>
> We began getting a baby-sitter one weekday evening each week and meeting for dinner near Larry's office. Each week we went to a different place. Sometimes we'd go to quiet, romantic restaurants with nice service, other times we'd try a noisy pizza parlor or even a subshop. The place never mattered as much as the process — it felt like we were dating again.

Developing and Renewing Friendships

Most new parents find that their friendships change when they become parents. Certainly, old friends still matter, but with a child as the focal point of their energies and activities, personal relationships receive less attention. New parents tend to gravitate, at least for a time, to other new parents. They are doing the same things, experiencing the same concerns, living on the same sleepless, no-time-for-myself schedule.

If you are a parent after prolonged infertility, you are probably all too familiar with the ways the arrival of a child can interrupt, or otherwise alter, a friendship. Chances are that it became difficult to maintain all of your relationships with your fertile friends, especially after they became parents. Hopefully, most of these friendships survived the crisis, but it must have been difficult to remain close with people who had two, even three children while you were struggling to begin your family. No matter how much you liked and cared about each other, your lives were in very different places.

Now you are in a different place again. Your fertile friends probably have older children. They may be involved with soccer and Sunday school while you are involved with diapers and binkies. Still there is more of an opportunity to reconnect: your daily lives may be very different but you do have parenthood in common. In fact, you may find that the differences in your children's ages are nice in some ways. Your friends can offer you their wisdom gained from experience and you can offer them the pleasures of being with a very young child again.

On the other hand, you may experience discomfort with your infertile friends. Having been there yourself, you know how painful it is for them to see you with your child, however pleased they may be for you. You can try to see them without your child but that is an unlikely option for many reasons, not the least of which is your need and desire to be with your child.

Talk with your infertile friends about their feelings and yours. What you are likely to find is that it makes sense to both of you to get together on occasion, but that, at this point in your lives, the differences in your circumstances interfere with your seeing a lot of each other. Remember that because parenthood, like infertility, involves a changing cast of characters, there is a good chance that some of your infertile friends will become parents soon after you do. You will have an opportunity then to renew your relationship and to meet on new terms—as parents.

Finally, you may find that this is a time in your life for new and fast friendships. New parents connect in childbirth/preadoption classes, at infant swims, in the park on a nice day, or in the pediatrician's waiting room. These fast friendships, which may or may not stand the test of time, are likely to offer you a great deal of support and companionship. Adults who are with a baby all day feel a need to talk with each other.

I found that my relationships were fluid when I first became a parent. Two women whom I met when we were all taking Pergonal became pregnant shortly after I did. When our babies were very young we saw a lot of each other and really enjoyed the time that we spent together. Later, when Jenny was a toddler, I felt closer to other mothers in my neighborhood. We got our children together for play groups and began taking them on outings. Now that Jenny is older and starting to have real friends of her own, I find that I am concentrating more on spending the time with people who are really my friends, most of whom I have known for years. I find that I've drifted apart from most of the women that I met in those early, intense months of motherhood.

The Obligation to Be Superparents

Most parents begin with high expectations for themselves. They look back on their own childhoods and promise that they will do better than their parents. They expect themselves to be patient, energetic, involved, creative, and loving. Infertile parents expect all this of themselves, and more.

While you were in the midst of infertility treatment, you probably made some promises. "If I am ever able to be a parent, I promise to be perfect. I'll never complain, I'll always be patient and available, I'll never, ever take my child for granted."

Now you finally have what you wanted for so long. To your surprise and, perhaps, embarrassment, you find that it isn't always so terrific. Certainly, you love and cherish your baby, but you are also tired, frustrated, and feeling at loose ends. Sometimes you even long for a few quiet moments to yourself. Then you remind yourself of your childlessness and recall the promises that you made. Soon you begin to feel like you've made a deal with the devil: you have made promises that you cannot keep.

Again, you envy your fertile friends. They can get angry, they can be frustrated, they can complain. They seem to have the option to spend less time with their child. They are not held to some unattainable set of standards. You envy the fact that it seems easier for them and you may feel some shame along with the envy. After all, you remind yourself once again, "This is what I wanted for so long."

I remember how much I longed for a good night's sleep. Each time I'd be settling into a nice, restful sleep, Jesse would awaken me. I'd hear him crying and I'd think, "Please, kid, leave me alone. I'm exhausted." Then I'd feel awful and I'd jump out of bed calling, "Mommy is coming. Mommy is on her way to the rescue. Mommy loves you." All my fertile friends had their children sleeping through the night long before Jesse ever did. They all said, "Let them cry. That's the only way you'll ever get some sleep." But how could I let him cry when I had waited so long for him and wanted him so much?

As an infertile parent, it is essential that you free yourself from any obligation that you feel to be superparent. You have a right to be tired, you have a right to want some time to yourself, you even have a right to resent the ways in which your long-awaited child has intruded on your life. Remember that when you are caring for a very young child, many of your personal needs—sleep, quiet time, recreation—go unmet. That you feel stressed by this does not mean that you love and cherish your child any less. It simply means that you, too, are a person with needs and this doesn't make you any less of a parent.

Parenting a child who is moving from infancy to toddlerhood is full of challenges, but it is also filled with rewards. It is a time of rapid change, of almost daily advances. Having lived your life on hold for so long, you are better able to appreciate the ways in which this is a time for exploration and adventure.

So many times, we just stand back and watch him in awe. We talk about what a little miracle he is. Each day, there is cause for celebration.

5

The Preschool Years

B Y the time their child is three, parents begin to realize that their "baby" is now a junior citizen of the world. Although the preschooler's proud declaration "I can do it myself" is seldom entirely true, a young child is capable of a great deal. Most three year olds are ready to go to nursery school, to make friends there, and to begin to explore the world outside their home.

The experience of watching a young child venture forth into the world and of assisting him in this process challenges parents. Most take pride and delight in their child's mastery, pleased that the child they remember as small and helpless is now able to do so much. At the same time, however, there is something very poignant about leaving your child at nursery school for the first time or taking her to a birthday party and realizing that she has reached an age at which parents are no longer expected to stay.

For infertile parents, a child's emergence in the world may involve some tugs and pulls. For one thing, infertile parents rarely, if ever, assume that they will have more children. Instead, they pass through each developmental milestone in their child's life knowing that they may not have another opportunity to experience it. While their fertile friends can celebrate toilet training and welcome the freedom that it offers, infertile parents may carry out that last empty diaper box with a certain wistfulness, wondering if they will ever again have an infant in diapers.

Do not be surprised if your young child's first school experience puts you back in touch with feelings of childlessness. Although you may have had her in day care or hired a baby-sitter when she was younger, you were acutely aware that much of the child care was to meet your personal or professional needs, not hers. Now, when she goes off to nursery school, it is different: she has a need to be with other children and to learn about the world outside your family. She is beginning a process that will continue for the next fifteen years or so: she is leaving home.

> I remember so well an experience that occurred on my daughter's third day of nursery school. I was on my way into school to pick her up when a woman stopped me and said, "Hi, I'm Kathy, Emily's mother. Emily and Sarah are friends." I was taken aback when she said this because up until that point, I had arranged all of Sarah's friendships. It hit me at that moment that Sarah was now capable of making friends on her own. I felt that she did not need me quite as much.

This chapter will discuss some of the issues that may be highlighted for infertile parents when their children are preschoolers, including:

1. holding on versus letting go
2. discipline
3. second-child infertility/second-child adoption questions
4. dealing with your child's curiosity and questions

Holding On versus Letting Go

Milestones can put infertile parents in touch with feelings of loss, with memories of childlessness. You may feel tempted to curl up in a ball with your child and wish that he would stay young forever. Most likely your better judgment as well as his forcefulness keeps you from acting on these feelings. Difficult as it may be, you recognize that he needs to move out in the world in order to grow and develop.

But there are decisions to be made about safety as well as emotional growth. How much should you let your child do? How much can you protect her from the real dangers in the world? Has your infertility made you overprotective or are you simply being prudent when other parents are careless?

I had a hard time last summer when my four year old was at day camp. It wasn't easy for me to send her in the first place since it meant giving up our summer afternoons together. I would have enjoyed having the time to go swimming with her, to have picnics, to spend time in the park. But I sent Chloe to camp because I felt that she would have a better time there than she would have hanging out with me.

Things went well until the third week of camp when Chloe came home with a notice about a field trip. The camp was taking her group to an amusement park. When I phoned to find out about the trip, I learned that they would be traveling an hour each way on a bus that had no seat belts. There was no way that she could go! I couldn't imagine putting my daughter on that bus—to say nothing of the possible dangers at the amusement park. Needless to say, it wasn't easy for me to tell Chloe that I would not allow her to go along with all her friends.

What upset me most about this incident was that none of the other parents seemed to notice. I was the only parent who kept her child home, perhaps the only one who even raised any questions about the trip. The incident left me wondering whether I am overprotective or whether other parents simply don't care. Of course I know that they care, but I wonder if they have any idea how precious all of our children really are?

As you struggle with holding on versus letting go, remember that this is part of a process that will go on for many years. Expect that there will be times in your and your child's lives when it will feel easier to let go and other times when you will feel more of a need to hold on. Expect, also, that certain situations will cause you to feel anxious and that others will be more comfortable. Try to be accepting of your anxiety and permit yourself to sometimes hold on more tightly than you feel is best. Your child will probably have a much easier time with a parent who experiences and expresses certain limitations than one who always attempts to comply with what seem to be external expectations.

I kept Chloe home on the day of the amusement park field trip. I explained to her that the bus ride made me nervous and offered to take her there another day in our fully seat-belted car. She seemed to accept this without question and welcomed a day at home with me. I think that we both enjoyed a day off in the middle of our fast-paced summer.

Discipline

It is during the preschool years that parents must begin to develop a style and a philosophy with which to discipline their children. This is never easy. It is one thing to have ideas in the abstract about discipline and quite another to face a real-life three year old.

Infertile parents frequently find disciplining to be a big challenge. They treat their long-awaited child like royalty. He is so cherished that you have difficulty holding him to normal standards of behavior. Sooner or later you realize that your failure to have reasonable expectations of him is doing him a real disservice.

> When Mark was younger I made some major mistakes in disciplining him — or failing to do so. Telephone calls were a prime example of this. He would be playing nicely and the phone would ring. As soon as I took the call he would interrupt me. Instead of setting clear limits and letting him know this was unacceptable behavior, I let him get away with it. I guess that what went through my mind was that he was more important than any phone call. That was true, but disciplining him was more important than always reminding him that he is the center of my universe.

> I look back with many regrets. At four, Eric is a little tyrant. I love him dearly but I also feel that I have failed both of us terribly by letting him control me. He is a difficult, demanding child who has not yet begun to deal with disappointment or frustration. If he doesn't have what he wants at any given moment he has a tantrum. Until recently I had this crazy notion that because I loved him so much, everything would fall into place.

Infertile parents often find that love is not only not enough, it can be too much. Love for an all-too-precious child can be blinding. Hence it is critical that you take discipline seriously from the time that your child is very young and see it as a central part of your responsibility as his parent.

Because consistency is a critical feature of effective disciplining, you and your spouse, as well as any other central caretakers, should talk together about how your child will be disciplined.

This should go beyond a philosophical discussion and focus on practical issues. You should clarify with each other, and later with your child, what kinds of behavior you will limit and how you will do so. Certainly you cannot predict everything that will come up, but it is much easier to make as many decisions as possible about punishment when you are calm, rather than leaving them to the heat of the moment.

Try as best you can to avoid idle threats. You will have very little credibility with your child if you are always threatening to do this or that but rarely acting on it. She will simply up the ante in her behavior if she knows that you will not follow through on your word. Because she has a substantial need to know that there are real limits, she is likely to push until she knows what they are.

When Nina was a baby I would try to prepare myself for the day when she would say that she hated me. I knew that it would happen because all kids say it to their parents in moments of anger. Nonetheless, I felt that it would be too much for me to bear because she was adopted. I thought that I would experience it as a rejection.

I think that there was a time when I let my fears govern my actions. I was overly indulgent with Nina because I wanted to convince her that I loved her — and convince myself that she loved me. Fortunately, I realized what was happening and toughened up before it was too late. By the time Nina was five, I was setting limits with her with regularity and consistency. And I was getting lots of "I hate you's" in return.

The surprise for me was that the "I hate you's" didn't hurt. By the time that they came I felt secure enough in our relationship to take them for what they were — momentary expressions of frustration. I could see that Nina "hated" me at those moments when I had to discipline her but that these episodes actually helped her to feel clear that I loved her. The disciplining that I once feared would interfere with our relationship has actually served to strengthen it.

Second-Child Infertility/
Second-Child Adoption Questions

Most infertile parents find that their delight in their first child is short-circuited early in their parenting experience because they begin to have concerns about a second child. But for many couples, these concerns rest in the background for the first few years while they take time to enjoy their long-awaited first child. Some couples happen into a pregnancy or an adoption before having to again embark on a real quest for a second child. This early arrival may pose some difficulties but it does spare parents the anxiety and the effort that many must reexperience the second time around.

For the couple who had difficulties the first time around, second-child infertility is especially painful because it revives unpleasant memories. Parents who had felt resolved with the arrival of the first child return to feeling helpless, out of control, at odds with their friends, their families, their faith, and sometimes, with each other.

Although couples with second-child infertility usually say that it is not as bad this time around because they are already parents, there are some ways in which already having a child adds to the pain. One is that parents identify with their young child's wish for a sibling. Johnny comes home from nursery school and asks why his friends are all getting babies. Susie says that she wants a little sister for Christmas. Infertile parents hear these requests as evidence that their child is suffering and their own pain intensifies. "We feel like failures as parents—we're unable to give our child what he wants and needs."

> When Seth was a baby, I joined a mother's group. We became very close, and I really enjoyed the times when we were together. Then, one by one, the other mothers began to announce their pregnancies. Suddenly, the group that had once been such a source of pleasure and support became something I needed to avoid. I was angry at the other women for having it so easy and at myself for again being different.

Second-child infertility is also difficult because it often brings the return of magical thinking. Parents look for a reason for their suffering and wonder if it is a sign that they have somehow failed as parents. "Perhaps this is some sort of punishment?" "Maybe we seemed ungrateful for our first child?" "Are we tempting fate to be seeking a second child when our first is so terrific?"

If you were able eventually to bear a child, you may not be sure that this is possible again and you may wonder about expanding your family via adoption or some other means. For you, the question that nearly all parents ask themselves, "Will we love our second as much as our first?" is especially pointed. You probably look at the child that you produced and wonder if you could ever love an adopted child in the same way. You may fear that you will always favor your biological child.

> We look at Davey and feel that adoption is out of the question. He is so special to us — so much a combination of the best of both of us. It seems like we'd be setting any adopted child up for failure — for a life-long message, "You're not as good as Davey."

For the couple who adopted their first child knowing or having since found out that they have a possibility of bearing a child, the question of how a second child will come to them is also vexing. With new diagnostic and treatment tools rapidly becoming available, these couples face questions about returning to medical treatment. To do so would mean returning to living life on hold and all the attendant anxieties. Nonetheless, old longings to bear a child who is genetically tied to them and to the generations that came before them often return with great intensity.

> Laura and I went through seven years of "unexplained infertility" before we adopted Ryan. Ryan is two now, and we adore him. He is truly our dream child. But as we begin to think about making him a big brother I find that old questions are troubling me. I've heard of a few people with unexplained infertility who've gotten pregnant with GIFT and wonder if we should try it. A part of me says that this time around some treatment will work. But then I look at Ryan and wonder what my wish for a biological child means or could mean to him. If we try GIFT, are we somehow saying that our adopted child is not good enough?

Some adoptive parents consider pursuing a pregnancy not so much because they feel a need to have a biological child as that they fear a second adoption. There is an element of magical thinking operating here. It goes something like this: "We were exceptionally lucky the first time around but we generally have bad luck when it comes to becoming parents. Our child is wonderful, but if we try to get a second child, we'll end up with a loser." To people who have already experienced so much loss, this can feel like too big a risk to take.

> When Charlotte was a year old, we were offered another baby. We were madly in love with her (and still are!) and knew that we wanted another child. We even felt ready. Still, the idea of another adoption was scary. She was clearly a member of the family, but it felt like a second adopted child would be a stranger in our midst. That was six years ago, and we are very glad we put doubts aside and adopted Justin. He is a terrific kid, and we have a really nice family. Still, if we wanted a third child, I expect that my fears and hesitations about adoption would return.

In facing second-child infertility, couples often find that they have to deal with "when is enough, enough?" questions. "How long are we willing to try for a pregnancy?" "How far will we go in trying the new technologies?" "How hard will we work for another adoption?" "D.I. took eight cycles the first time; how long are we willing to try this time around?"

As with primary infertility, couples find means for making decisions. Most find that they reach a point at which life can no longer be left on hold. If their chosen path to parenthood is not working out — even if it was already their second choice — they consider other options. Because they already have one child, some decide to abandon all efforts to expand their family. Others feel, as they may have the first time around, that their main goal is a child. They are willing to move on to a second or even a third choice in order to have a family.

> Peter and I were devastated when we first learned that he had azoospermia. We very much wanted a child and we wanted it together. But after much sadness and soul searching, we settled on an alternative that we felt we could live with: we took Peter's best friend up on his offer to biologically father our child. Nineteen artificial inseminations later, our daughter Cathy was conceived.
>
> Cathy is now two, and we very much want another baby. We've tried donor insemination again for several months, but our friend has moved away and we are using frozen specimens. As much as we appreciate his valiant efforts, we're getting discouraged. We don't think that the frozen specimens are traveling well and fear that we are all wasting our efforts. Also, Laura is getting older, and we're more eager for her to have a brother or sister.

Peter and I are now talking about adoption. We had started to look into it when Cathy was conceived and again, it is beginning to feel right. I have had the opportunity to be pregnant, we have had a child with known and familiar genes, and now it is time to expand our family.

As you take steps to expand your family, be prepared to get little support in your endeavor. Expect people to understand very little about second-child infertility. Expect them to tell you you are lucky to have had or adopted one wonderful child. "Count your blessings," they will tell you. "You have a child. You are a family. What is all this about wanting more?"

The world is remarkably insensitive to infertile parents who want to have a second child. If you previously conceived, your doctor is likely to tell you that you have nothing to worry about: "It happened before, it will happen again." If you adopted, you may find that some agencies will not place a second child with you: "There are too many childless couples out there; consider yourselves lucky to be parents." Or, if they will place a child with you, it is on their terms, at their timing.

Expect yourselves to be in a very lonely position. Your fertile friends are breezing along having second and third children, and they don't really know how to deal with your distress. Your infertile friends envy you and cannot comprehend how you can long for a second child when they don't even have a first. Your parents tell you that one child is enough, never mind the fact that they had three or four or more. Meanwhile, with a young child in day care or nursery school, you are constantly having to deal with pregnancies or with new arrivals.

As you face the stress and the isolation of second-child infertility, try to sort out your priorities. If you are clear that you do want to add another child to your family, then which is more important to you: how he comes into the family or when he comes? If you identify your priority, then you will at least have some control of one aspect of your situation.

If having a child who is born to the two of you is very important, for whatever reason, then try not to focus on issues of spacing. Undoubtedly you have some ideas about what ideal spacing would be, but infertility should have taught you that "ideal" is not a way for you to think when it comes to having children. To predetermine how far apart your children should be is likely to simply add stress to your marriage and to your relationship with your child who will wonder if he has done something wrong or otherwise failed you.

Your children will have a sibling relationship no matter how close or far apart they are in age. Certainly, the difference in their ages will have an impact on that relationship but so will any number of other factors. Remember that the five or seven or ten years between them now, which may seem like such a long time, will not matter very much to them when they are adults. Furthermore, you may discover that there are actually some advantages to brothers and sisters having several years between them.

If age, career, or some other personal matter make it very important that you have your children close together, then you should be prepared to move rapidly to a second-, even a third-, choice route to parenthood. To put your lives again on hold, when spacing is a real priority, will cause you a great deal of stress. You should focus instead on the fact that your goal is to expand or complete your family. Again, your children will have a sibling relationship no matter how they enter the family.

Finally, try to bear in mind that families are formed in all sorts of ways. When you set out to be parents way back when, you probably had some notion of your perfect family. That notion should be long since gone. Fortunately, you live in a society that has grown accustomed to all sorts of families: blended families, step families, mixed race, multicultured families. Whenever, and however, your family comes together, all of you will indeed be a family. Hopefully, that will be something that you can celebrate, feeling enriched and not totally depleted by the surprises you encountered along the way.

Dealing With Your Child's Curiosity and Questions

Curious George is the now classic story of a monkey whose curiosity gets him into all kinds of trouble. Small children identify with George's curiosity; they know what it is like to be filled with questions. Although parents may share their children's fascination with George's escapades, they also think the book communicates an important message: children are sometimes too curious for their own good.

The little "monkeys" that we raise are filled with curiosity. Most parents recognize that exploration and investigation are among the most pleasurable—and most essential—activities of a preschooler. Still, it is not easy to be with a little person who is attempting to circumnavigate the dentist's office or to measure the length of the living room with a roll of toilet paper. Nor is it easy to field the multiple questions that a preschooler asks.

Most young children are very curious about the origins of life. They want to know how babies are created, where they grow, how they were born. They are curious about their own bodies, and about their parent's. They want to know about the anatomy of children of the opposite sex. Their questions are often confusing and difficult for their parents who are unclear what children should know, what children can understand, what information should be offered, and what should be withheld.

For parents after infertility, the natural curiosity of a preschooler can be especially confusing. If you had a baby after years of infertility, you may still feel some conflict about conception. After all, you were probably taught that conception was a natural event, one that occurred as a normal result of a loving union. "First comes love, then comes marriage, then comes . . ." and so forth. Now, you look back and know that babies don't always come from "doing what comes naturally." Your own little "Curious George" is the result of complex medical/surgical interventions.

If you adopted your child, used D.I., or a surrogate, you probably have a stronger response to your child's questions. Not only do her questions bring back some unpleasant memories of your own struggle, but they also raise real dilemmas about what she should know. You may feel very strongly that you don't want to create and perpetuate a family secret, but you probably recognize that at three or four, there are many aspects of the new facts of life that your child could not begin to understand.

Certainly, the experiences of adoptive parents differ from those of D.I. parents, and the experience of D.I. parents differ from those who conceived with IVF or GIFT. However, the challenge that all of you face is to respond to your children in a way that will foster their growth and enhance your relationship with them.

First, be prepared for questions. Remember that your little explorer's curiosity will not be limited to the contents of your purse or your medicine cabinet. Questions about "where did I come from?" are inevitable. Think ahead with your spouse about what your child should know and when he should know it. Realize that you can always change your mind, but that it is important to have an answer that you are comfortable with.

Second, be sure to listen to the question. You may have an answer prepared, but it may not be responsive to the question at hand. Don't answer your child out of your anxiety but rather try to understand what he really wants to know. Listen to the context in which the question arises: is he really curious about whether he grew in your tummy, or does he simply want to know how babies are born.

> When my daughter was four years old, she asked me how she was born. Instead of answering her, I went into a long explanation about how she grew in the "other mother's" uterus. She nodded as if she understood, and I felt that she was not traumatized by the fact that she was adopted. Then, a few days later, she told me that she was the only one in her nursery school who grew in a uterus — all the other kids came from tummies. I had managed to do what I most feared: to convey to her that she was different.

Third, remember that questions and answers will be part of an ongoing dialogue. Your children will not ask questions once; they will ask them many times, in many ways. If you make "mistakes," you will have second chances. Finally, pay attention to the context in which questions arise. The process of talking with your child may be as important as the content.

> My daughter always asks her most serious questions before she goes to sleep at night. At first I thought that drowsiness loosened her up and enabled her to ask questions that at other times were too difficult. More recently, I realized that bedtime is a time when she feels especially close to me. We snuggle up together. She is able to talk with me about difficult subjects during this time because she feels so secure.

The preschool years, for all their challenges, are also a time of great pleasure for most parents. Although your child is still very dependent on you, he is also developing and mastering new skills. You are likely to find that you enjoy his company more in certain ways: he can walk, talk, tell you what's wrong . . . and what is right. She says things that are funny and clever and loving. You can travel with your preschooler without taking along a truckload of diapers. You can eat in a restaurant without cementing all the utensils to the table. To your wonder and delight, you have a little companion who is actually good company. The two of you can have fun together and can appreciate and celebrate milestones, past and present.

6

Kindergarten and Beyond

All I really need to know I learned in kindergarten.
— Robert Fulghum

K INDERGARTEN is a time when children begin to learn how the
world works. They learn about rules and regulations, about
schedules, about sharing, and about acting responsibly. For them,
kindergarten is a time of discovery and growth.

Parents frequently greet kindergarten with mixed emotions. It
puts everyone back in touch with feelings about their own school
experiences. They recall early images of themselves, their families, and their teachers. Parents watch their children go off,
clutching their lunch boxes and book bags and remember a time
when they, too, became citizens of the world.

For infertile parents, a child's entrance into school may rekin-
dle feelings of loss. By now, you have had some experience with
separations from your child, but kindergarten feels different in
several ways. For one thing, it is not optional. With preschool or
day camp you always had the option, however remote you kept
it, of pulling your child out and keeping him at home with you.
If you didn't like his teacher or his counselor, you could change
programs. What is different about kindergarten, even in private
school, is that others really do have jurisdiction over much of
your child's life. You have input, your ideas and preferences are
acknowledged, hopefully even welcomed; but your child is now
part of a larger society.

The following are some of the things that infertile parents
think about when their children enter school:

1. fears and feelings about loss revisited
2. privacy and the boundaries of the family
3. talking with your child about sexuality
4. your child's entrance into the larger society

Fears and Feelings about Loss Revisited

The theme of loss—real, feared, and imagined—runs through the experience of most infertile parents. However, there are several pivotal points at which it is likely to intensify. A child's entry into school is one such milestone.

In sending your children off to school, you not only turn them over to institutions, but you also begin to release them "on their own recognizance."

Parenting a kindergartener involves a series of judgment calls. Parents try to determine what their children are capable of as well as recognize what is beyond them. There is a danger of assuming that they can do more than they are able, but there is also the risk of holding them back.

For infertile parents, these judgment calls present a special challenge. You decide, for example, that your six year old is capable of walking to school with the little girl next door. There are crossing guards along the way and there are no busy streets to cross. Then you think about the cars that whiz around corners and picture your child stepping off the curb at the wrong moment. Or, you worry that she will be distracted by her friend and fail to pay attention when she needs to.

> When Robby was in second grade, it occurred to me that I could probably leave him at home for brief periods of time while I went out on an errand. He knew not to touch any appliances, and I could lock the door and instruct him not to open it. I could teach him how to handle phone calls and how to dial for emergency help. He would probably be safer, I reasoned, than he would be in a car with me. Still, I had a terribly unsettled feeling. What if something went wrong? What of the emergency that I could not foresee? What if tragedy struck while I was standing in a line buying donuts? All of my happiness could be gone in a flash.

Use your child as your guide. More than anyone else, she will help you determine what she is ready to do. As you begin to give her more responsibility at home, you will see how she reacts to it. Can she remember to make her bed in the morning, or does she have to be reminded daily? If you give her a small allowance, how does she handle it? If you tell her that she has to remember when her library books are due, is she able to follow through or do you find yourself with overdue books? These seemingly simple, age-appropriate tasks provide a good deal of information about how a child is learning to take responsibility.

Don't be reluctant to consult your child's teacher. She should have a clear sense of how your child functions in the world when you are not around. You may be very surprised at what you hear. The child who needs to be prodded to do her chores at home, may be exceptionally responsible at school. The little girl who can't get along with any of the friends you invite over to play, may simply be exhausted by her burgeoning social life at school. The teacher's observations should help guide you in distinguishing those areas in which your child needs a good deal of supervision from those that she is prepared to handle more successfully on her own.

Finally, be sure to talk with friends who have traveled this road before you. Children are all different, as are parents, but friends you respect and trust can be immensely helpful. Without dictating your behavior, they can let you know how they handled situations that confused or challenged them.

I have two friends each of whom has three children. Their children are all older than mine. I call my friends my "local wise people" and I turn to them regularly for advice. They probably think nothing of the information that they give me, regarding it as simplistic and old hat. But for me that is not the case at all. Between them they have launched six children in the world and I find it very helpful to hear how they did it.

Privacy and the Boundaries of the Family

When our children enter school, they become public people and we become public families. School registration forms ask us all sorts of things about them, and about ourselves. As participants in a larger system, we are obliged to respond to the questions, but for many parents after infertility, they stir up feelings and concerns. For example, the question that appears, in some fashion, on most school forms—"Was there anything unusual about your pregnancy or your child's birth?"—is likely to puzzle and trouble many infertile parents. Do you want to tell a school that your child was conceived by IVF, or that you spent your pregnancy on bedrest, or that you used sperm washing and intra-uterine insemination (IUI)? Most likely not. Nonetheless, the question stirs up feelings.

Adoptive parents in particular are confounded by this sort of question. Many wonder whether it is in their child's best interest to tell the school she was adopted. On the one hand, this information may help teachers to be more sensitive to the child, especially when the class is studying families. On the other hand, there is the risk that the information will somehow be used against your child. Perhaps a teacher will have some bias about adoption and will inappropriately see some aspect of behavior or school performance as the consequence of adoption.

> Abby's public school registration form included a simple question that threw me. It said, "Is there any other information that would help us to better serve your child?" A simple question, but for me, the answer was complex and unclear. Should I tell the school that Abby was adopted? How would that information be helpful? Might it be harmful? How would the school react if I didn't tell them and they found out in some other way? Since I regard it as Abby's personal information, I felt that it was her business and not mine to tell people. At the same time, however, she is only a little girl and there are many important decisions that I do make for her. Should this be one of them?

Another way in which questions of privacy and the boundaries of the family come up for adoptive parents has to do with other children knowing the special circumstances of your child's arrival. Some other parents will probably tell their children that your child was adopted and these children will, in turn, talk with your child. You are then faced with your child's reaction to the encounters that she has with other children, encounters that she may or may not tell you about.

> When Anna was younger, my friends were careful not to talk about her adoption with their children, knowing that they might then say

something to Anna that would be hurtful. Now she is older, understands that she was adopted, and her friends understand what adoption is. Their parents sometimes ask me if it is okay now to tell their children that Anna was adopted. They seem surprised when I reply that it isn't—that I feel that it is Anna's personal information and that it is for her to decide what she wants to share about herself. Fortunately, others seem to be respectful of this—the very fact that they ask reflects sensitivity to the situation.

As your child's world expands, and he becomes more aware and more knowledgeable, there will be more situations in which privacy is an issue. You won't necessarily know how to handle a particular situation, but it may be helpful to set up certain guidelines for yourself:

1. If you are asked about personal information, consider whether you are obligated legally, or otherwise, to answer it. If not, is there some other clear purpose at hand? If you are not clear why someone wants to know something, find out before telling.
2. Think twice before volunteering information about your family. Is there a real reason why you are offering it, or are you simply giving in to the anxiety of the moment?
3. Consider this an evolving process. As time goes on, you can always decide to be more open about your family. What you cannot do is to take back things you have already told people or institutions.

Talking with Your Child about Sexuality

Around school age, most children become very curious about where babies come from. Speaking with children in a way that answers their questions without confusing them is a challenge to all parents. For parents after infertility, talking to a curious young child can be a formidable task.

If your child came to you through special circumstances—adoption, donor insemination, surrogacy, even IVF—then you have probably given this subject a good deal of thought. You have undoubtedly struggled with what to tell your child and when to tell her. Hopefully, you have arrived at answers with which you feel comfortable. The problem is that you do not know what her questions will be.

> My daughter, Lucy, is adopted. When she was four, she saw a picture of Jack and me on a vacation in Amsterdam several years before she was born. I told her that "Daddy and I took a trip to a far-away place." A few weeks later, we were driving home from her preschool and she said to me, "Was I in your tummy when you went on your trip?" My first reaction was, "There it is, there's the question I have been anticipating for so long." I was all set to tell her about her adoption but paused and reminded myself to listen to her question. I simply said, "No," and asked her why she wanted to know. Lucy's answer surprised me. She told me that one of her friends from school was going to Venezuela to visit her grandparents. The teacher had explained that Venezuela was far away and had asked the children where they had traveled. Lucy had been wondering if she had ever been to Amsterdam.

If you gave birth to your child you may be surprised to find yourself uncomfortable when she asks you how babies are born. After all, you did achieve a pregnancy (or more than one) and you had the chance to experience the miracle of birth. This should be an opportunity to reminisce about an experience that you cherished. Still, you find yourself curiously unsettled by her question. The joy is there, but you also remember the horrible struggle. Dr. Linda Hammer Burns tells the following story of her own experience:

> When my daughter was six her friend's mother became pregnant. My daughter was very curious about this and wanted to know how babies got into Mommy's tummies. I tried some standard explanations about the meeting of egg and sperm, but none fully satisfied her curiosity. Finally, I described to her, as simply as possible, what a man and woman did together. She was incredulous and said to me, "That's awful—how many times do you have to do it?" To my complete surprise, I burst into tears. When my daughter saw the tears she asked what had upset me. I explained to her that it still made me sad to remember how long and how hard Daddy and I tried to have her. I told her that some people make love once and get a baby and that others have to try and try and try for one.

Discussions with your child about conception and pregnancy are further complicated by the fact that she gets input from outside your home. There will be discussions in school, usually as early as kindergarten, that focus on the family. You must present information at home that is consistent with what she learns in school. In this regard, it can be helpful to talk with her kindergarten teacher early in the year to get a clear sense of what your child is likely to hear in school. Telling the teacher about special circumstances in your family may help her to handle the complicated material with sensitivity.

Finally, you should anticipate that your infertility may have left you feeling that your sexuality is damaged. A part of your life that once felt natural, comfortable, and pleasurable was disrupted. It may have happened years ago, yet remnants of the damage remain and may unconsciously or unintentionally emerge at unexpected moments. The thermometer no longer sits on your bedstand but you still remember its awful presence.

Your Child's Entrance into the Larger Society

Most new parents are delighted by their child's abilities. From the time they first begin to speak, our children captivate us with their cute expressions and their remarkable perceptions. Most parents come to believe that they have extraordinary children — bright, talented, unique.

When your children enter school, you will probably find that they are not as extraordinary as you may have thought. This realization can be somewhat sobering, especially after infertility. Like all parents, you may be a bit surprised, even disappointed, to learn that Susie, whom you thought was so bright, is only in the middle reading group. And Paul, who was such a "jock" at baby gym and swim, is actually pretty slow on the soccer field. Those of you who adopted your children may find that some old questions about genes return.

Both of my children are adopted. My daughter, Karen, is nine and has always been a super student. She was identified as gifted in first grade and has been doing advanced work ever since. When my son, Michael, began kindergarten last year I somehow assumed that he would follow in Karen's footsteps. As it is turning out, Michael is a much more middle-of-the-road student. That is fine with me, but at first it was sort of jarring. It reminded me that I can make few assumptions about how my children will perform at any given activity based on how my husband and I do and based upon each other. To the extent that genes are determinant we can make few predictions.

When your child enters kindergarten, don't be afraid to acknowledge some disappointment. Remember that years of trying to become a parent promoted fantasies of a dream child. If you were to have imagined yourself with a kindergartener, the child probably would have had certain features that felt particularly appealing or important to you. You may have imagined a little basketball player or a beginning ballerina or a child who could read Shakespeare on entering school. Now you see, probably more than before, that your real child is not at all the child of your dreams.

This is the time that you will begin to understand who your child really is. You will be able to see his areas of interest and ability and can help him develop them. You will be able to help him distinguish between things that he avoids because he feels he is not good at them and things that simply don't interest him. This is a critical time in your child's life because it is the time at which he begins to compare himself to those around him. In order to help him with this, you need to feel comfortable and accepting of who he is.

I had a dream child. She was a little tomboy, the kind of girl who played little league and soccer, who liked horses and dogs, whose idea of a good time was going fishing with my father. My real daughter, whom I gave birth to after seven years of trying, is interested in dolls and pretty clothes. She can't play little league because they don't allow dresses and party shoes on the ball field. She won't go fishing because it is "dirty and smelly and slimy." My dream child is someone I would have liked to know and enjoy. My real child is someone whom I adore beyond all measure.

In summary, it is in the kindergarten year that many parents come to fully appreciate the complexities of parenting. Love matters; love is important; but we must parent with our ears and our minds as well as with our hearts. We need to think, and puzzle, and find the best answers that we can to help our children to grow, to keep them safe, and to teach them to develop and maintain good judgment.

7

Latency Age

T HE years between ages seven and twelve are usually referred to as latency age. Gone, or greatly diminished, are the tensions and conflicts of early childhood — those of adolescence have not yet heated up. The latency-age child is interested in the world around him and he is interesting to be with. For parents and their children, this is a time of greater freedom, discovery, and growth.

Infertile parents report feeling less aware of and less affected by their infertility during their child's latency years. Many of the feelings that were so powerful, such as the "obligation" to be superparents, have subsided. Feelings of being different from other parents have lessened as talk among parents has moved away from labor and delivery and "ideal spacing" and on to soccer and little league, to how you get your child to clean her room and do her homework. Infertile parents of latency age children appear to remember their infertility, but they do not experience it with such intensity.

> I wear my infertility like a badge of honor. It is a battle won. I have lived through it and I am a better person for it.

> I have matured since infertility and have grown because of that process. The pain of infertility has found its proper niche and I have integrated it into my life. It is part of who I am, but not all of who I am.

Many parents say that their self-esteem has been restored. They no longer feel damaged, defective. Their sexuality, assaulted by infertility, is at least partially repaired. Still, there are certain concerns that arise during this time, including:

1. continued vulnerability to separation and loss
2. acknowledging and accepting a child's strengths and limitations
3. putting closure on their fertile years

Continued Vulnerability to Separation and Loss

The latency-age child is someone who is beginning to separate from his family, as well as represent it in the world outside the home. This may be a difficult time for parents if they have remained vulnerable to separation and loss. Some of the major separations that begin in kindergarten continue as children have overnights, go on school field trips, perhaps even travel by bus or subway alone. This is the time when some children spend as much as eight weeks away at summer camp. For parents who have held on tight or who have resisted the urge to do so, this time can pose real challenges.

> Steven is eight now — and I have come a long way from where I was a few years ago. He now spends nearly every school vacation at my mother's house, about a two-hour drive from here. I still have a hard time with it, but he is very cute about it. He says, "Mom, I need to get away. Relax, you'll be okay."
>
> I am okay, but I still struggle with feelings of emptiness when he is gone. Maybe it would be different had we been able to have another child, but seeing as he is the long-awaited only one, it is very difficult. I don't think about accidents and injuries — I just feel his absence.

Infertile parents of school-age children are aware of their children's need to separate. Painful as it is, they recognize that separation promotes growth and that it is something they must deal with and not avoid. Whereas infertile parents of younger children often speak with pride of how their children rarely if ever stay with baby-sitters, as their children get older these same parents are pleased when they are able to let go.

We were having dinner last week at a nearby Chinese restaurant. As we were finishing the meal, my eight year old asked if we could go next door to an ice cream shoppe for dessert. I said yes, and then I had a great idea. I said "How would you like it, Shelley, if I gave you the money and you went by yourself?" She may have hesitated for a split second but then gave me a delighted *sure!*

I had a mildly anxious few minutes and then went next door. Shelley was already waiting by the door. She had a smile on her face that was bigger than her ice cream cone. I told her how proud I was of her. I didn't tell her how proud I was of myself!

At the same time that they recognize the need for their children to separate, infertile parents recognize that they have more to worry about.

As the mother of a rapidly maturing six year old, I recognize his need to have me let go. He needs to know that I have confidence in him and that I recognize his capabilities. Still, my infertility has taught me a difficult lesson: *Things go wrong.* Before infertility, I believed in statistics, in the law of averages, in the sense that "it will probably be all right." I no longer feel that way. I now know that bad things really do happen to good people and I feel an urge to try to protect against them.

If you are struggling with questions of what it is reasonable and safe for your latency-age child to do, remember that your task is complicated by the times in which we live. The world was a lot simpler when you were her age. Dangers existed but chances are that your parents didn't have to give a second thought to sending you on an errand or allowing you to ride your bicycle to school. Kidnappers, drug dealers, and drunk drivers existed in those days, but they are a more substantial cause for concern today. Infertility makes you no more likely to be their victim, but it has taught you that bad things don't just happen to someone else.

Infertile parents of latency-age children are keenly aware of the passage of time. They are aware of how rapidly their children are growing and they see and feel the limits of their time together. Feelings about separation and loss can be heightened during this time as they look toward the future.

I am ever aware of how quickly time is passing. It feels like yesterday that I brought my first baby home from the hospital, and he is now eleven. It is hard to believe and to accept that he will be leaving home in six years. It is equally hard to believe that my daughter, my "baby," is now nine and that my time with her at home is half over. I am grabbing for each moment as it passes.

Acknowledging and Accepting a Child's Strengths and Limitations

By the time a child is in first or second grade, he has certain fairly well-defined areas of interest and ability. Some children are good on the soccer field; others are much more comfortable reading a book. Some children struggle with the simple math that they learn in first and second grade, while they have classmates who bound forward to multiplication and division. Parents realize that their children are not necessarily what they wanted or expected they would be.

> My eight-year-old daughter, Allison, taught me an important lesson. I am someone who loves ballet and who always looked forward to having a daughter who would also love ballet and who would be better at it than I was. I started Allison's dance lessons when she was four and took great pleasure watching her learn and progress. Then, when she turned eight, she sat me down and gave me a nice "talking to" . . .
>
> "Mom, I have something to tell you. I know that you love ballet but Mom, I don't. Ballet is just not my thing. Mom, I go to my own beat."
>
> I was disappointed not to have a ballerina but proud and pleased to have a little girl who goes "to her own beat." Allison told me something that I certainly needed to hear: she is her own person and not the confirmation of my dreams and aspirations.

Infertile parents sometimes find that their self-esteem, so battered by infertility, has been inappropriately tied up with their children. They have used their children's abilities—real and imagined—to feel better about themselves. As these children emerge as their own people, their parents can feel sad, even angry.

I realized, when my children were six and seven, that I was trying to use them to repair some of the damage to my self-esteem. When they did well, I was proud, pleased, and happy. When they messed up, or acted up in some way, I experienced it as a real narcissistic injury. Before infertility, I was not a person whose self-esteem was particularly vulnerable. Now I have to be careful to avoid putting my children in a position where their job is to make me feel better.

Infertile parents who have used their children to manage problems in self-esteem face a real challenge during latency. They must recognize that their children are already pressured by the world and that they do not need the added stress of performing in order to meet their parents' expectations. Letting go of the image of the exceptional child can put some people back in touch with feelings of loss.

It was very hard for me, at first, to accept the fact that my daughter is an average student. When she was very young, she seemed exceptionally bright. She walked early, talked early, knew her alphabet, and could recite nursery rhymes at a very young age. She was good at sports and her memory was astounding.

As a third grader, she is doing fine. Her report cards say that she is performing at or above grade level. But she is, by no means, outstanding. I see that some of her friends are more capable than she is, and I have mixed reactions. I worry that I might have done something wrong or that I could have done something better. I admit also, that I feel impatient with her and I catch myself telling her to try harder. At the same time, however, I am forcing myself to accept the fact that she is who she is and not who I want her to be.

For adoptive parents, the task of accepting their children for who they are has an added challenge. It is during latency that a child's abilities, interests, and intellect declare themselves. Adoptive parents, who probably wondered in what ways their children would and would not be like them, now confront the realities. Highly intelligent parents, for example, may find that their child simply is not as bright as they are. Musically talented parents may discover that their child has no musical ability. "Couch potatoes" may discover that they are parenting an athlete. Hopefully, parents are able to accept these differences with some degree of comfort and not experience them as but another loss.

Before we adopted, I worried a lot about how bright our child would be. Then, when Nina arrived, I forgot my concerns and believed that she was a very bright kid. It has dawned on me over the last few years since she has been in school, that she is actually not all that bright. I'm happy to discover that, for some reason, it no longer matters.

We probably all know people who make the mistake of trying to live through their children, sad individuals who maintain very little identity of their own. Their children suffer and many are prompted to take extreme positions in order to let their parents know that they are separate individuals. Now, while your child is still young and closely tied to you, is an excellent time to let her know that you respect and admire her individuality. This comes up not only in your reactions to the work she does at school but also in the other messages that you give her. If you allow her to select her own clothes, to decorate her room, to decide which after-school activities she will participate in, you communicate to her that you view her as capable of making decisions for herself and that you recognize that your way isn't necessarily best for her. Hopefully, you are enabling her to be like you in those ways that she chooses, never forcing her to declare differences simply as a means of separating.

Putting Closure on Their Fertile Years

At some point all women face the realization that they have reached, or are rapidly approaching, the end of their fertile years. For most women this is a difficult time, but it is an especially powerful turning point for infertile women, who have gone through so much to bear children, with or without success. For many, this experience coincides with their child's latency-age years.

Infertile parents often speak of an ongoing longing for another child, even if their family is in many ways complete. Those who conceived, as well as those who never did, acknowledge the fantasy of an unexpected pregnancy. Some even admit to risking pregnancy at a point in their lives when another child would pose major problems.

As I approached forty, I realized that I was getting very careless with birth control. We had managed to have three terrific children after many years of infertility, and now I was tempting fate by risking—almost trying for—another pregnancy. After one "pregnancy scare" I made the amazing decision to have my tubes tied. Difficult as it was, I realized that this was the only positive way in which I could take control of my fertility.

It has been over a year since my tubal ligation. It was the right decision and one that I can live with. Still, when I see a new baby the longing returns. When I know that I am ovulating the fantasies of conception come back.

Some infertile mothers experience more than just a fantasy of an unexpected pregnancy. Some tell of renewed efforts to have a baby. Old feelings about infertility, seeming long since put to rest, return as people make that one last best attempt at a pregnancy.

I went through several years of infertility; when I was nearing thirty, we adopted our son and then, two years later, we adopted our daughter. I enjoyed their early years so much and felt so satisfied that I believed I was "resolved." When I was in my late thirties, I began to read and hear about all the new high-tech treatments for infertility. I began wondering whether our situation was so hopeless after all and I began thinking a lot about a baby. We ended up reopening the whole painful kettle of worms, even to the point of undertaking IVF four times. In some ways, this go-around with infertility was even more painful than the first. Not only did we have all the hope and disappointment to deal with but we also had the pain of a now eight and ten year old who wondered—and asked—"aren't we good enough?"

When I was thirty-eight I had a "surprise" pregnancy. My older son, whom we adopted, was eleven at the time and my younger son, who is our biological child, was eight. For several years, pregnancy and raising another child had been very far from my mind.

Somewhere around my thirty-eighth birthday, I began to have fantasies of a baby girl. I had originally wanted to have a daughter, but had put that desire to rest years before. Infertility had taught me to be very grateful for the children I had and had warned me not to covet my neighbor's little pink dresses. But there I was at thirty-eight, happily back at work, with two growing sons and I was thinking about girl's names!

For several months this remained a fantasy. Then, over the fourth of July weekend, I began to suspect that I might actually be pregnant. My period was late, and I was feeling a bit tired. I tried not to think about it for a few days but when a week went by with no sight of blood, I did a home pregnancy test. To my amazement, it was positive.

Three weeks later, I miscarried. For me, this was a devastating experience. I felt that I had lost more than a chance to have a daughter (I will never know if the fetus was a girl but I believe that it was)—I lost my chance to master the mysteries of reproduction. True, I had been pregnant before, but it had been with tremendous effort and dramatic interventions. This had been my one opportunity to simply "happen into pregnancy." It had felt so "normal" to buy a home pregnancy test. The miscarriage simply confirmed my sense that my body doesn't work right after all.

If you are revisiting old feelings about fertility and reproduction and attempting to say good-bye to them at the same time, give yourself some sense of control. You can do this by imposing some time limit on how long you will attempt pregnancy, not leaving it to the harsh reality of menopause to make that decision for you. Remember that you cannot count on most physicians to be much help to you in this decision, and expect that they are likely to offer treatment as long as you are willing to accept it.

For some of you, revisiting old issues does not involve taking action. Old longings to experience pregnancy or to be pregnant again may resurface, but they are just that—old, sad longings. They need to be viewed amid the reality of your real family life, which may, indeed, be full and complete, hopefully even abundant with riches.

Hence it is often during their child's latency years that infertile couples come to grips with the boundaries of their families. For some, especially those who have not had a biological child, this can be a difficult experience, one that brings back some of the old pain of infertility. However, for many, the excitement and the satisfaction of parenting a latency-age child can take away the sting. For these are, indeed, the years that many parents have looked forward to and anticipated. Their latency-age child offers them good companionship as well as the opportunity to relive some aspects of their own childhoods.

8

Adolescence

P ARENTS do not usually look forward to their children's adolescence. Parenting an adolescent involves frustration and
anxiety, sleepless nights, empty refrigerators, borrowed clothes,
and borrowed cars. Parents who have two or more children stum-
bling through adolescence wonder if they should pack their bags
and take an extended sabbatical. Many might seriously consider
such an escape if they didn't have to worry about the condition
of their house and car on their return.

A history of infertility offers no dispensation from the stresses
of adolescence. In fact, many infertile parents face additional
challenges during this time. For example, those who adopted
their children recognize that this is a particularly rough time
because their children's quest for identity is complicated and
compromised by the absence of known biological connections.
No doubt, identity questions must be all the more complex for
D.I. and surrogate offspring.

This chapter will take a brief look at the experience of parents
of adolescents, with special attention to some of the ways in which
a history of infertility may continue to affect their feelings and
actions. Areas of concern include:

1. feeling a loss of control
2. enabling a child to explore and develop his identity
3. physical changes—in yourself and in your child
4. dealing with sexuality
5. continued feelings of separation

Feeling a Loss of Control

Parents of adolescents often feel a loss of control. While they can set standards of behavior within their households, they are also at the mercy of the outside world. Parents of adolescents worry that their children will be tempted by drugs and alcohol, or pressured by academic demands and the promises of life in the fast lane. Parents of past generations had to worry about their children going off to war; parents today confront the terrifying specter of acquired immune deficiency syndrome (AIDS).

The loss of control is a familiar experience for infertile parents. When you were going through infertility treatment, you felt that you were no longer in control of your body. If you went on to pursue adoption, D.I., or surrogacy, you knew that others now had a large measure of control over your life. When you finally became a parent, you may have tried to regain some sense of control.

Now you have an adolescent. Now the little child who you lovingly knitted sweaters for is walking around in two left sneakers, laces untied. Now the child that you helped cross the sidewalk is out driving with friends at night. Now the child that you patiently helped with his science project is talking about quitting school and taking a sailboat around the world. Now you feel a loss of control.

As a parent of an adolescent, you need to distinguish those areas from which you should step aside and allow your child to make decisions (and perhaps mistakes) from those areas in which she very much needs—and wants—your guidance. Some parents make a mistake trying to exert too much control, but others make the mistake of saying and doing too little. Parenting an adolescent involves judgment and action, as well as patience and trust.

> When we found out that Justin was having problems with drugs, I was really angry with myself. I felt that Bob and I had taken too much of a laid-back, permissive approach. Because Justin is an excellent student and so capable in many ways, we let him take charge of too much of his life. I looked back and realized that there were clues along the way that told us that he needed some guidance and some limits.

Parents after infertility can use their earlier experiences with loss of control to advise them as they face some of the challenges of parenting adolescents. Hopefully, your earlier experience helped you see that loss of control is never absolute, that there are ways in which we can and must gain mastery over even the most seemingly out-of-control situations.

> The impact of my infertility on my parenting has, by no means, been all bad. It isn't the biggest part of who I am as a parent, but it is there and it offers me some coping skills. These skills have been particularly helpful as my children have grown older. Now when I walk into my teenage daughter's disaster zone (her room), I remind myself of how out of control I felt before I had children. This perspective helps me: it keeps me from "losing it" over the small things.

Enabling a Child to Explore and Develop His Identity

Adolescence is a time for exploration. Difficult as it may be for parents who feel that they know who their children are and who they should become, adolescents themselves are uncertain and confused. Most feel a need to consider several possibilities for themselves and many go so far as to try on an assortment of identities.

It is a challenge to all parents to stand back and let their children find themselves. Even those who have "good kids" who don't drink or take drugs have to deal with behavior and attitudes they find upsetting or objectionable. Certainly there are circumstances that call for parental intervention, times when children are crying out for guidance and for limits. Parents need to be able to identify these instances as well as to let go during the many times when there is really nothing they can or should do.

> I have now survived the adolescences of my three daughters, and it has not been easy. Our oldest is serious minded, straight, hard-working. Sometimes I felt like she was driving herself too hard — that she was missing out on some good times. My second daughter

spent her teenage years looking and acting like a freak. One day her hair was pink, the next she had a green "mohawk." My youngest was a cross between the two, not bizarre in her outlook or appearance, but hardly conservative. Now as they enter adulthood, they are three lovely young women. The oldest is in law school, the second is in art school, and their baby sister is hoping to become a veterinarian. They have made choices for themselves that are not the choices that I would have made for them, but they seem content.

For those infertile parents who are also older parents, a child's search for identity can be especially challenging. You may find yourself feeling an enormous generation gap. Those of your fertile friends who had their children when they were young may be involved in personal exploration that is not all that different from that of their adolescents. Still young, they look ahead to many child-free years of opportunity. They may be considering career change or advancement, or perhaps even a move to another city or state. Their youth may facilitate their explorations.

As an older parent, you are in a different place. Chances are that you are feeling very "middle-aged." Rather than looking with your adolescent at a world of possibilities, you are preparing to face years of physical decline. If you spent years pursuing fertility, to the point of having compromised other pursuits, you may now look back with a sense of longing and regret. You wonder where all the years went.

> My big regret is that we didn't get started sooner. Peter and I were married a long time before we had any idea that we wanted kids. We have thoroughly enjoyed raising Adam, but the feeling of time lost has never gone away.

If you adopted your child, then his search for identity presents further challenges. Much as you may support, even encourage, his need to explore his biological background, you can also feel vulnerable and threatened. You may believe that he needs to search in order to consolidate his own identity, but you may still experience the search as painful.

I am a psychologist and much of the work that I do involves helping people to figure out who they are and what they want for themselves. I am also the adoptive mother of two late-adolescent daughters, one of whom wants to search. To my surprise and shame, I am having a very hard time with this process. I believe that a search would be good for her and that she may need to do it, but it makes me feel frightened and somewhat abandoned. I don't want her to know that I feel this way, nor do I want to influence her decision or that of her sister.

Your adolescent's search for identity may feel less unsettling to you if you are able to identify the issues that it touches in your own life. If, for example, you find yourself having a strong reaction to the decisions your child is making, or considering, about college, career, life-style, think whether you are responding because of your own dissatisfactions. You made some choices, actively or passively, that have shaped the course of your life. You may need to use this time to review and reassess them.

Physical Changes—In Yourself and in Your Child

Adolescents pay enormous attention to physical appearance. Their parents not only have to deal with pink hair and green mohawks, but they also have to deal with boys wearing one earring and girls wearing several. The same parents who once took pride in dressing their three year old in her best, frilly party dress now consider themselves lucky if, at fifteen, she agrees to wear shoes when she goes out with them.

For adoptees, concerns about physical appearance are all the more complex. Adoptees want to be accepted by their peers, but they also think about and long for a physical connection to another person. Some of their preoccupation with appearance may be an expression of these longings for physical connectedness and of their acute awareness of how different they look from other members of their families.

My daughter is constantly in front of the mirror, struggling with her appearance and complaining that it is not right. I know that it is normal for adolescents and for girls, in particular, to be bothered by the way that they look and to wish that they could make changes. Still, I can't help but wonder where adoption fits in and if she is expressing something about her adoption. I wonder if she is looking in the mirror, longing to know one person who really looks like her.

As a parent, you probably recognize that a struggle with appearance is a necessary part of identity formation. Nonetheless, your child's preoccupation with how she looks may be difficult for you. If you are an older parent, you may be dealing with changes in your own appearance. Gray and thinning hair, more wrinkles, less muscle tone—daily reminders that you are getting older. It may be especially hard to listen to your child's concerns when you are troubled by the changes in your own body.

If you adopted your child, her wish for physical connectedness may resonate with your own longings for generational continuity. This was something you probably felt at the time that you adopted, but it may feel different fifteen years later. You may have fewer surviving relatives and your own illnesses or injuries may have put you more in touch with your own mortality. You may be surprised at how powerfully old feelings return.

> I thought I had made my peace with my inability to have children and I felt delighted with the two sons who we adopted. But as my sons grow into men, so different in physical appearance from the men in my family, I find that old thoughts about what it would be like to have a biological child creep back in and pester me.

As parents of adolescents you are also experiencing physical changes that go beyond appearance. Menopause is a difficult time for many women, and is all the more stressful for infertile women, whether or not they succeeded in bearing a child. It marks the last good-bye to fertility, the final letting go of certain dreams. Women who felt that they made peace with their infertility years earlier may find that powerful feelings about it return during menopause.

> My son Dan, whom I gave birth to after seven years of infertility, is now ten. I have enjoyed the past ten years and have felt none of the anguish that I experienced during the long trial of my infertil-

ity. But now I am visited by menopause and I find that some old feelings are back. I feel barren and empty, and sometimes I lie in bed at night with a quiet ache.

Menopause was cruel but I also feel grateful to it. I realize now that it happens for a reason. Or at least it did for me. Were it not for menopause, I would have kept on trying forever. I think that had my menopause come in my sixties, I would have spent another ten or fifteen years quietly hoping for a miracle birth.

Menopause is unfortunately not the only physical change that confronts parents of adolescents. As you enter your forties, you are likely to find that illness and medical problems are all around you. Friends are getting sick, some with chronic conditions, others with life-threatening illnesses. Gone is the innocence of youth, the feelings of invulnerability. You realize that as devastating as infertility was, it was but one of the many ways in which our bodies can betray us.

In the year that I turned forty, my mother became terminally ill, a friend's sister died of breast cancer, a cousin was diagnosed as having M.S. My infertility had caused me to struggle with my own mortality but the full reality of it didn't hit home until that year. It was sobering to realize that anything could happen and to know how little control I had.

As you face some of the harshest realities of middle age, you will undoubtedly have feelings and reactions to your adolescent. He is strong and youthful. She is filled with energy. You want them to take care of their bodies, and you worry when you feel that they are being neglectful. You may feel angry, at times, for the ways in which they take good health for granted.

Try to accept these reactions as part of the separation process. Your adolescent is moving ahead with his life and you, with yours. You have a right and responsibility to advise your child about health, safety, and nutrition, but in reality, there is only so much you can do. Some of your energies are better spent working on your own body and improving your sense of well-being. If you do not already get regular exercise or participate in a sport, it is not too late for you to get started. Taking up tennis or joining a basketball league might bring you some initial aches and pains, but it should also offer you a renewed sense of physical mastery.

Dealing with Sexuality

Parents of adolescents have always had to adjust to and help their children with their emerging sexuality. Teenage pregnancy has long been a concern, as has venereal disease, homosexuality, and promiscuity. However, these issues are all now secondary to (but often related to) the dread on the minds of all parents: AIDS.

In addition to educating and reeducating your adolescent about the dangers of AIDS, you probably have ideas and concerns about their emerging sexuality. Your experience with prolonged infertility — and its outcome — has left you with some lasting feelings about your own sexuality. Most likely, you still feel damaged, defective, unable to "do what comes naturally."

If you eventually succeeded in conceiving and carrying a child, you are likely to have some concerns about your child's reproductive ability. Your infertility experience has undoubtedly familiarized you with all the things that people do that can compromise their fertility. The Pill, the intrauterine device (IUD), sexually transmitted disease, repeated abortions, and drug and alcohol use have all been implicated in impaired fertility. You see the need not only to educate your child regarding AIDS, but also to teach her to take care of her reproductive system as best she can.

You may worry that even with education and caution your child will experience infertility. Perhaps your son will be subject to a disease or injury that will affect his sperm production. Perhaps your daughter, who so resembles you physically, will also have irregular periods. Worse still is the fear that you did something that will alter or compromise their fertility.

I am a DES daughter so I know that parents can unintentionally do things that prove harmful to their children. I took Clomid to conceive and to establish a pregnancy. My doctor assured me that this was different from DES, that Clomid-HCG could not affect my child. But then again, DES was touted as the wonder drug of the fifties.

Now, as my daughter approaches puberty, I wonder and worry. I believe that what I took was safe — otherwise I wouldn't have done it — but I can't help but wonder.

Adoptive parents often have an additional set of concerns as their children approach adolescence. Adolescent adoptees have been known to "act out" their need to have a biological connection through teenage pregnancies. Pregnancy can be used as a vehicle to connect them with a biological relative as well as a means of identifying with their birthparents. It is not uncommon for adolescent, adopted girls to become pregnant, have the baby, and then place the baby for adoption, a sequence that is most likely an effort to gain some mastery of their own early experience.

Parents cannot stop their children from acting out. If your adolescent was adopted, you may have to spend some anxious years, hoping that she will not feel a need to become pregnant. Perhaps you can help her to deal with her feelings in other ways by talking with her about her wish to see and know more about her birthparents. Remember that adoptees feel a divided loyalty. She may call you names, figuring you can take it, but never mention her curiosity about her birthparents for fear that this will really hurt you. If she can talk with you about her longings and perhaps even find support and help for a search, a teenage pregnancy may be less compelling.

Although the struggles of adolescent, adopted girls are more apparent, boys also wrestle with feelings about their adoptions. You may find that your son is spending a lot of time with a friend or girlfriend who was also adopted. Be prepared that he, too, might act out by impregnating a girl. He is likely to be less articulate of his curiosity about his birthparents, but that does not mean that he is not thinking about them and struggling with questions of identification and allegiance. For boys it can be especially difficult because, in most instances, more is known about the birthmother than the birthfather. Moreover, birthfathers are often portrayed as "no good," "irresponsible," "careless," characteristics that are especially troubling to a young man who is growing up and searching for positive identifications.

As an adoptive parent, you might try to dispel some of the myths about birthfathers. Even if you know little or nothing about your son's birthfather, you might still talk with him about his fantasies. You may be able to help him see that his birthfather was probably not an ill-intentioned or reckless person. He was prob-

ably young and confused himself, trying to find his way in the
world. Your son may be able to identify with his birthfather's pre-
sumed youth and confusion, and hopefully this understanding
will help him make better choices for himself.

Continued Feelings of Separation

By the time their children reach adolescence, parents have been
dealing with separation in one way or another for many years.
Still, it takes on a new perspective when children begin to drive,
to earn money of their own, and to make decisions about college.
Parents of adolescents have to really face the fact that they are
leaving home.

Your feelings about separating from your adolescent will be
determined by many factors: your relationship with your child,
your own life circumstances such as health, career, marital status
and satisfaction, and your own experience leaving home. It will
also be affected by how many other children you have at home.
Parents who have several children, and who watch them leave one
by one, have a very different experience from those who have one
child.

If you have a small family because you were unable to have or
adopt more children, this may be an especially difficult time for
you. As your child prepares to leave home, you may find that old
issues about family boundaries resurface. Should you have made
more of an effort to expand your family? Did you "quit" too soon
because it was the expedient thing to do? You may find that you
envy your friends with several children: they seem to have more
of a revolving door than an empty nest.

A history of infertility by no means assumes a small family. Perhaps, as a result of infertility, you took a "more the merrier"
approach, spending the last fifteen years or so with a home filled
with children. Having been childless for so long, you may have
chosen to immerse yourself in parenting. For you, the prospect
of an empty nest may raise some serious questions about your
future. Who will you be and what will you do without your children? Is there anything else in life that could possibly give you as
much pleasure as raising your family? Will you ever get over this
feeling that someone is missing?

For months I started to cry every time I set four places at the dinner table and realized that there were now only three of us. I
thought I'd be better by the time that Tommy came home for
Thanksgiving break, but my sadness persisted. It seems like yesterday that I was picking him up at nursery school.

As you struggle with separation, you may see some of your fertile friends having an easier time with it. They may also experience a good deal of pain, but they are looking forward to
child-free days. For them, being without children does not represent emptiness, defect, loss of control; they can recall and recap-
ture the freedom they felt and enjoyed before they had the
responsibility of children.

One of my close friends told me that he plans to set limits on his
children so as to prevent them from moving back home after college. He says that he had known people who have had their adult
children return home for extended periods of time and that he
and his wife are looking forward to their years together without
the children. I felt really sad when I heard this because it is so
much the opposite of how I feel. I am so afraid of the loneliness,
of how I will feel when the children are gone, that I can imagine
going to some lengths to actually urge them to come home.

As the parent of an adolescent, you need to actively prepare
yourself for what life will be like once your child leaves home.
Ideally, this is the continuation of a process that began many
years ago. Still, this is a very different process now, as your child
applies to college or explores jobs away from home. Now you
need to think, in a very practical way, about how you will spend
your time and your energies once she is gone. Perhaps you can
see this as an opportunity and not as a burden.

It was very difficult for me when Joshua decided that he wanted to
go away to prep school. The decision made sense in many ways — it
was the school that my father and grandfather had attended — but
his leaving left me feeling at loose ends. Then I began thinking
about flying. I had always wanted to learn to fly. I had always been
too busy to learn to fly. I had always felt that it was an idea whose
time would come. The time had come.

By the time your child reaches adolescence, your infertility has presumably taken its place as part of your history. And like other pieces of personal history, there will be times when it steps forward and participates in your current experience. Hopefully, you will be able to make some good use of it. Perhaps as you remember an earlier time when you felt a loss of control, you will feel equipped to cope with similar feelings as they arise during your child's adolescence.

Parenting an adolescent is filled with challenge, but there are some rewards as well. As your child struggles to discover and establish his identity, you may find some nice surprises in what emerges. The same teenager who walks around in tie-dyed, untied sneakers and a green mohawk writes a sensitive and perceptive essay for her college application. The same rude-mouthed kid who calls you names and criticizes everything about you, cooks dinner for you on your anniversary. And when you see the parents of one of your teenager's friends, they tell you what a pleasure it is to have your child visit their home.

Know that if your child did not feel so close to you, she would not need to work so hard to separate.

9

The Legacy of Infertility
One Family's Story

I see infertility as a life-cycle problem. It doesn't go away when
you have a child or when you raise that child. It sits there,
somewhere in the background. It comes up again when you
have — or don't have — grandchildren.

AT first it seems odd to hear Terry speaking so personally
about infertility. Terry is the mother of three young daughters, all conceived with ease. Her pregnancies were uncomfortable, but they were not complicated medically. She had an
unplanned pregnancy that ended in an early miscarriage and
another unplanned pregnancy that she elected to abort. Terry is
a woman who is familiar with the benefits, as well as some of the
special challenges, that come with being fertile. Even as she
speaks of infertility, she has an infant at her breast.

How is it that Terry can speak so personally about infertility?
Surely it is not a problem that has interfered with or in any way
compromised her own ability to build her family.

I grew up in the shadow of my mother's infertility. It was not some-
thing that she spoke of often but I always knew that it was there.
When I would ask her about it, she would avoid the subject. But
I knew that she spoke with other people about it.

Terry goes on to tell her mother's story. She was a bright,
capable woman who spent twelve years trying to conceive. The

time was the early fifties, and even though her mother sought the best medical care, little was known about infertility.

> My mother lived in a time when all the women had their children early in their twenties. So by the time that she was in her early thirties, all of her friends were busy with growing children. My mother dealt with her circumstances by carving out a new life for herself, one that was different from the one that she had planned on. She went back to school, completed a Ph.D., and entered medical school. She and my father got an apartment in Back Bay and became active in the arts in Boston.
>
> Around the time that my mother turned forty, she had some irregular bleeding. She went to her doctor who reportedly said to her, "I'm tired of your fibroids, I'm tired of your endometriosis, you've got a fast-growing tumor and your uterus has got to come out."

The "fast-growing tumor" became Terry. Although her mother agreed with her doctor that it was finally time to be rid of her uterus, she did consult with another doctor before undergoing surgery. To her complete astonishment, he had a different diagnosis: pregnancy.

> I believe that her pregnancy with me came at a time when she no longer wanted to become pregnant. By forty she had established a life for herself that she found satisfying. In those days it was weird to be a pregnant forty year old. The other forty-year-old women had long since had their children. My mother felt odd and different and I think that had abortion been more accessible, she would have chosen to end the pregnancy.

Despite her ambivalence about the pregnancy, Terry's mother went on to become a fine and loving mother. Nonetheless, Terry feels that difficulties stemming from the infertility remained. Often Terry had the feeling that she had once had more siblings and that she had killed them. She felt guilty about this and felt that she should not enjoy being an only child at their expense. How had she managed to survive when they did not? What was so special or so powerful about her? Terry remembers going through childhood with feelings and questions that she could never discuss with her mother.

Terry also remembers looking forward to being a mother herself and feeling that this was something else that she could not share with her mother. She felt that it would be too painful for her mother to have to recall her own longings.

> Although I identified with my mother in some ways, I did not anticipate that I would be infertile. Instead, I expected that I would have babies when I wanted to and that my fertility would separate me from my mother. When I did become pregnant, I said very little about it to my mother and we kept our distance. I missed being able to share the experience with her, but I understood that it was painful for her. When each of our children was born, my husband was the one who phoned my parents.

Terry's mother is now in her mid-seventies. The daughter she waited twelve years for is nearing her thirty-sixth birthday. Though separated by several hundred miles, mother and daughter visit often. When Terry and her husband want to have a few days away, they call on her parents to come and take care of the children.

> My mother and I came together after Rachel, my youngest daughter, was born. Mom came to help out with my older daughters while I was in the hospital and stayed for another week after I returned home. One morning we were all sitting at my kitchen table. My mother looked at each of my daughters and then at me. Then she said the most incredible thing. "To think that all these girls came from inside me." Amazing words from a woman who had seen herself as barren for her entire life!
>
> I guess that in some way my fertility has helped my mother to no longer see herself as a woman with a faulty womb. The fact that I had daughters, that all of us originated from her eggs, has been affirming. My mother is beginning to take real delight in her grandchildren. The woman who stood a bit aside when Hannah, our oldest, was a baby, now joins in with the feedings, the changings, the play, and the discipline. She is beginning to act like she feels she belongs.

Part

II

10

Domestic Adoption

Last Sunday night after Michael's seventh birthday party, I was picking up his room as he brushed his teeth. I said casually, "What was your favorite present?"
"You were," he answered.
"I was?" I asked.
"Yes, because you adopted me when I was zero."
I said, "You were my favorite present ever."

Jenny and I were in the pediatrician's office yesterday and there was a mother with a newborn. Jenny, who knows she was adopted and who understands what that means, began to ask me how babies are born. Suddenly I felt very sad. How strange that I could be there with the child who I love and cherish, still longing to have a full belly.

THESE are voices of adoptive parents. Most often they are couples who came to adoption with difficulty and after much disappointment. They wanted to have a child together and most went to great lengths to try to accomplish this. Although there are exceptions—those couples who were always comfortable, perhaps even enthusiastic, about the possibility of adoption—most people who eventually adopt struggle long and hard with whether this second choice is really second best.

I remember worrying a lot about whether we would feel like long-term baby-sitters. We imagined that it would always feel like we were taking care of someone else's child. Looking back it's hard to imagine that we could have felt that way.

Despite their questions, many infertile couples wade their way through a complex emotional and logistical process and become adoptive parents. Once there, they look back and wonder what all their questions were about. Most discover — to their relief and surprise — that adoptive parenting feels a good deal more comfortable than they had anticipated.

In the presence of a real child, couples are better equipped to understand and deal with some of the special challenges they face as adoptive parents. These challenges are complex and varied and are the subject of several books (see Resources and Readings). This chapter will simply present an overview of some of the themes that are likely to come up for adoptive parents and will identify issues that may arise in their families, including:

1. authenticity
2. ambivalence
3. talking with children about adoption
4. talking with others about adoption
5. questions of nature versus nurture
6. the relationship — in fact or feeling — with the birthparents
7. accepting and dealing with the normative crises
8. the need for a support group.

Authenticity

In the beginning, adoptive parents often have difficulty believing that they are real parents. In a sense, this is not surprising since they, like all other first-time parents, have spent many years not being parents. It is hard to imagine that anyone who has spent thirty to forty years or more not being a parent is likely to feel immediately comfortable in this new and enormously challenging role. However, biological parents feel less vulnerable in this regard, because they know that there are no other "candidates for the job." For newly adoptive parents, the fact that there are "other parents" out there serves as a threat to their sense of authenticity.

As time passes, adoptive parents report that questions of authenticity diminish or disappear entirely. The many and varied activities of daily parenting go a long way toward convincing them that they are very much "real mothers" or "real fathers." How can you help but feel like a real parent when you are getting up in the middle of the night to comfort a child frightened by a nightmare, or you are rushing home from work mid-morning because you just got a call that your son forgot his lunch? How could you doubt your role as parent when you are filling goody bags or sewing the Halloween costume that your junior designer created? Nonetheless, the way that adoption is viewed in our society—as something that is different and somewhat less than biological parenting—perpetuates the feeling that adoptive parents are not quite as real.

> I'm taken aback by the occasional, but still troubling, comments about her "real parents." I don't think people mean anything by it, but who do they think I am? Just the lady that fixes bloody noses and changes poopy diapers? I try to shrug off the references to "real" parents but they still leave me feeling uncomfortable. I guess that they tap into my lingering fears that she will someday feel that I am not her real mother.

Real parents is not the only term that troubles and confuses adoptive parents. Rather, adoption is surrounded by language that undermines the reality of the parenting and challenges the strength of adoptive connections. For example, well-meaning friends and family will make reference to having "one of your own," implying that adopted children are somehow not really yours, or they will say something about her "natural" parents, suggesting that adoption is somehow unnatural.

Until recently, adoption professionals did little to remedy the semantic difficulties in adoption. The terms *birthmother* and *birthfather* are now widely used, but not long ago people stumbled over *biological parents, surrendering parents,* and *the girl* when referring to the birthparents. Similarly, there are a host of unpleasant terms used to describe the process by which a child comes to be adopted: *given up, surrendered,* and *relinquished* all have negative connotations. These terms and the general absence of a clear and accepted language of adoption, have contributed to the uncertainty that newly adoptive parents have felt about their roles.

Ambivalence

All parents are ambivalent. All parents have moments when they hate their children, moments when they wish they could take a vacation from parenting. For adoptive parents the issue of ambivalence can be more complicated.

Adoptive parents have the option of "returning" the child that they adopt. While few exercise this option, or even seriously consider it, all know that it is there. Having it there can make the normal ambivalence that they feel more stressful.

It is the unthinkable. How could I ever consider returning the child who we worked so long and hard for? The child who we wanted so much? Of course I want her! Still, there are times when she exhausts me. I admit that at those times the thought of giving her up passes quickly through my mind. When it does, I feel frightened. I wish that option was never there.

Talking with Children about Adoption

Dr. Joyce Pavao, a psychologist who works with adoptive families, believes that there are certain "normative crises" that arise in all adoptive families. In most families, the first of these comes when parents begin to talk with their children about adoption.

When they are thinking about adopting, or preparing to adopt, couples often worry about how they will raise the subject of adoption with their children. Once they become parents, this seems less problematic. Adoption-related discussions are no longer something they are thinking about in the abstract, but rather they are part of a developing and enduring parent-child relationship. Nonetheless, there are certain things that all adoptive parents should consider as they prepare to talk with their children about adoption.

The first consideration for all adoptive parents is the age and developmental level of their child. A preschooler can learn the word *adoption* but has very little, if any, grasp of what it means. A six or seven year old understands how babies are born and can comprehend what adoption is. But it is not until a few years later that he realizes the loss that he has suffered. And it is a few years after that before a child understands the legal system and can view adoption as a lasting, legally secure relationship.

Probably as important as the child's level of understanding about adoption is the parent's level of comfort. Parents who have grappled with the loss involved and who have struggled with the ways in which adoption is different from biological parenting seem comfortable talking with their children. They have the sense that adoption discussions, challenging as they may be, occur in the context of a rich and resilient parent-child relationship.

> Before we adopted Amanda, I imagined that she and I would have these "big discussions" about adoption—formal conferences that would convene periodically. What has happened is something very different and ever so much more fun. Adoption comes up often one week and then not at all for several months. When we do discuss it, I always feel that it is in the broader context of our life together. It came up a few weeks ago because we met a family with four obviously foreign-born children. Then it came up this week because Amanda was talking about names and she asked me who had named her.

No matter how comfortable they are with their child and with the subject of adoption in general, some adoptive parents still face a very difficult task. Some parents have information they wish they did not have to tell their children, that they wish they could protect them from. These are parents whose children were conceived as a result of rape or incest or were abandoned, or they are children who have some problematic medical or psychiatric family history.

For these parents, talking about adoption involves talking about some very unsettling subjects. Aware of the dangers of keeping secrets, parents struggle with when and how to best share this information with their children. In her book, *Making Sense of Adoption,* adoption writer and educator Lois Melina offers useful instruction on how to talk with children about these and other complex subjects. She advises parents to pay careful attention to their child's age and level of understanding and to think carefully about the phrasing they use.

Some parents make use of the many children's books about adoption when they are talking with their children. Others find that there are enough adoption-related messages in popular children's stories such as *Superman* or *Peter Pan*. For them it seems somewhat forced or artificial to seek out special books on adoption.

> I have never bought my children any of the children's adoption books although I hear that some of them are quite good. It's not that I avoid them — or the issue — but rather it seems like adoption is everywhere. Both Sesame Street and Mr. Rogers did nice features on adoption that my children saw and enjoyed. Then my son got very involved in *Superman* and I realized that it is one of the most wonderful adoption stories of all. Superman's parents, who love him dearly, give him up so that he can lead a better life. I was delighted when my son decided to be Superman on Halloween; what a nice identification for a child who has been adopted.

There are also a number of real-life events that prompt and promote discussions about adoption. One event that is likely to prompt conversations about adoption is a child's entrance into school. Parents are often concerned that someone at school will reveal that the child is adopted. Consequently, many parents feel that they should give the child this information before someone else does.

> I was very glad that I had told Beth that she was adopted before she went to school. On the second day of school we had an interview with the school psychologist. With Beth right there he asked me how my pregnancy was. I tried to send daggers through my eyes when I said to him, "There was none!"

Adoptions in the family or the neighborhood are other events that are likely to promote discussions about adoption. One of the advantages of parents remaining in contact with other adoptive parents or infertile friends is that they are likely to know other people who are in the process of adoption. Their children have the opportunity to see families go through the anticipation and excitement of an arrival. These children see that adoption is a commonplace event and get the important message that they are not alone in being adopted.

By the time they are school age, most children want to have a pet. Obtaining a pet and bringing it home can certainly trigger off many adoption feelings and memories. Parents enjoy their children's excitement and enthusiasm as they become the newly adoptive parents of a puppy or a hamster, a kitten or a turtle.

> My five-year-old daughter came home from kindergarten and asked for a hamster. I was anything but thrilled with the idea until we went to the pet store and got Lucas. But to my surprise, I had fun watching Caroline become a proud "Mommy." And within a few hours I was totally attached to Lucas.
>
> While I hesitate to mention my daughter and a hamster in the same breath, Lucas's arrival brought back some happy memories and introduced some adoption talks. That night, when our exhausted little pet was sitting quietly, Caroline, the new and over-involved mother said, "Maybe Lucas is feeling sad—maybe he misses his first Mommy." From there we were able to move very comfortably into reminiscing about her arrival and the first days we spent together.

Talking with Others about Adoption

Before becoming parents few people realize how public their lives will be once they are "with child." An adult alone on a street or in a supermarket is never stopped by a stranger unless someone is asking for help or directions. By contrast, an adult with a young child, especially a new baby, is a public person. People do not hesitate to stop and comment, to try to play with the baby, to ask personal questions.

Newly adoptive parents find that they must distinguish between privacy and secrecy. Many feel compelled to respond to a stranger's, "Oh, what an adorable baby" with, "Yes, we adopted him" or to answer, "You look so thin for a new mother" with, "I wasn't pregnant, we adopted our baby." In an effort to avoid secrecy and the attendant sense of shame many newly adoptive parents relinquish privacy.

> I look back now and laugh at myself. No sooner would someone comment on my baby—as they inevitably did—than I would blurt out, "she's adopted." It was a real compulsion with me—kind of a

diarrhea of the mouth. I'm pleased to say that I've gotten over that
need. Now I simply smile and say "thank you."

Adoptive parents must also distinguish between acknowledging differences and insisting on them. In his landmark 1964 book,
Shared Fate, H. David Kirk found that adoptive families did better
when they were able to acknowledge differences rather than
reject them. However, many adoptive parents, in an effort to
follow Kirk's advice, end up going too far and doing what Dr.
David Brodzinsky has called "insisting on differences." These
families talk about adoption too much, conveying the message
that adoption is, indeed, *very* different.

Most adoptive parents realize that there is usually no reason to
tell strangers on the street that their child is adopted. But what
of others? Should they tell their child's school? What about day
camp? Should they mention it to the parents of their children's
friends? These are among the many questions that adoptive
parents consider as their child begins to interface more with the
world outside their home.

> I was really troubled by my daughter's elementary school admis-
> sions form. There was a direct question on it, "Is your child
> adopted?" I am in no way ashamed that she is adopted but I also
> feel that it is our business and no one else's. So I answered "No"
> to the question and ever since then I've felt very uncomfortable. I
> don't like to lie and I keep wondering if anyone at school has
> figured out the truth.

> I feel very strongly that I do not want to tell Tessa's school that she
> is adopted. My wife is a teacher and she has told me about the ways
> in which some teachers are biased against adopted children. They
> tend to see a lot of what goes on as the result of the child's adop-
> tion. We are very open about the fact that Tessa is adopted but I
> feel that we cannot be open and honest with her school.

Adoptive parents are concerned that information they tell
others about their child may be repeated back to her in a way that
is hurtful or harmful. Other children can be very cruel—intentionally or unintentionally—and often their parents demonstrate
even more insensitivity. Most adoptive parents recognize that

they cannot shield their children from cruel commentary but that by paying attention to who and what they tell, they can help to limit what is said.

> My daughter came home from school and said that one of the other children said that she was sold. I asked her how she responded and she said, "I told her that I was not sold, that I was adopted." I asked her how the other child responded to this, and she said "She told me that even if I'm adopted, I was still sold."

In the beginning, many adoptive parents are surprised at how challenging it is to keep their child's personal information private. While acquaintances would not ask most people about the specifics of their family backgrounds, people do not hesitate to ask a lot of adoptive parents, "What do you know about her background?" "Do you know how old her birthmother is?" "Do you know where they live, if they went to college, what their medical and psychiatric histories are?" Few pause before asking these and other equally intrusive questions.

Again, personal is personal. What is personal is not necessarily a secret but it is private. People may feel that they have license to ask all sorts of questions but that does not mean that adoptive parents are obligated to answer them. To the contrary, many adoptive parents feel that they have a responsibility to their child to protect his privacy.

> At first it was awkward, especially with our infertile friends. We were delighted with all the information that we got about Seth's background and wanted to tell everyone how lucky we were. But we felt that we owed it to him to wait until he was old enough to understand and appreciate what the information meant. If at that time he wanted to tell people about his ancestry that was fine — but that was his place, not ours.
>
> Anyway, it was easier said than done. We found that the response that we developed for most people — "We're pleased with Seth's background, but feel that it is private" — just didn't feel right for our infertile friends. We had all shared so much together and now it felt like we were suddenly changing the rules. We stewed about it and then concluded that we had to put Seth's future feel-

ings first. We had every right to tell the world the details of each IVF attempt, but we did not have his consent to publicize his history.

Another reason why some adoptive parents are reluctant to talk about their child's history has to do with their awareness that adoptive parents are sometimes told what the teller feels they want to hear. Adoptive parents realize, when they begin to compare notes, that many other adoptive parents have also been told that their child was born to an attractive and bright college student and her medical school boyfriend. Some adoptive parents are troubled by this and feel that they are being duped in the same way that adoptees were when they were told, years ago, that their birthparents were killed in a car accident or in the war.

Adoptive parents have to educate people about adoption. Adoptive parents who may not otherwise be activists are sometimes troubled by the things they hear from people who are not personally involved with adoption. They are troubled by the language that is used, such as *real parents,* and by the bias that people sometimes demonstrate. Adoptive parents sometimes feel compelled to protect and defend adoption and other adoptive families.

> I was with some of the mothers of Laura's classmates. They were talking about one of the other children, who is adopted. Unaware that Laura is also adopted, they were blaming some of the child's problems on her adoption. I found myself in a real bind. I didn't want to tell them about Laura because I felt that it was invading her privacy and also because I feared that she, too, would be treated with prejudice. At the same time, however, how could I stand by and let ignorant people malign adoption?

> As an adoptive father I try to teach people gently how to talk about adoption. Since my wife and I had a baby together after we adopted, people will frequently comment that "we're so lucky to have one of our own." I try not to put them off but explain that whether you bear or adopt a child it is your "own." Similarly, when someone will say, "Oh, they look so much like brothers" I say, again trying to remain calm and gentle, "They really are brothers." I believe that people are not ill-intentioned, but rather they are unfamiliar with adoptive relationships.

Questions of Nature versus Nurture

When they are considering adoption, couples often struggle with the question of how much impact they will have on their child's personality, character, intelligence, and interests. They wonder which characteristics can be influenced environmentally. A long-standing fear among adoptive couples has been that they will end up with a "bad seed."

> We worried that we would provide a loving and intellectually stim-
> ulating home but that we'd have a child who still couldn't thrive
> there. We feared that we would get a child of limited intelligence
> who simply didn't fit in. We feel grateful to have ended up with a
> son who is certainly as bright and talented and curious as any child
> who we could have produced, but I can still understand why we felt
> as we did ahead of time.

Although adoptive parents know that much of parenting is "nurture" and not "nature," there is growing evidence supporting the significance of genes. There are large, ongoing studies in Sweden and Finland of identical twins reared separately. These studies have revealed that genes influence a wide range of human characteristics.

What does this mean for adoptive parents? How do they react to the widely-publicized findings that children come with a genetic package that guides them in many areas of their lives? Ahead of time, many couples find this notion frightening. For some it brings back old fears of the "bad seed," and prompts them to revisit some of their concerns about adoption. Nonetheless, most couples do go ahead and adopt. Once their child is in their home, the role of genes usually becomes a diminished concern. Like other parents, adoptive parents recognize that their children come into this world with certain characteristics and abilities and that one of the tasks of parenthood is to help a child enjoy and make the most of what she was given.

> I have read some of the recent studies about the influence of gene-
> tics and find myself curiously unphased by them. I suppose that

this is because my children are my children, whatever they may or may not have inherited. Sure, if I were to dwell on it, I could become frightened that my daughter has some dread disease in her family background or that my son will never be much of a student. But as much as I am a worrier, I can't think of it that way. They are my children and whoever they are and will become, they are part of our family. Part of the fun of parenting is watching children emerge as real people.

The Relationship—In Fact or Feeling— With the Birthparents

Joyce Pavao notes that when you adopt a child, you enter into some relationship with the child's birthparents: they are, and will remain, part of his family. What adoptive parents need to figure out—and this is usually an evolving process that occurs over time—is what the nature of that relationship will be. Sometimes they are able to do this in active collaboration with the birthparents; often it is a something that they must sort out on their own.

A discussion of open versus closed adoption—and all the ramifications of each—goes far beyond the scope of this book. However, because they are two very different experiences, it is important to pause here for a moment and briefly mention the key differences between them.

A closed adoption, which, until very recent years, was the format of most nonrelative adoptions in this country, involves anonymity. In a closed adoption, efforts are made to protect the confidentiality of the birthparents and the adoptive parents. The premise here is that this will make it easier for both sets of parents, as well as the child, to go on with their lives. Neither set of parents will have to fear interference from the other. And children, presumably, will not be confused as to who their parents are. Birthparents and adopting couples who have a strong need for privacy or who feel that this format will help them establish clear boundaries in their family choose closed adoption.

Open adoption, which has become much more popular in recent years, rejects the idea that anonymity is helpful in adoption. Birthparents and couples who choose open adoption believe that both families will feel more comfortable knowing each other. Birthparents take comfort in knowing and often choosing the parents of the child they conceive and carry. Adoptive parents feel reassured to know their birthparents as real people and not to have them sitting in the background as some dark mystery.

When they are deciding on an agency or other adoption program, couples give a great deal of thought to what form of adoption best suits their personality and family styles. Although infertile couples often approach adoption fearful of the birthparents, many find that as they proceed with the process, their fears diminish greatly or vanish. Some couples discover that as time goes on, they are more comfortable with greater openness.

The degree to which an adoption is open or closed will influence the discussions that parents will have with their children regarding the birthparents. Parents who know the birthparents or who have substantial information about them can feel more comfortable filling in the pieces of a real story when they feel their child is ready to hear them. Parents who know little if anything about the birthparents face the more difficult task of having to respond to their children without answers.

> For me the hardest part of the discussions with Emily is the lack of information. Since she is only seven, I don't think she is ready or able to handle a lot of details about her history. Still, I wish that I had a few more basic facts, such as her birthparents' first names and perhaps, their occupations. It's very hard having Emily refer to her birthmother as "the other lady," and I don't feel much better calling her "your birthmother." I find it very hard to explain to Emily that I really don't know the names of the two people who played such a vital role in all our lives.

Whether they pursue open or closed adoption most adopting couples find that they develop very positive feelings toward their child's birthparents. In fact, these positive feelings may be an essential ingredient in the adoption process because they set the stage for a strong, positive attachment to the child. What most adopting parents realize is that just as they have suffered the loss of their biological child, so, also, have the birthparents suffered the loss of *their* child. Theirs is, indeed, a shared fate.

> My most poignant moment was when I was the tooth fairy for the second time. The first time my daughter lost a tooth I was too busy adjusting to my new role as tooth fairy to give much thought to her first parents. But the second time around was different. I was standing there in the middle of the night, holding a tooth that I had no idea what to do with, and I realized that there were some people out there who would probably be thrilled to have it. It was very hard having no means of sharing it with them.

Some adoptive parents acknowledge that along with positive feelings toward the birthparents are some uncomfortable and competitive feelings. They admit to fears that if their children ever search they will find parents they like better. They identify the traits in themselves they see as least desirable and imagine that the birthparents would be better in these areas.

As adoption is changing along with definitions of family, adoptive parents are exploring new ways for them to relate with birthparents. Groups such as Adoptive Parents for Open Records, Inc. (APFOR), a nationwide volunteer organization of adoptive families, are working toward helping adoptive parents and birthparents to better integrate their roles in a child's life and with each other. APFOR supports open adoption as well as open records, feeling that this is a vital means of promoting the dignity of all those involved in the adoption process. APFOR tries to dispel what it considers to be common myths in adoption—that birthparents should be feared, that a child who grows up in a loving home will have no need to search, that adoptive parents can "replace" birthparents.

In thinking about birthparents, adoptive parents should also be aware of groups such as Combined United Birthparents (CUB), an organization of birthparents committed to adoption reform. CUB focuses on protecting the rights of birthparents and works actively toward adoption reform. Like APFOR it is working toward changing adoption practice, hoping that removing the aura of secrecy will help all those involved in the adoption process.

Accepting and Dealing with the Normative Crises

Today's adoptive parents clearly work hard to do it right. Keenly aware of the mistakes of past generations, couples adopting today try to be open and honest with themselves, as well as with their children. Most have worked hard to resolve their infertility before moving on to adoption.

Neither the efforts of adoptive parents nor their enlightenment can protect them and their families from the difficulties inherent in adoption. Joyce Pavao calls them the normative crises to dispel the myth that something is wrong in adoptive families. But the fact that they are normative does not lessen the pain involved.

The first normative crisis commonly arises when parents begin to talk with their child about adoption. Parents who feel comfortable with the subject and with the way that they tell their child may be surprised by the child's reaction. Dr. Pavao points out that as adults we have no way of predicting how a child will understand or make sense of information that is given to her.

A second normative crisis often arises when children enter grade school. This is a time when a number of adoptees are thought to have learning problems. Many are now being diagnosed as having attention deficit disorder (ADD). These children need to have a good assessment by someone who really understands adoption and adoptive families. Some adoptees do have ADD or other learning problems, but some of what parents and teachers see may have more to do with the child's confusion about adoption. A child may be so distracted by internal questions that he is unable to focus. Or a child may have certain learning problems specifically related to adoption. Dr. Pavao tells the poignant story of an adopted child who had difficulty learning subtraction. When this was explored, it turned out that the boy was so afraid of things being taken away that he could not learn to subtract.

The third major crisis time in adoptive families is in adolescence. Here adoptees are struggling to establish their identities amid divided loyalties. While nonadoptees must sort out how they are like their parents and how they differ, adoptees face the ever-so-much-more-complicated task of sorting out who they are in relationship to their birthparents as well, parents whom they, most likely, have never known. This process is painful for them and for their adoptive parents, who find that old feelings about authenticity and infertility reappear.

> The last few years have been very painful for me. First I lost both my parents. Then my sister died, leaving me with no close blood relatives. Soon after that, my husband and I were divorced. He remarried and went on to have a child with his new wife. Then I remarried, and my new husband and I decided that we too would try to have a child. In the midst of all this, my two children, whom we adopted as infants, hit adolescence.
>
> In the past year, my children have grappled with questions of identity. My daughter goes out of her way to dress and act as different as she can from me. My son is less polarized, but he too makes an effort to state who he is and is not.
>
> I know that much of what my children are going through is normal adolescence, but still I feel that for all of us things have gotten jumbled up. My renewed efforts to have a baby, which included IVF and GIFT, met with no success and left me feeling all the more damaged and defective. The birth of my former husband's new baby left me sad and envious and seems to have stirred up feelings in both my teenagers that they aren't good enough. And their increased efforts to separate have confronted me, in a most painful way, with the differences between us.

The next crisis point usually comes around leaving home. Dr. Pavao reports that some adoptees are so paralyzed by the threat of loss that they cannot leave home at all. They can express this in a range of ways. Some choose maladaptive means, such as acting out in a way that makes it impossible for them to leave, and others are more straightforward, choosing a college or a job that is close to home. Some adoptees express their ambivalence about leaving home by electing to go far away.

> When it came time for Steven to pick a college, I was surprised to find that the same kid who would never leave home to go to summer camp, even though he loved sports, was eager to go to school in California (we live in New York). I felt that he was making some

kind of statement to himself and to us that he needed to get very far away in order to find himself. I was not at all surprised when he stayed there only one semester and then transferred to one of our local commuter schools.

Another crisis in adoptive families comes when children marry and consider having families of their own. For many adoptees this is the time they feel a need to search. The prospect of a pregnancy or the birth of their first child prompts some adoptees to feel an intense longing to know someone who is physically connected to them. Some adoptees undertake a full-fledged search for their birthparents; others take more gradual, hesitant steps.

Each of these pivotal points in the adoptee's life stirs up feelings for adoptive parents. It is a challenge to all adoptive parents to respond empathically to their children when they are feeling so vulnerable themselves. This is where the concept of a shared fate can be especially helpful.

Adoptive parents, their child, and their child's birthparents do, indeed, have a shared fate. Had any of them had their first choice in life, they would not be together in the adoption triangle. Birthparents would not have chosen to have children they could not raise. Adoptive parents would have preferred to give birth to their children. And adoptees would surely not volunteer to live with the identity confusion that accompanies the knowledge that you have been adopted.

When they are at odds, when the going gets rough, adoptive parents and their children can hopefully find some comfort in feeling that they came together through fate. Unlike biological families, which are formed without question, adoptive families are usually the result of a great deal of pain and soul-searching. Like biological parents, adoptive parents often feel that fate brought them their child. They find that theirs is a special kinship.

Ahead of time I pictured it as almost an adversarial process. I had the strange idea that my adopted child and I would be opponents: that the fact of her adoption would prevent us from ever having a close relationship. Now that we are in it together, I realize that the fact of her adoption, while problematic in some ways, does not put a wedge between us. Rather, it is something we have in common. We came together after each of us had suffered an enormous loss. That we survived the loss and became a family is something that we will always share and which, I believe, will help us to stay close.

It has not been easy and I have surely felt angry and cheated many times along the way. "Why me?" I have asked. "Why him?" How did we end up together and was this ever meant to be? "Why us?"

Yesterday was one of those days when I had my answer. It had been a particularly rough day and I was crying when Doug walked in the house. He's been difficult and defiant lately, so I wasn't exactly pleased to see him. I expected that he'd only say or do something that would make things worse. But that was not what happened. When he saw me crying, he came over, put his arm around me and said, "Mom, it looks like you need a hug. Mom, I hope you know that I love you."

It has not been easy, but the rewards are there and they are sustaining.

The Need for a Support Group

Although adoption is common, perhaps increasingly so, adoptive parents are still in the minority. They still feel different from other parents and many find it helpful to have ongoing contact, either formally or informally, with other adoptive parents.

Some adoptive parents have no difficulty finding a support network. They meet other adoptive parents when they are in the process of adopting and they maintain those relationships over time. Depending on their children's ages and their own life-styles, they may get together socially as couples, or form a mothers' group or a play group with their children.

When I was going through infertility, I joined a RESOLVE support group. I became very close with several of the women in the group and after the group officially ended, our subgroup decided to continue meeting together on our own. Then I adopted Megan and was afraid that they would not want me to continue. In fact, the opposite happened! Others saw me as a trailblazer and wanted me to be there as they, too, got ready to move on to adoption.

As it turned out, we were all mothers within a year. Since then we have continued to meet, sometimes with all of our children, sometimes just women. Our children are growing rapidly and now we are all beginning to make plans for second adoptions. We moved from a group of women talking about Pergonal shots to one talking about homestudies. Now we talk about the things about adoption that concern us, as well as about those that delight us.

Adoptive parents, who do not have a natural peer group, as well as those who wish to be more active in adoption, may be interested in joining an adoptive parents organization. The Open Door Society in Massachusetts is one such organization. It offers meetings and social gatherings for adoptive parents, as well as an informative newsletter. Another increasingly active and involved adoption organization is Stars of David, now with chapters in most states and in twelve foreign countries. Since December 1984, Stars of David has served Jewish and partly Jewish adoptive families. These are but a few of the many groups that adoptive parents have formed to find companionship and to share their experiences.

Adoption is undoubtedly complicated. Those involved in it come with a history of losses, the legacy of which plays some part in their experience together. Adoption in our society also carries with it a history of misunderstanding, deception, and prejudice. Nevertheless, things are changing. Today's adoptive and birthparents, together with some pioneering professionals, are working actively to remedy the problems in adoption practice — in its language, its customs, and its stigmas. Living in a society that has an increasing capacity to accept differences, adoptive families are discovering that underneath a bedrock of shame are kinships to celebrate.

Rob and Jane:
From Generation to Generation

When I was trying to conceive, I used to cry over what it would mean to Rob if we didn't have a baby together. I felt that as an adoptee he had a special need to have someone in this world of his own flesh and blood. I felt that he would feel a profound sense of loss if we adopted. What I didn't foresee was how affirming it would be for him to have a child enter our family the way that he had entered his.

Rob and Jane are now the proud parents of Ruthie and Alex, ages five and three. Both children came to them through private adoption. Ruthie arrived after a long, difficult struggle with infertility that included surgery and the use of potent fertility drugs. Somewhere along the way, Rob and Jane both reached the point at which they felt it was time to move on to adoption.

> Among the fears that we had about adoption was that it would take forever. I had worked in a family-service agency that did adoptions, and I remembered couples waiting five, six, even seven years for a white baby. I had visions of that happening to us. We were delighted when we contacted a lawyer specializing in private adoption and he told us that it would take six months to a year. We were all the more pleased when he phoned us with a baby three weeks later!

Rob and Jane have many joyous memories of Ruthie's arrival. However, both agree that their favorite moment came when they phoned Rob's mother and told her the news. Not only was she thrilled to be a grandmother, but she was especially touched that her first grandchild was adopted. She told Rob and Jane that it took her back thirty-four years and helped her to relive Rob's arrival.

> I felt that it did something for Rob as well. He had always heard the happy stories of his arrival but this was his opportunity to really feel the pleasure that his parents felt when he entered their family. I think that this is one of the reasons that he and Ruthie have such a special bond.

Jane looks back at this juncture and wonders why it ever felt so important to her to have a biological child. She feels that her family history, as well as Rob's, makes her well suited to be an adoptive parent. As the daughter of two holocaust survivors, she has no medical history on any of her relatives other than her parents.

Whenever I go to a doctor I am always troubled by the questions about inherited conditions. I have to tell them that I don't know whether any diseases run in my family because no one lived long enough to get them. In this regard, I'm very much like Rob: I have no idea what I did or did not inherit.

And Rob adds

I agree with Jane that it is very strange to go to a doctor and have them ask those questions. It was always especially hard for me because my brother, Ted, was born into our family when I was five. When my mom would take us to the doctor I felt really funny. She'd go on about the family history with no mention of the fact that I was adopted.

As an adult this took a nice twist. Ted and I were talking about a medical problem that he had and he told me, in a completely off-hand way, that he always included my medical history when he was having a physical. I laughed about this, but it really touched me. I realized then that both he and my mom felt so connected to me that it barely occurred to them that we had different genes.

Jane and Rob identify the day that they took Ruthie to the *mikvah* (Jewish ritual baths) and had her converted to Judaism as another high point in their lives. While neither is an especially observant Jew, they do feel that Judaism is their link with the generations that came before them as well as with those that will follow. Having Ruthie officially converted was a way of establishing and affirming her place in their extended families. They both feel that it will be important for Ruth and Alex to have religious educations and to grow up with strong and clear Jewish identities.

Perhaps it wouldn't matter so much to us had they not been adopted. But because we converted them we can never take their Judaism for granted. We see it as a gift that all of us share and feel that religious observance will be strengthening and sustaining in our family.

Rob and Jane feel very grateful to his parents, now both deceased, for providing them with a model by which they can handle adoption in their family. His parents were always open and enthusiastic, so much so that it would have been hard for Rob to grow up not feeling good about his adoption. He remembers how his mother told and retold of the joy that she felt when he arrived.

Rob has not felt a need or interest to search for his birth family. However, Jane teases him about the career that he chose: genetics. She feels that he found a creative and adaptive way of dealing with his feelings about his own adoption.

> I feel that we bring a history and a legacy from our families that makes adoption very comfortable for us. When Ruth was a baby I made up a song about adoption that I began to sing to her. "This is who we know who's adopted . . ." Whenever I get to the end of the long list of adoptees who we know, including, of course, her father and brother, she adds my name. Ruth has a hard time understanding that a member of her family could NOT be adopted.
>
> I feel confident that Ruth and Alex will grow up with a strong sense that being adopted is a very natural way to be. We feel very grateful to our children's birthparents, and to the lawyers that helped bring them to us, for making all of us a family.

11

International Adoption

We really enjoy being an international family. Sure people
stare at us when we go places, but we don't mind it. We feel
that they are simply curious or quietly admiring.

When Ian was a baby we were wheeling him in his stroller and
a woman stopped us and said, "Oh what a beautiful baby! How
much did you pay for him?" It was so absurd that all we could
do was laugh.

THESE are voices of parents who have adopted internationally.
Usually they are people who enjoy and celebrate differences. Often they have lived abroad and feel a tie to a particular
culture. Or they have read and studied about a part of the world
and feel drawn to it. Faced with infertility, they see foreign adoption as offering them new, often unanticipated opportunities.

Even before we learned of our infertility, we thought and talked
about international adoption. I had spent some time in South
America while I was in medical school and left there feeling a special connection to the children. I can remember having fantasies
then, as a young and single medical student, of adopting a child
and bringing her home with me.

Not all couples who are excited by the prospect of an international family go on to adopt children from another culture.
Some realize, when they think seriously about it, that they are not
equipped to parent a child who will always look different from

them. For some this has to do with anticipating how they will feel when their child is an adolescent or adult. They can imagine themselves with a cute little Asian daughter, but get stuck when they try to picture her as an adult. Others decide that much as they would welcome a foreign child, the communities they live in, or perhaps their families, would be rejecting of the child. Finally, there are those who conclude they would have difficulty raising a child with a dual cultural identity.

> Liz and I were both very excited by the prospect of adopting a child from India. We both feel an interest in and tie to Indian culture. But all four of our parents are alive and well and sitting by the pool in Florida. When we told them of our plan they made it clear that the child would not be welcome at the condominium.

> We wanted to adopt internationally but had a hard time figuring out how we would integrate another culture with our strong Jewish identity. We know people who have done it and we even spoke with them. But for us it felt like it wouldn't work. We couldn't imagine helping a thirteen-year-old Korean or Colombian son prepare for his bar mitzvah.

Hopefully, couples who do go on to adopt internationally have carefully considered all of these issues and have concluded that none are sufficient reasons for altering their course. Those who decide to make a lifetime commitment to a child need to be well aware of the challenges involved. This chapter will identify some of the special features of international adoption, including:

1. adopting an older baby or older child
2. the long-distance journey
3. raising bicultural children
4. dealing with society's reactions
5. medical concerns
6. international sibling group adoption

Adopting an Older Baby or Older Child

Although some prospective adoptive parents prefer to adopt a child who is not a newborn, most couples considering adoption want to begin with a very young baby. This is not always possible with international adoption, both because most of the children available for adoption are not newborns, and also because delays in immigration advance the age of the child.

> For many reasons we really wanted to adopt from Korea. It was therefore very upsetting for us to learn that the program we were working with defined a "baby" as any child under two. We knew we would be disappointed if we got a child that was over a year. But feeling that we had no choice, we went ahead and applied, hoping for the best. The "best" did happen and we got Jared when he was eight months old.

> We received word that Marianna was ours when she was three months old. We were initially ecstatic, but our happiness faded when we learned that it would be at least six weeks before she could leave Peru. When six weeks turned into nine weeks, I felt really frustrated. I can remember spending the summer walking around with a picture and envying the other mothers who were out with their babies. It was so hard to think that Marianna was also waiting and to know that the wait was probably harder on her than it was on me.

International parents have feelings not only about what they have missed out on but also about what it means for their children to spend time in an orphanage or foster home. Those who try to adopt them at a very young age often fear that there will be consequences for their children as a result of the delays.

> Christopher was fifteen months old when he came to us. We noticed early on that he seemed to have no separation anxiety—he went so readily to strangers. That behavior may have been adaptive for him in the orphanage, but it was not appropriate once he had a home. It took him about six months to develop enough of an attachment to us that he had a hard time leaving us. When it finally happened, we were glad to see it!

Another reason why families adopt a child who is older than they would have preferred has to do with the ages of the parents. Some intercountry programs set a limit on the age of the parents, saying that there cannot be more than forty years, for example, between either parent and the child. In such circumstances, a couple in which either parent is forty-three would have to adopt a child three or older. For some couples this involves a compromise they do not feel prepared to make, and they decide to adopt through a different intercountry program or to adopt domestically. However, many couples find that once they struggle with the question, they are able to accept the age limitations and adjust to the prospect of parenting an older child.

> At first we felt angry and resented the "age discrimination." It felt so unfair, especially after all that we had been through. But realizing that there was little we could do to change the rules, we decided that the best thing we could do for ourselves was to accept them. We began thinking of some of the advantages of starting out with a toddler and actually got into the idea. When our daughter arrived, at two and one-half, we felt ready, prepared, and very excited.

The Long-Distance Journey

An international placement is often completed in one or two years (it varies from country to country and program to program), not a terribly long time for an adoption. However, the process of adopting internationally can be complex and stressful. Couples may have to travel to the child's country of origin, and some are forced to involve themselves in legal and bureaucratic complexities. It is not unusual for a couple to end up spending several weeks, perhaps even months, away from home, waiting to bring their child home with them.

Although the adoption process does go smoothly for some, others encounter obstacles. Couples have been known to be assigned a baby who has a serious medical problem they were not prepared for. Adoptions have also fallen through due to some political upset or unrest or for other, often less clear, reasons. Parents sometimes come home with a different baby than originally assigned.

> To this day we have no idea what happened to the little boy from El Salvador who was to be our son. This is painful, because as much as we are a family—complete and happy—we still care for him. It seems like a strange twist of fate that the political situation

in his country prevented us from getting to him. We think about whether we might have rescued him and brought him to a better life. We wonder where he is and we hope that he is well.

Because their journey to parenthood can be arduous and span many miles, parents who adopt internationally frequently refer to their families as miraculous. They do not take their children for granted, nor do they take the fact that they found each other and came together as a family as a given. They are acutely aware that there were many other possible endings to their story.

When I look in the mirror and see myself with Elena I feel that it is amazing that we are together. I think of all the other lives she could have led, all the other children who could have become ours, all the miles that each of us traveled and realize that this is, indeed, a miracle.

Raising Bicultural Children

Couples who adopt internationally do so with appreciation—and usually enthusiasm—for the importance of maintaining their child's dual cultural identity. They are people who are interested in other cultures and who enjoy learning about the history and customs of their children's countries of origin. They see their children's knowledge of their cultural background as central to the formation of a strong and cohesive identity.

At seven, my daughter feels a great deal of pride in her Colombian background. She likes to try Colombian foods, wear Colombian clothes, and she plans to begin studying Spanish in a few years. I enjoy her enthusiasm and hope that it will offer her a very solid foundation as she develops and explores her identity. Since it will be very difficult for her to search for her biological parents, I am glad that she feels such a strong sense of roots in her Colombian background.

International parents find different ways of acknowledging and maintaining their child's other heritage. For some, this is a very active process. Foods and clothing from South America or India or Korea become part of home and family life. Others invite their children's other culture in more occasionally, perhaps on holidays or when they are getting together with other international families. Whatever their style, most parents of foreign-born children see themselves in a process that is ongoing and evolving, in which they are exploring how to best integrate two cultures.

International families often make a point of getting together with each other, either in organizations such as Latin American Adoptive Families (LAAF) or informally, with others they met through their agency or in a preadoptive parents group or class. Many feel strongly that both they and their children benefit from these visits.

> It has been very important for us to get together with other families with Korean children, more so for our kids than for us. We enjoy getting to know other adoptive parents but find that for our children, the gatherings are much more than a social event. For them these times offer an affirmation that there are lots of other international families. They are so reassured to meet other kids who look like them and who have parents who look like us. For them the gatherings say "You are not different; we are not different."

Dealing With Society's Reactions

Couples who adopt children of another race anticipate that others will notice, question, and comment on differences. Those who go ahead with an international adoption generally feel equipped to handle the responses of others and prepare themselves for the fact that some exchanges may be upsetting. Nonetheless, they may not appreciate how public they will be once they have a child.

> I knew that it would be difficult, but I don't think that we were ever really prepared for just how difficult it would be. My wife and I are both fair, with blue eyes, and we have four Korean children. Wherever we go and whatever we do, people stare. We've learned to accept it and regard it as part of being who we are—an international family. Still, there are times when I do wish that we could go someplace and not be looked at, that we could occasionally resume our identity as private citizens.

Parents of foreign-born children must not only prepare for the comments, questions, and looks they will get from other adults, but they must also figure out how they will deal with the things that people will say to their children. Parents of Asian girls, for example, have noted that people often react to them as though they are "cute little Oriental dolls." Some worry that their daughters will try to act like little dolls in an effort to please others.

Parents of foreign-born children are sometimes surprised by the racism that exists within our society. While most of the comments they get simply reflect people's curiosity or ignorance, occasionally there are commentators who are deliberately cruel. Parents need to find ways of protecting themselves and their child from these comments.

> For the most part, strangers, as well as friends, have been supportive of the way that we have formed our family. When we are out together, people will stop us and make comments, usually saying things like "You have beautiful kids" or "We have good friends who also have Korean children." I find them intrusive, but most of the time I feel that they mean well. But then along comes someone who takes me completely off guard and says something horrible. I try to tell myself that some people are simply ignorant, but their comments do hurt and I wonder how they will affect Anna when she gets older.

Parents of foreign-born children also have to deal with the fact that society responds differently to young children than to preteens and adolescents. When their children are young, these parents may field frequent comments and questions of curious strangers, but often they also have a sense that their children are accepted. In fact, some report that friends and neighbors are enthusiastic about their children, eager for their own children to have multicultural friends. However, things can change as children get older. Foreign-born adoptees may get a more mixed reception when they reach adolescence.

> My son had a wonderful experience in elementary school. He had lots of friends and did well academically. I felt that he was accepted for who he is and that people did not make much note of the fact that he is Korean. Therefore it was a real shock for us when he

entered high school. Some of the mothers of girls in his class phoned me and made it clear that although Craig is a nice boy he had better not have any ideas about dating their daughters.

It was a shock to Marcy to go away to school and find that the other kids saw her as an Asian. It was not that we denied her Korean background in our family but we live in a small, primarily lily-white New England town where there are not many Asians. We made some efforts to introduce Korean culture into our home, but mostly we lived as a white family. When we traveled, people would sometimes look at us with curiosity; but in our home town, we were simply accepted as a family—a socially active and prominent family.

   When Marcy arrived at college, the other students did not react to her as an upper middle class New England WASP. Instead, they thought that she was an immigrant from Korea or, some thought, Viet Nam. I think that for several months it jolted her identity: Marcy realized that part of separating from us involved making a major shift in her perception of herself.

Medical Concerns

Parents of children adopted internationally sometimes face some special challenges medically. There are specific medical problems that are associated with different countries. For example, Korean children are sometimes Hepatitis-B carriers, and children who come from South and Central America may have parasites. Couples adopting internationally should know that their child could have medical problems that will need to be attended to shortly after arrival.

   International parents face the additional challenge of raising children who come with an incomplete medical history. In some instances adoption agencies are able to provide parents with an extensive medical history on their children, but for others information is scanty. Often parents adopt children whose age and birthday is unknown. Furthermore, international parents seldom have the opportunity for medical updates. As their children grow, there is limited access to information about conditions and diseases that may be inherited.

The first challenge that we faced after Alana's arrival was trying to determine what grade she belonged in in school. Certainly there were questions about language and her learning level, but we also faced the more basic question of trying to figure out her age. The records from the agency were entirely unclear. Fortunately, doctors at Children's Hospital (in Boston) were able to determine her age for us through tests and physical examination.

Parents of foreign adoptees usually accept their lack of medical information. In fact, some state that they were actually drawn to foreign adoption because of the anonymity that it offered and recognize that an absence of information often accompanies anonymity. But even those who would have liked to know more seem to have developed some degree of comfort with circumstances.

Our infertility taught us that life is unpredictable. None of us ever know what is really going to happen and those that think they do suffer from an illusion. So who is to say that it helps to know that you may have inherited heart disease or diabetes? We try to eat well, live wisely, and to be prepared to handle as best we can any medical curve balls that come our way.

Although there are difficult aspects of international adoption, couples who begin or expand their families in this manner are usually very enthusiastic about the choice they have made. Life has taken them down roads less traveled and most feel lucky to find themselves there. They find that international adoption has enriched their lives in unexpected ways.

Suzanne and Bill:
Some Unexpected Pleasures

In a strange sort of way, I'm glad that I was infertile. Had I not been, I would never have lived such an interesting life.

The interesting life that Suzanne refers to has centered around the adoption of her older child, Alex, from Paraguay. Suzanne notes, with some curiosity and amusement, that she had never even heard of Paraguay five or six years ago. Now she has not only traveled there, but she has an expanding network of families who also have children from Paraguay.

> When we first returned from Paraguay, I made contact with one couple in a nearby town whom I had heard had a daughter from Paraguay. The following year we got together with four families. This Sunday, I'm having a barbecue for thirty families, all of whom have children from Paraguay!

Although Suzanne and Bill are delighted with their family, which also includes Lissa who was born to them last year, they acknowledge that it was not easy getting to where they are now. They married when Suzanne was twenty-one and Bill was thirty-nine, and because of Bill's age, they began to try to have children immediately. What followed was five years of frustrating and demoralizing efforts at diagnosis and treatment.

> They never really found much of anything wrong with us, which may explain why I did eventually become pregnant. We went through the GIFT procedure twice, and I had husband insemination many times. Over time we became very discouraged. I had always liked the idea of adoption and with Bill over forty, I felt strongly that we should not delay. Five years into infertility, I began calling around and initiated a serious look into adoption.

Suzanne explains that they chose a program in Paraguay largely because it predicted placement in approximately one year. They were ready to become parents and did not want to wait several years for an adoption. Foreign adoption had the added appeal of being more anonymous, something that Suzanne preferred, having heard some "horror stories" of American birthmothers who changed their minds.

> While we are glad that we adopted from Paraguay, the process itself was difficult. We applied, received an assignment very promptly, and then waited six months until we could go and get our son. The wait was complicated by the fact that every time we would call the agency, we'd get what proved to be false hope. They were constantly telling us that we would be on our way to Paraguay shortly, but, in fact, there were constant delays.

Suzanne goes on to say that the trip to Paraguay and the return home with their new baby went very well. Friends and family were supportive and enthusiastic. Still, there were a few comments that were hard to take. Suzanne is a nurse and a couple of the doctors she works with said some especially insensitive things. One, who was foreign born himself, asked her how she would communicate with her foreign baby. Another introduced her to some colleagues with the comment, "Suzanne's son is adopted and her daughter is her own." While she is able to laugh about these remarks, Suzanne acknowledges that they hurt.

> We are blessed that our children actually look alike. Nonetheless, I do worry about how Alex will feel when he is older. I hope that people have the sense to stop making dumb comments when he is old enough to understand what they mean.

Suzanne loves to talk with other couples considering Latin American adoption. She remembers how scary it was for her and how foreign it seemed. Having been to Paraguay, and traveled a great distance in other ways as well, she enjoys encouraging others to do the same. "I would have missed out on some wonderful experiences had we not decided to adopt a Latin American baby. I never realized how glad I'd be about it."

Marsha and David:
Gefilte Fish with Soy Sauce

> When we decided to adopt from Korea, I remember thinking that our son would be coming to the right home: we love Asian cooking. This was a boy who would be raised on an assortment of Chinese, Japanese, Thai, and Korean cooking. Of course, there would be a smattering of Jewish cooking thrown in. I always get a kick out of seeing him put soy sauce on his gefilte fish!

For Marsha and David it has been very important to integrate their son Jed's Korean heritage with their Jewish backgrounds. They report that prior to his arrival, they had not been observant nor had they been members of a synagogue. It was when they

became parents to a two-and-one-half-year-old Korean boy that
they decided to join a synagogue and participate more actively in
their religion.

> People still look at us when we walk into the synagogue as a family.
> My husband and I and our daughter, all tall and fair, and our nine-
> year-old Korean son. But I think that he looks adorable in his
> *yamulka!* I have also been comforted to see that there are a number
> of other children in the congregation who are clearly not Jewish
> by birth. Last week when I took him into Hebrew school, there was
> a little black boy in his class.

Now nearly seven years into it, Marsha and David are very
pleased with their decision to adopt. Putting them more in touch
with their own religious heritage is just one way in which it has
enriched their lives. However, they acknowledge that it was not
an easy choice for them. As the proud parents of a bright and
talented, sweet and easy little girl, it was hard for them to imagine
expanding their family by adoption. They were afraid that they
would adopt a child who would ruin everything.

Marsha describes her movement toward adoption as an emotional process. She says that she could think of many reasons not
to adopt but that when it came down to it, she decided on the
basis of her feelings. She had reached a point, after several years
of infertility, at which she could no longer attempt another pregnancy. She realized that it was time to move on to another means
of parenting.

> The hard part was convincing David. He adores Allison, our
> daughter, and could not imagine loving a second child as much.
> He was especially afraid of adoption, afraid that an adopted child
> would not have the great start in life that Allison had had — good
> genes, good looks, good prenatal care. I took a very calm approach
> with him, introducing the subject gradually, but consistently. Little
> by little, he began to be interested.

Marsha goes on to say that once they had decided to adopt,
both she and David felt clear that they preferred an international
adoption. They both felt very comfortable with the idea of a multicultural family. They had lived in Asia, had traveled extensively,
and regarded the prospect of an international family as exciting.

Once we had decided to do a foreign adoption, we looked into a variety of programs. We decided on Korea for many reasons: we liked the particular program we could go through and we felt very comfortable with the culture. The next question for us was whether to request a boy or a girl (or make no request regarding sex).

In those days the Korean program permitted applicants to specify a boy or a girl. Since I had always wanted girls and had no real interest in a boy, I assumed we would request a girl. Then some things happened that changed our minds. One was that we began thinking about how different our two girls would look and thought that might be hard for our second daughter. The other factor was that we heard that an overwhelming number of couples were requesting girls and that the Korean government was beginning to object to this bias. We made an about-face and decided to adopt a boy.

Another part of the decision for Marsha and David was to decide on the age of their child. They realized it really did not matter to them to adopt an infant but it did matter that the child was healthy. When they filed their application, they specified that they wanted a healthy boy under the age of three. Eight months later Jed arrived: he was two and a half.

He spoke no English when he arrived, but that was not a problem. He learned simply by our talking to him. I found that he began to understand what I was saying very quickly and that it took longer for him to begin to speak in English. His first sentence was "cold toilet."

Marsha says that one of the hardest parts of adopting Jed was dealing with Allison's reaction. She had been an only child for eight years, and although she said that she wanted a little brother, she had a hard time when he arrived. Marsha remembers Allison saying some horrible things to her little brother, but also being the proud and caring older sister.

When she wasn't being impossible, it was really cute to see the two of them together. Allison was very good with Jed and very sweet when people looked at the two of them and said, "Is that your brother?" Allison always said that of course he was her brother and seemed puzzled by people's questions. I think that the experience was great for her. It taught her about prejudice at a very early age, about family loyalties, and about dealing with differences.

Marsha says that as Jed's mother she has certainly had to deal with differences. She has become accustomed to being out with Jed and having people come up to her with comments and questions. She says that sometimes this is difficult because she is busy focusing on the errand she is doing or on her conversation with Jed. A stranger will come up to her, out of the blue, and interrupt everything.

Marsha says that she has learned to handle these interruptions but that she realizes that as Jed gets older, the challenges will become all the more complex. People are still reacting to him as a cute little boy, but it will be harder when he is a teenager. She has heard stories from other mothers of foreign-born children, of the prejudice and racism that emerges when their children reach adolescence.

> Fortunately, I realized when we adopted that we would always be an inter-racial family. I am grateful that I learned something about dealing with others when Jed was still too young to really understand. Now that he is older, it is getting more complicated and I can only anticipate that this will continue as he matures.

Although she anticipates challenges, Marsha remains very positive about their decision to adopt. She says that both she and David have found some unexpected delights in having a foreign-born child. She feels that the fact that they were encouraged by their agency to have few expectations for their son helped a great deal.

> It gave us license to have more joy with him. We are able to enjoy most everything about him. We are taking great pleasure in watching him grow and develop. He is bright and interesting and always happy.

International Sibling Group Adoption

For a variety of social, cultural, and economic reasons, sibling groups do become available for adoption, and agencies do attempt to keep them together. Although many prospective parents would not consider a sibling group, feeling that one child is enough of an adjustment, there are some couples who are open to or even intrigued by the prospect of an instant family. Perhaps it is some of the same adventurous spirit that draws people to international adoption that also interests them in sibling group adoption.

Couples arrive at the decision to adopt a sibling group for a number of reasons. For some, there are concerns about their age and perhaps about finances. Adopting a sibling group may be the most practical and expedient way for them to form a family. Others are attracted to the idea that their children will grow up with their biological relatives and feel that this opportunity will remove much of the sting of adoption. Still others come across the question of adopting a sibling group on their adoption application and indicate that this is something they would consider, assuming that they will never be faced with a real decision.

However they come to it, the sudden arrival of two, three, four, or more children is an enormous adjustment for any couple, especially those who are new to parenting. The fact that there are major cultural differences makes this all the more challenging. Parents discover that they have ingenuity and stamina beyond what they might ever have imagined.

Craig and Pam: "We Always Knew We'd Have a Large Family"

When I was growing up in a small town in the midwest, I never would have pictured myself where I am now: the proud and exhausted father of four Korean children. Even when we decided to adopt our first child, an infant son from Korea, I never would have dreamed that within three years he would have three *older* siblings. I have learned that life is full of unexpected twists and turns, disappointments and delights.

Craig and Pam knew from the time that they first met they would have a large family. This was something that was important to both of them, and so it was clear that it would be a priority in their lives. Whatever obstacles they had to overcome, they would somehow manage to have several children.

> When we learned that Pam was infertile, we decided not to spend endless time pursuing infertility treatments. We had known several couples who had done so and from our point of view, it ruined their lives. Besides, there are thousands of homeless children out there, looking for homes and parents. We felt that it would be immensely satisfying to open our home and our lives to some of them.
>
> Although we were open to all sorts of children, we very much wanted the experience of having a baby. We felt strongly that this was how we needed to begin our family and so we applied to adopt an infant. We chose a Korean program because we were both interested in the Korean culture and because we knew some other families who had adopted from Korea.

Craig and Pam's son, David, arrived from Korea when he was three months old. He had not been with them very long when they began thinking about a second child . . . and third . . . and fourth.

> As much as we enjoyed David's early months and years, we did not feel compelled to have another baby. Because we knew that we wanted to have several children and because we were both getting older, we began thinking about adopting an older child. Then we learned that sibling groups were available. After considerable thought—and some long talks—we decided to apply to adopt a sibling group.

Craig says that they were very excited when they learned that they would be able to adopt two sisters and a brother, then ages eight, five, and three. Adopting a three year old meant that David would have a brother the same age as he was. Adopting an eight year old and a five year old meant that David would go from being an only child to having two older sisters. There would be big changes for everyone!

> I suppose that we broke all the rules. We "twinned" and we adopted children who were older than our son. But we have never been

ones to stick to the conventional route and this felt to us like the best way to build our family.

Craig and Pam continue to feel that they chose the best way to build their family, but they also acknowledge that it hasn't been easy. Rebecca, Tia, and Jesse arrived speaking no English. Rebecca made it clear that she was not happy to have left Korea, that she did not want to learn English, and that she wanted to have very little to do with her new family.

We tried to be very patient with Rebecca and give her a lot of space. We understood how difficult it was for her and tried not to expect her to adjust rapidly. We felt that she had enough to contend with having to enter a new school just three weeks after she arrived and didn't want to put additional pressure on her.

As it has turned out, Rebecca, like her younger brother and sister, have adjusted well to their new home and country. They all attend Korean language school and enjoy maintaining some Korean customs, but they are also full-fledged American kids.

When we go someplace as a family, people always stop and look. Most of the time, I feel that they are just being curious: they are surprised to see so many kids. Sometimes they stop us and ask things like "Are they really brothers and sisters?" or they look at them and then at us and strain to try to find a physical resemblance. Occasionally someone says something rude, but by and large I feel that our family is, and has been, well received.

Craig and Pam look back on their decision to adopt a sibling group with pleasure and with some amusement. They remark about how organized they thought they were and note that they had no idea how much work and how time-consuming four children would be.

We've been lucky in that each of our children has chosen to go into crisis at a different time. I don't know what we would have done had they decided to "fall apart" simultaneously. What we've found is that it is very challenging and exhausting but that there is an ever-present light at the end of the tunnel.

Lynn and Carl:
"Never Take More Children
Than You Have Hands to Hold"

When the question on the adoption application asked how many children we were willing to take, we had something to talk about. We had already decided, given Carl's advancing age and the fact that we wanted more than one child, that we would be willing to take siblings. But did that mean two or were we willing to be really adventuresome?

Lynn and Carl chose adventure and responded to the question by saying that they would take up to six children. The only stipulation that they made was that one of the children had to be a girl and that one had to be under the age of two. As it turned out, they became the parents of three daughters and one son. Their children were one and a half, four, six, and eight when they arrived.

We realize, in retrospect, that we made a mistake on the application and that we were lucky that things turned out as they did. We think that it is a mistake to ever take more children than you have hands to hold. We ended up with one child per hand but we could have found ourselves in trouble!

For Lynn and Carl, parenthood has been a real adventure. Carl had been married before and has three biological children, all of whom are now in their late teens. But he notes that his earlier experience as a father was very different than his current adventure.

For Lynn and me it's been a great experience becoming sudden parents to four Korean children. We had traveled in China and felt some strong connections to the Asian people. Hence it was not difficult to make the decision to do a Korean adoption. What we didn't know at the time was how exciting it would be to have a sibling group.

Lynn and Carl have now been parents to Sarah, Jessica, Seth, and Maggie for two years. They applied for adoption in early

October, three years ago, received an assignment at the end of the next January, and waited until July for their children to arrive.

> The time between January and July passed very slowly for us. We knew that our children were in an orphanage waiting for us, and it was frustrating that we could not all be together. It was a very strange feeling to be writing and sending pictures to children that were ours but whom we had never met.
> Eventually we received word that the children would be permitted to emigrate. We wanted to go to Korea to travel with them, but others discouraged us, saying that we would have to be very well rested when they arrived here. As it turned out, we were very glad that we did not try to make the trip since it ended up taking the children three days to make the journey. They were bumped several times from flights. It seems that everyone in the world comes before children who are being adopted.

When the children finally arrived here, their new parents were waiting with open arms and hearts, fortified, as best they could, with sleep. As predicted, they needed to be well rested, because one of them had to be awake at all times for the next few days. Their children were not only suffering from jet-lag but also from complete culture shock. They had never before seen hot and cold running water. They were entirely unfamiliar with common kitchen tools and perplexed by utensils such as knives and forks.

> Fortunately, Carl's teenage daughter, Allison, came to the rescue. Allison came over one evening when we were having pizza for dinner. She walked into a scene in which there were four crying children, frightened that pizza was poison. Allison sat down, began gobbling up slices of pizza, and four curious little copycats followed suit. From then on, pizza has been their favorite food and it is sometimes difficult to get them to eat anything else.

The pizza story is but one example of the Americanization of Lynn and Carl's children. Although they arrived speaking no English, they have learned the language quickly as well as most of the styles and customs. Lynn recalls their citizenship day as one of the happiest days of her life—and theirs. It was a great pleasure to see the pride that the children felt as they became American citizens.

Things are going very well now, but I don't want to pretend that it has always been easy. It's been exhausting and there have been some difficult times. For me, the toughest part was with our oldest daughter, Sarah. She gave me a rough time in the beginning, competing with me for who was going to be mother to the other children and acting bossy and defiant around me. Things changed a lot after the first year and she and I have grown very close. I guess that she acted like a little mother because she felt so much need for a mother.

Lynn describes the town that they live in as "yuppish" and says that the people there have been welcoming of their children. The schools were very responsive, although they were not exactly sure what to do with children who arrived on the first day of school speaking no English. There are other Asians in town and other families who have done foreign adoptions, and so there have been few if any problems associated with being an international family.

We have so much enjoyed being an international family that we have formed a group with other families that we call *The Sibling Group Group*. Our group is made up of families who have also adopted siblings. There are others with Korean children, but there are also families with children from Guatemala, El Salvador, and other South and Latin American countries. We have one family in the group who adopted a sibling group of six and others who have adopted two sibling groups. We get together in the winter for a "Mom and Dad's night out" and we have family activities such as picnics and holiday parties. We are a support and social group and we try to be there to offer advice and comfort for couples who are awaiting the arrival of their children.

Lynn and Carl are enthusiastic about their decision to adopt a sibling group. More experienced and more rested than they were two years ago, they acknowledge that they didn't anticipate how tiring it would be. But they also acknowledge that rest was not what they were looking for when they set out to become parents. For them, parenting has been a wonderful adventure, "one which gets better and better all the time."

12

Raising Biological and Adopted Children

I am always moved—and a bit amused—when people comment on how much my daughters look like each other. Strangers have no idea that one was born to me, and the other adopted.

I have three sons, two by adoption and the third by birth. My oldest has brown hair, my second is a redhead, and the third is a blond. People often look at the three of them together and say that they look so different from each other. I respond to them matter-of-factly and say "Yes, I know." I'm pleased that I've grown comfortable leaving it at that.

I really don't think that much anymore about our daughter being adopted. I don't think of her any differently than I do our son. Both children are miracles—our daughter because she came to us when we wanted her so badly, and our son because he was born against all odds into our lives.

THESE are voices of parents who have both biological and adopted children. Although there is little or no evidence to support the old folk wisdom "adopt and you'll get pregnant," there are, indeed, many families that have one or more biological children after adopting. Most often there is a medical explanation for this: either a treatment that didn't work in the past is now successful or a new diagnostic tool/treatment has become available. However, there is also a small group of couples who, for some unexplained reason, do have a miracle pregnancy after having been told that they had little or no chance of bearing a biological child.

There are also families who have one or more biological children and then find that they are not able to have another. Sometimes this is due to infertility; other times to age, some mishap during labor and delivery, or the discovery of a genetic disease. Whatever the reason, these families are also formed with biological and adopted children.

Some couples, though few, choose to form their families through birth and adoption. These are likely to be people who are very comfortable with differences or they have some personal or historical reason for wanting to adopt. Some may have been adopted themselves. Others have lived in a foreign culture and feel a special connection to the people there. Still others want to offer a home to a child who is without one. Whatever their reasons, these couples do not usually have a history of infertility. Because they have not had to deal with the disappointments and frustrations of infertility, and because they have "blended" biological and adopted children by choice, they will not be included in this discussion. This chapter will focus, instead, on those parents who did not choose, as their first choice, to build their families by adoption.

The following are some of the special concerns of families that include biological and adopted children:

1. identifying, acknowledging, accepting, and (hopefully) celebrating differences
2. arrival order and position in the family
3. family planning

Identifying, Acknowledging, Accepting, and (Hopefully) Celebrating Differences

In *Shared Fate*, H. David Kirk examined patterns of adaptation in adoptive families and concluded that those who acknowledge differences generally demonstrate better overall adjustment than those who attempt to avoid or deny them. Parents raising both biological and adopted children undoubtedly face a special set of challenges, especially with regard to acknowledging differences. Not only are they dealing with how they differ from nonadoptive families, but they are also dealing with how they differ from other adoptive families as well. Moreover, they must deal with the differences that exist within their own families — with what it means to raise children who came to them in different ways.

Parents who have both biological and adopted children have frequent reminders of differences. The following are some of the differences they encounter. In each instance, what is important is not that the difference exists, but rather how the parents and children feel about it and react to it.

First, there are differences in appearance. Families who adopt transracially anticipate these differences, but those who adopted children of their own race frequently hope that the child will blend with the rest of the family. When the rest of the family includes a biological child, the issue of blending becomes more complex. Although there are some families in which siblings — biological and adopted — look remarkably alike, or in which the adopted child looks very much like one of the parents, it is not unusual for the adopted child to look different from the rest of the family.

Differences in appearance seems to be of more concern to families who have a biological child first and then turn to adoption than it is for those who adopt first. Families who adopt first report such strong attachment to their adopted child, and such surprise at the pregnancy that follows, that they do not focus a great deal on differences of appearance. By contrast, parents who have a biological child first frequently mention appearance as one of their reservations regarding adoption: they express concern that they will adopt a child who will look strikingly different from the rest of the family, perhaps so different that it will prevent him or her from "fitting in."

My wife and I and our seven-year-old son are all tall and lean. We had great fears when we applied to adopt that we would be "matched" with a baby who was destined to be short and fat. We

felt that this would never work for us. We could accept differences
of coloring or hair color and we could accept a child who looked
very different from us ethnically. What we struggled with—and
decided to insist upon with the agency—was body type. We felt
that we had to enter into an adoption anticipating that our child
would have a stature similar to the rest of us.

In the early years of parenting, parents are likely to think about
differences on birthdays. With a biological child, a birthday is
uncomplicated. Parents remember their child's arrival and celebrate how far all of them have come since that time. They have
no feeling of discontinuity.

With an adopted child, birthdays remind parents that they
were "absent at the creation." Except in those instances in which
the adoptive parents were present at the birth, there is a missing
period in the child's life. Whether it be three days, three months,
or three years, parents have feelings about this and are likely, at
least initially, to connect more to the date that they adopted their
child than to the child's birthday. Although this feeling of discontinuity diminishes over time, adoptive parents are unlikely to
ever feel completely connected to their child's birthday. Moreover, birthdays are a reminder of the other set of parents who,
wherever they are, are commemorating the occasion in a very different way.

> By now I am certainly familiar with Lauren's birthday. I've been
> through enough goody bags and created enough Barbie cakes to
> feel thoroughly familiar with her birthday. But it was not that way
> for her first, and I believe, even her second birthday. In the early
> years, I had vivid memories of the day we received the call that she
> was coming and joyous memories of her arrival day. Those were
> the days that mattered to me, but I put them aside because I felt
> that her birthday was what mattered to her. I celebrated with her,
> knowing it was hers.
>
> Later, when Lisa, our biological child, turned one, I noticed how
> different it felt for me. Her birthday was a day that we had really
> shared together: it was ours.

Some adoptive families do celebrate their child's arrival date as
well as their real birthday. Families who adopted an older child,

who can remember the day that he joined their family, find that this is a nice occasion for them to share together. Most note that it is different from birthdays in that it is a more private celebration.

> Mark was born in February and adopted in August. He was two and a half at the time and he remembers a little about his arrival. We have two celebrations each year. On his birthday we have a regular party with his friends. His arrival day celebration is always a family affair. One year we went to a Korean restaurant but he prefers to grill hamburgers and hot dogs and to feast on chips.

An arrival-day celebration also helps families with biological and adopted children equalize memories. Although they are unlikely to emphasize the joy that they felt around their biological child's arrival, it becomes easier to treasure those memories as a family if there is comparable joy conveyed in remembering the adoption.

Families with both biological and adopted children note that increased openness in adoption has also helped equalize memories. With birthparents no longer being kept in the shadows, many adoptive parents have the opportunity to participate, in some way, in their child's arrival. Even if they are not present at the delivery, many are in close contact with the birthparents. For these adoptive parents, their child's real birthday is an occasion about which they have very vivid and fond memories.

> We adopted our daughter, and I gave birth to our son, one year and two days later. As joyous as my own delivery was, I remember, with equal delight, watching Sybil, our daughter's birthmother, give birth to her. It was a homebirth, which made it especially nice for all of us. The intimate sharing that occurred among all of us is something that I will always remember and treasure.

Religious celebrations are other occasions that prompt parents to note the differences in their children's backgrounds. There are instances when a family adopts a child whose religious background is the same as their own, but most often this is not the case. Parents frequently adopt a child of one religion and convert the child, usually as an infant, to their religion. Then they have the experience of raising a child who is a convert.

> Each Christmas my two young daughters try to rebel against our Jewish household. They usually cordon off a room or two and declare it Christian territory. They put a paper wreath on a door, post drawings of Santa Claus, and hang tinsel and fake Christmas lights. I always find their efforts amusing, particularly since they bring back memories of my own childhood longings to be Christian at Christmas time. However, with my older daughter Sharon, there is an added twist since she was actually born to a Christian mother and converted to Judaism when she was three weeks old. At those moments when she expresses her wish to be Christian, I wonder if we took something from her against her will. By contrast, my younger daughter Cathy's religious affiliation is much more straightforward. She was born a Jew, and being Jewish is an important — and automatic — tie that she has with her ancestors.

Some families who have biological and adopted children are dealing with the added dimension of racial and cultural differences. Parents may have adopted a foreign-born child and then conceived, or they may have decided to expand their family internationally when they found they were unable to have more biological children. These parents have had a private piece of their lives made public: people look at them and conclude that their children joined their family in different ways. Often this invites commentary or questions.

> Occasionally I come upon really rude people who say horribly insensitive things in front of my children. But more often than not, I find that people are not ill-intentioned, they are simply curious. They see us together and wonder how we came to be a family. If I'm in a bad mood or have had a difficult day, I can have a hard time being patient with them. But more often than not, I am able to accept their curiosity. I try to help educate them that there are many different and creative ways in which families come together.

Differences between biological and adopted children are evident, also, in terms of interests and abilities. With biological children, parents are likely to anticipate, correctly or not, certain abilities and talents. Even things that may not be inherited are credited as being passed from one generation to another. In fact, one of the dangers of a biological connection is that parents may close off options for their children because of the assumptions they make about them. Parents who have both biological and adopted children sometimes find that adoption opens them up to new possibilities for all of their children.

> We have four sons. Our older two boys are adopted and our younger two are our biological children. Our older boys are big, sturdy, and athletic and have been so since they were small babies. Our younger boys, who are now only five and seven, are built as we are—small, scrawny, and not athletic. However, I watch our younger boys look up to their big brothers and imitate them. I won't be at all surprised if the little ones decide to pursue sports so that they can be like their big brothers. What a surprise this is for my husband and me—we never pictured ourselves the parents of athletes!

> I am a scientist and the father of two boys, ages eight and three. Our older son is our biological child and our younger son was adopted after several years of secondary infertility. Before Jed, our younger boy came along, I had very set ideas about how Mitchell, our older, would perform. I expected him to do very well in school and assumed that he would be a junior scientist. I had no such expectations of Jed.
> I have discovered many things in the past three years, both about myself and about others. Among the most important has been the realization that I cannot control or determine who my sons will be. Having Jed and letting him be himself has helped me to also allow Mitchell to also be himself. As it turns out, Mitchell has little interest in science, at least at age eight. I feel some disappointment about this but I also feel reassured that he will not grow up feeling trapped, as some kids do, by a demanding father.

The most complicated area of difference is that which involves differences of feeling toward the children. Parents who have a biological child and then adopt inevitably fear that they will love the adopted child less than the child born to them. Parents who adopt and then find themselves pregnant have a similar worry. Do parents who have both biological and adopted children actually favor their biological children, or is this fear ill-founded?

Some parents insist that there are no differences. Others say that the question is simply too difficult to ask, let alone answer. Still others say that they do experience differences but are confused by them, since there are always so many other variables at hand.

> For a long time, I wanted to believe—and to have others believe—that I loved them both equally. And the truth is that I do adore both of my daughters. Still, there are differences in the way that I feel about them and I cannot disown those differences.
>
> With Vicki, my older (and adopted) child, I welcome closeness but I never assume it. When she is affectionate, I find that I am touched by it and somewhat surprised; for as wonderful as she is, and as close as we are, there is always a certain distance between us. I can never quite assume that we are a unit.
>
> With Karen, my younger (and biological) child, there is no question of our connection. She can be difficult and demanding but she is mine. That never gets challenged.
>
> The differences that I feel make it much harder for me to separate from Karen than from Vicki. I worry more about her safety, have a more difficult time letting go. By contrast, it is easier for me to get angry with her than with Vicki. There is neither the fear that my anger will cause her to leave me, nor the guilt that perhaps the anger is somehow related to lingering feelings about infertility.
>
> I am not sure what all this means. For all that I know, my feelings may be related more to birth order and differences in the girls' temperaments than to adoption. But I'm afraid that with adoption in the picture, I always think "adoption" without weighing other factors.
>
> I am also not sure what affect these differences will have on each of my daughters. Vicki may actually have an easier time in life *because* I don't need her to be so close to me. Karen may grow up resenting me for holding on so tight. I only know that it does make me uncomfortable to think that adoption may be influencing my behavior and attitudes in ways that could compromise my relationships with my daughters.

Unlike those parents whose children were all born to them—or all adopted—parents with biological and adopted children grapple with the issue of adoption as a variable. Some say that they scrutinize their reactions to their children, wondering when they are influenced by other factors such as birth order, temperament, behavior, interests, and appearance, and when they may be reacting to the fact that one child is adopted and another is not. They report feeling more comfortable with other factors as variables and say that it is upsetting to think that the fact of an adoption may be influencing them. Mothers seem to struggle with this more than their husbands, most likely because they are the ones who have experienced pregnancy.

> When we adopted our older son, Ricky, my husband had a more flexible job situation than I did. He was able to stay at home most of the time with Ricky while I continued at my full-time job. Their relationship grew very strong and solid during that time.
>
> When I became pregnant two years later, Jeff was immersed in a new job, and for many reasons it seemed to make sense for me to stay home. I had the intense bonding experience with Peter, our younger son, that Jeff had had with Ricky.
>
> My sons are now five and two. I love them both, but I feel like I want to inhale Peter. My love for him is boundless. Perhaps it was the time that I spent with him in his first few months that has made the difference. Still, I worry that the real reason is that he was born to me. I could never admit this, not even to my husband.

> I know from my friends who have two or more children that it is normal to have different feelings toward your children. I have a good friend, for example, who freely admits to me that one of her daughters drives her crazy, and that the other can do no wrong. When I think about it, it would be impossible, unnatural, and boring for us to have the same feelings toward each of our children. Still, with one child who is adopted and another who is not, I have a very hard time sorting out my feelings. When my son who is adopted upsets or annoys me, I can't help but feel some guilt. I may have very substantial reasons for being upset with him, but I inevitably ask myself if I am giving him a hard time because he is adopted. By contrast, when my daughter, who was born to us, acts like a pest, I feel a tinge of relief; it feels easier and safer to be angry with her.

Differences are real, and parents who are able to acknowledge them seem to feel more comfortable in their relationships with their children. By owning differences, they minimize the possibility that their children will play on them. Should the children say such things as "You love Johnny more than you love me because he is your real son," "I was the one who was born here," or "You're not my real brother anyway," parents will not be confused and guilt-ridden. Having dealt with their own feelings honestly, they feel better equipped to help their children deal with theirs.

Arrival Order and Position in the Family

Parents of both biological and adopted children have thoughts and feelings about the order in which their children joined the family. For example, when a biological child follows an adoption, parents sometimes feel that the natural birth order has been interrupted. Their biological child was the first child born to them, but he is the second or even third child to arrive in the family. Is he responded to as a second or third child, or does he also bear some of the rights and burdens of a firstborn? Similarly, their adopted child may have been the first to join their family, but was the second or third born to her birthmother. These alterations in the natural order of things give parents pause. Some find what has happened confusing.

> I am the older of two daughters. My mother was also the older of two daughters and now my adopted daughter, Meg, is the older of two daughters. She and I struggle, much in the tradition of the struggles that I had with my mother and that she, reportedly, had with hers. Meanwhile, Liz, my younger daughter, but also firstborn to me, escapes the struggles. She gets away, as I perceive it, with all the tolerance accorded to second-born girls in our family. This all seems to me to be an odd twist of fate. I wonder sometimes, how Liz and I would have done had Meg not joined our family before her?

Parents who adopt first and later become pregnant often feel comforted by the fact that their adopted child will always be their "firstborn." To the extent they worry that they will favor their biological child, they feel their adopted child has a certain security and status by virtue of position. On the other hand, there is the issue of choice: would they have adopted had they known that they would be able to bear a child? Will their adopted child wonder about this as well?

Some parents who adopt first and later bear a child come to these experiences with a complex legacy: they may have lost other babies or they may have medical or genetic conditions that advise against pregnancy. Most likely, these experiences have influenced the ways in which they view adoption and biological parenting. Adoption may be the safe alternative to a problematic situation; the subsequent birth of a healthy biological child, a miracle.

> We had lost two babies—both stillbirths—before we turned to adoption. When adoption brought a healthy baby boy into our lives, we could not believe our good fortune. When I conceived a year after his arrival, I was frightened and very tentative. I expected that that pregnancy would bring another loss. The birth of a healthy baby—another son—was an incredible surprise. I think that it was initially easier for me to bond with our first son because I was not so fearful of losing him.

Parents who had a biological child and later adopted frequently recall that it was a very difficult decision. They remember looking at their biological child and feeling that she would be a hard act for any second child to follow. They worried that it was a real set up for an adopted child. They worried also that they would bring in a stranger who would ruin all their lives.

Despite their reservations, many couples decide to expand their families through adoption. After much soul-searching, they reached a point at which adoption began to feel right. Most report that this was not a rational decision: there were all sorts of compelling reasons not to adopt. Instead they say their adoption decision was ultimately made for emotional reasons.

> For a long time I had serious reservations about adoption. I couldn't imagine getting excited about an adoption in the same way that I'd been excited when I was pregnant. It felt all wrong. But time passed, and gradually things changed. Recently, I was surprised to find that I was actually happy when my period came. At this point, I'm really looking forward to adopting, and I don't want anything to get in our way—even pregnancy!

I went from not really wanting a second child to several years of infertility in which I very much wanted another child. Then I had an ectopic pregnancy and realized that "enough was enough": what mattered was having another child and not necessarily having another pregnancy. I was ready to look into adoption.

It was one thing for me to think about adoption and another for my husband to consider it. He is a geneticist, and for him the decision to adopt was like climbing Mount Everest. Had I listened to all his rational reasons not to adopt or had he remained focused on them, we would never have our son. But the fact is that adoption is really an emotional decision. None of us adopt for logical reasons; we adopt because it is something that we feel we want to do.

Parents who adopt a child after having a biological child also identify advantages to this family constellation. They point out that their older children are usually eager for a sibling. For parents this is a comfort: if they feel ambivalent about adoption, they are reassured by their belief that their child will undoubtedly gain by having a sibling.

Another advantage of adoption after biological parenting has to do with expectations of children. Parents who have a biological child first and then adopt point out that adoption has helped them to lower their expectations. They report having put a lot of pressure on their older child because of his known genes and say that they ease up with their adopted child, whose talents and intelligence are presumably unclear. This can ultimately be helpful to both children because the process helps parents to realize that children are who they are and that there is only so much we can or cannot expect of them.

I think that the key to parenting my younger daughter has been lowered expectations. I expected so much of my older daughter who, after all, inherited all of our wonderful genes. Then she was an only child for several years and that only added to the picture. When Dara finally came along, I was much more ready to see her for who she was. Whatever she did brought us great joy. I was able to delight in her without worrying that she should be doing better and achieving more. It has been a refreshing change and I have noticed that, in the process, I have eased up on Kim as well.

A third advantage to adopting after having a biological child has to do with the parent's sense of security. Having "produced" a biological child, there is no question that they are "real" parents. Unlike parents who adopt their first child, these couples probably do not struggle with questions of whether they were meant to be parents. Because they know firsthand what "normal" parenting is, they are less likely to attribute the daily stresses and strains that occur between parent and child to adoption.

> Having given birth to my daughter helped me to feel more confi-
> dent when my son arrived from Korea. Some of the things that
> upset other adoptive mothers who I know did not trouble me
> because I had been through similar experiences with my daughter.
> I knew that they had nothing to do with adoption and that they
> were simply part of normal parenting.

Finally, parents who adopt after having a biological child feel their decision is a positive statement about adoption. They feel both of their children will know their parents chose to adopt; it was not something they had to do in order to become parents. They feel this positive view about adoption conveys an important message to their children. It reflects a willingness to accept differences and a belief that life sometimes offers us alternate means for reaching our goals.

Family Planning

A major concern for parents by birth and adoption has to do with family planning. Parents in these blended families are often uncertain about how large their families should be. Some who conceive after adopting one or more children feel that they have enough children but that they have not had enough pregnancies. They struggle with whether to have another child because they have such a strong desire to reexperience the magic of pregnancy, labor, and delivery. Others adopt a more-the-merrier approach to family planning, thinking "Now that we have a family that is so different from the one that we had originally envisioned, why not add more children?" They have an abiding faith that things work

out, that you add your children when and how you can, and that
children, however they come to you, are truly a blessing.

Confusion about family planning as well as years of suffering
from infertility make it exceedingly difficult for infertile parents
to use birth control. How can they possibly prevent a pregnancy
when they struggled so long and hard to have one and when they
cherished the experience when it finally happened?

> I am the contented mother of three children, two by adoption and
> the third by birth. I thoroughly enjoyed their early years and am
> now rolling with the punches of their adolescences. Motherhood
> is, and has long been, the most satisfying experience I have known.
> Still, I am certain that I do not want to have any more children.
>
> For several years now my husband and I have dealt with the
> painful question of birth control/voluntary sterilization. It has
> been very difficult for us, in part because we don't even know if we
> could conceive again. Perhaps our concerns are over nothing,
> perhaps we are hopelessly infertile and should be grateful to have
> succeeded with one pregnancy. However, because we could not
> consider abortion after infertility and because we do not want any
> more children, we feel obliged to take steps to prevent con-
> ception.
>
> Having encountered problems with the common forms of birth
> control, we have had to face the fact that the answer for us may lie
> in voluntary sterilization — either for him or for me. Each of us has
> scheduled — and canceled — the surgical procedures that would
> enable us to put all these questions behind us. Having worked so
> hard to have a family, and having cherished them so much, it
> seems impossible for us to take the step that means once and for
> all, never again.

> When I had a pregnancy "scare" after years and years of infertility,
> I was embarrassed to tell my infertility specialist that I didn't want
> another baby. He said something to me that I found to be very wise
> and comforting. He told me "Remember that infertility is being
> unable to conceive when you *want to.*"

Although it complicates their lives in some ways, parents whose
children came to them through birth and adoption feel blessed.
Most would not have planned things this way, but many feel that
they have happened upon a very special way to build a family.

Not only have they experienced the pleasure and satisfaction that comes from having biological offspring, but they have discovered that love and attachment grow from more than genetic links. It is the daily ritual and interaction of family life, the sibling battles and the sibling bonds, that make them a family.

> Yesterday my five year old said "I've been thinking about who I look like." I was taken aback for a moment by her comment since she does look a lot like both my husband and me and since her sister, who is adopted, looks somewhat different. I was afraid that there had been too much commentary about who looks like whom and that this would cause Jessie, our adopted daughter, to feel hurt. But then Ericka, our younger, went on. "Mommy, I think I look just like Jessie."

> When our son arrived from Korea, our daughter, who was nine, was impossible. The little princess, who had been the center of our universe, was now dethroned. She was angry and hostile and at one point she told us to "send the little bastard back to Korea." But things changed, and in time she grew to be a loving and devoted older sister. Now, when people ask in puzzlement "Is *he* your *brother*?" she responds with great pride and a touch of indignation, "Of course *he's my brother*."

Judy and Alan: "A Bad Case of Nerves"

> I can remember sitting at my window and watching the mothers and their babies out walking on a spring day. I would sit there and sob, feeling like I was the only one in the world deprived of a baby. The pain was so intense at times that I wondered how I would survive it. It all feels like it was yesterday.

In fact, it was not yesterday. Over twenty years have passed since Judy and her husband, Alan, went through infertility. In the interim they have raised two sons. Their older son, Ricky, now twenty, came to them through adoption when he was four days old. Their younger son, Jeffrey, now fifteen, was born to them. Judy smiles and says, "I had two more children than I once thought I would have." Then she adds wistfully, "But I never used up my nurturing. I would have loved to have had more children because I had more mothering in me."

When Judy and Alan married they planned to have several children. Judy was an only child and looked forward to a large family. Alan, though looking forward to a career in finance, saw himself as a family man. Soon after the wedding, when both were in their early twenties, Judy and Alan tried to conceive.

> Eight months went by without a pregnancy. I hurried off to my gynecologist who did a test or two and then declared me "too nervous to have a baby." I don't think that he even tested Alan but he seemed certain that his diagnosis of excess nerves was an accurate one. He recommended that we contact the Jewish adoption agency.

Judy and Alan applied for adoption and were told that they would have to wait about a year. Normally it took less time, but they were "a special couple who will get a special baby." So with their diagnosis of bad nerves and the pronouncement that they were special, Judy and Alan resigned themselves to a long wait. And as the agency had promised, their special baby, Ricky, arrived one year later.

Both Judy and Alan remember Ricky as a very easy baby who immediately endeared himself to them. He was beautiful, he was calm, he was adaptable. They took him everywhere and felt thrilled to be his parents. Still, Judy acknowledges that she continued to feel damaged, defective, even sick.

> He was everything I could have ever wanted in a child, but he reminded me of everything that I wanted to forget about myself.

When Ricky was a year old, one of Judy' friends insisted that she seek further work-up for her infertility. It was then that Judy learned that her "bad case of nerves" was actually two blocked tubes, a benign tumor, and endometriosis. She underwent surgery to reconstruct the tubes and was told that she had at best a 50 percent chance of conception. When nothing happened she and Alan decided to go ahead and adopt again—privately this time.

The second adoption attempt turned out to be a disaster. We located a pregnant woman and got very excited and involved. Then she delivered a healthy baby girl and decided to keep her. We were both devastated. I remember Judy walking around and saying that she was ready to give up, neither pregnancy nor adoption was worth the pain involved. Three weeks later she missed her period.

Judy and Alan had only a very brief time to celebrate her unexpected pregnancy when their worries began anew. She started to spot very early in her pregnancy and was instructed to spend the first three months in bed, not an easy task for a mother of an active four year old. Things did get easier midway through the pregnancy but Judy and Alan had learned to expect disappointment. They remained guarded and hence, they were somewhat prepared for the next challenge that they encountered:—premature delivery.

Jeffrey was born six weeks early. His lungs were underdeveloped. He had trouble sucking. He was small and scrawny and simply not ready to be born. The baby that I had waited eight years to give birth to had to remain in the hospital while I went home.

Fortunately, Jeffrey did do well, and despite his prematurity, he thrived. But he was never the baby that Ricky had been. Never easy, never adaptable, never pretty.

And yet, I inhaled him. He was a funny looking little being but he reminded me of everything I liked in myself. I felt feminine. I felt attractive. I felt whole again.

Over the years Ricky has remained the handsome, competent, easy older brother, and Jeffrey has been the cute, impish, somewhat immature younger son. Alan and Judy wonder how much the differences in their personalities are innate, how much they may have to do with birth and adoption, and how much is birth order. Would their older child, however he came to them, always be the strong, responsible caretaker? Would their younger son always be the baby, even if he hadn't had such a suspenseful start? These are questions they will never be able to answer.

Judy and Alan feel that their sons have never paid a lot of attention to the fact that they are not biological siblings. What has seemed to be of greater importance in their relationship is the fact that they are five years apart in age. Because Ricky was always mature for his age and Jeffrey was always a late developer, the age span seemed even greater. Ricky was a great baby-sitter for Jeffrey, but when he got older he came to regard his younger brother as something of a pest. Jeffrey depended on Ricky; but when he realized that Ricky was going away to school, he did a lot of growing up.

> I have always seen milestones as opportunities. Ricky's leaving home, while painful, was an opportunity for all of us to grow. But the real pivotal event in his life — and in many ways in all of ours — was his bar mitzvah.
>
> Both Alan and I come from families who have long been active in our synagogue — the oldest and largest Reform congregation in the southeast. My great, great grandfather was the president of the congregation, and Ricky is named for him. My father and grandfather, and Alan's father and grandfather, were all trustees of the synagogue. Hence, it was a very important event in both of our families for Ricky to be bar mitzvahed there. It was especially significant because despite all the involvement that our families had in the synagogue, there had never been a bar mitzvah on either side of our families.
>
> As I see it, Ricky was able to use his bar mitzvah to affirm his identity. Separate from us, separate from his birthparents (who are also Jewish), but connected to all of us, he stood before the congregation. I cried through all of it but they were truly tears of joy.

According to his parents, Ricky has never been particularly curious about his adoption. He has never spoken of searching for his biological parents. Nonetheless, when it came time to select a college he decided to go far from home. He lasted only a semester there, and then he transferred to a school much closer to home. His parents had the sense that his first school had been selected for its distance — that his journey there was his quest.

At twenty Ricky is a handsome young man. His parents are also very attractive, but Ricky looks nothing like them. Nonetheless, people stop Ricky and say, "You're the spitting image of your Dad."

Jeffrey, by contrast, *is* the spitting image of his father. "A clone from day one." Judy and Alan wonder sometimes what this is like for Ricky—to look different than his father and to have a brother who is such a chip off the old block.

> Despite all his strengths, I think that Ricky is really less self-confident than Jeffrey. Whether this is the result of his adoption, we will never know. He is a strong person, with a clear mind and with integrity, but he does lack a certain confidence that we see in his younger brother.

While they wouldn't have planned it this way, Judy and Alan feel enriched having had their sons come to them in two such different ways. Judy feels that the experience of adoption has made it easier for her to separate from each of her children.

> When you adopt a child, you have to confront the fact that you can't take full credit for this child. This acknowledgment forces you to separate from that child. Having that experience helps you to separate from a biological child as well. In the end, our children—however they come to us—are separate from us. Adoption has helped me to accept this.

Liz and Craig:
An Unplanned Planned Family

> When we were first married, my husband Craig and I were in the Peace Corps in Peru. Our closest friends there gave birth to their first child and then adopted a Peruvian baby. To us this seemed like the ideal way to build a family. We decided that when we were ready to become parents, we too would have our first child (or first two) and then adopt a South American baby.

Liz and Craig have formed their family as they had hoped, by birth and international adoption. However, things did not happen in the sequence that they planned. Their adopted children, now fourteen and thirteen, came to them after several years of infertility. Their biological child, now seven, was one of those miracle babies who came along when hope was gone.

Liz looks back now and feels that she and Craig had the right idea eighteen years ago when they were enthusiastic young Peace Corps volunteers. Having an international family has been immensely satisfying to them. She has thoroughly enjoyed her children and celebrates the different ways that they came to them.

> Sure there are times when people say rude or insensitive things to us. Certainly there are instances when adoption is difficult to deal with. But all in all, these have been wonderful years. We live in a small town where we are active and involved citizens, and our children have been welcomed and embraced by the community. The town has watched them grow up.
>
> When they were very young the town paper did a feature story on adoption and included pictures and quotes by our two older children. I was really pleased by that. Now my daughter is in high school and my son is finishing up junior high. Both continue to receive a lot of positive attention and support. They have good friends and do well in school.

Liz acknowledges that having a biological child turned out to be more important to her than she had anticipated. When she was pregnant, people showered her with gifts and celebration, conveying that this was indeed a very special pregnancy. She reports having had a mixed reaction to this: on the one hand, she was touched by their excitement and enthusiasm; but on the other, there was a message that this baby was somehow more valued than her others.

When asked if they feel different ties to their biological child than they do to their Indian-born adolescents, Liz and Craig speak openly about attachment. They speak of feeling close and committed to their older children, but feeling a more intense connection to their youngest.

> I puzzle sometimes over the differences. I wonder if it is really birth and adoption that make a difference or whether it is birth order. I have the most difficulty with my oldest. She and I recreate many of the same struggles that I had with my mother. I have the feeling that I would have trouble with any eldest daughter, no matter how she came to me. Similarly, my youngest stirs up all the feelings that I think I would have had with any youngest child, particularly a girl. I find her cute and cuddly and want to keep her close

to me. Is it because she was born to me or is it because she is my "baby"?

Liz says that the children don't pay a whole lot of attention to the different ways they came to the family.

> Martha, our oldest, does ask questions about India and about adoption. Jesse, our son, voices no questions, but perhaps that is because Martha asks them for him. Lisa, our youngest, will occasionally tease the others by saying she was born into the family, but these remarks are part of the bantering that goes on—back and forth—among the kids. When she pulls this line, Martha and Jesse are quick to respond by reminding her that they got here first.

Liz and Craig are pleased with the family they have and have therefore taken the question of birth control very seriously. Unlike some other infertile parents who feel unable to use birth control and who are willing to have more children than they'd planned on, Liz and Craig feel they owe it to themselves and to all of their children to be very careful about family planning. Because they could not imagine undergoing an abortion, they have felt a real responsibility to prevent further pregnancies; an ironic position to be in after several years of unexplained infertility.

Liz and Craig look back on their Peace Corps experience and on the dreams that began there with a sense of satisfaction and of gratitude. Infertility robbed them of certain choices and added stress to their lives, but it did not prevent them from building the family that they had imagined. Many things in their lives have changed, but their preference for an international family has remained strong.

13

Donor Insemination

I had a miracle baby long before anybody ever heard of IVF or GIFT, and I can't tell anybody about it.

I feel like I am masquerading as a fertile woman. No one has any idea what I went through to have this baby.

We live with some questions that are too difficult to think about. I think that they are best left untouched.

THESE are voices of people who became parents through donor insemination. To the rest of the world they and their families look perfectly "normal." In many instances no one ever knew that they were infertile. Those who told friends and family there was a problem may have let people conclude that it was treated successfully. Even many of those who had acknowledged there was a serious male factor later went back over their tracks to erase any clue that they had turned to donor insemination. Most donor insemination parents live with a secret.

The secrecy adds stress to the experience of donor insemination parents. This chapter will focus primarily on that issue: what it means to live with a secret. However, it will also touch on other of the important features of D.I., some of which are outgrowths of or related to secrecy. They include:

1. secrecy
2. isolation and poor access to a peer group
3. when and how to talk with a child about D.I.

4. donor anonymity
5. the question of an "unequal" relationship
6. the wish to use the same donor for a second child
7. the need for support and advocacy groups

Secrecy

The secrecy begins with the procedure itself. Most physicians and programs practicing D.I. instruct couples to keep the fact of D.I. a secret, even from their obstetrician, their families, and eventually the child. Programs go to great lengths to keep couples from identifying each other and block off all access to donors. When women conceive they are sent off to busy obstetrical practices for routine prenatal care.

> My pregnancy was an exceptionally difficult time for me. My friends and family where thrilled for us, since they knew we'd wanted a baby for so long and assumed that our problem had been resolved. My doctor congratulated me and sent me on to a regular OB who had no way of knowing what I was worried about and why. And since I was concerned for my husband, who had already been through so much, I avoided telling him of my pain. Feeling bound to secrecy, I kept the fears to myself. No one knew how terrified I was that I had done something terribly wrong, how much I feared that a mistake had been made, how worried I was that something unexpected and awful would come out of me.

Secrecy is not something that most parents through donor insemination welcome nor necessarily support. Some actively reject secrecy and are open about the choice that they have made. Some are quite public about their decision, taking active steps to change the long-held doctrine that theirs is a situation that should be shrouded in secrecy. However, most D.I. parents accept that they must live with some degree of secrecy and deal with it as best they can.

Most D.I parents deal with the secret by defining its boundaries. While some may accept the recommendation of their physicians or their donor programs to maintain total secrecy—to the point of even keeping the truth from their child—most conclude there are some people that must know.

D.I. parents have varying ideas and feelings about who should know. Many agree that their child should know, but some feel that until the child is told no one else should have this personal information. Others choose to limit the telling to a few close family members and friends, feeling that it is impossible to maintain these intimate relationships with a secret lurking in the background. Others feel that they will tell or not tell people as it feels comfortable, making the decisions as they go along.

> We felt clear from the start that we wanted our parents and our siblings to know. It would have been too difficult to live with a family secret. When they all reacted enthusiastically, we began to tell a few friends. It was at that point that we decided we needed to close ranks for a while. We didn't want to look back at any point with regret, and felt that we could always tell more people but we could never erase the ones we'd told.

> I have told only my parents and my sister. It has been difficult but I feel that the circumstances of Andrew's birth are his business and no one else's. To tell anyone else ran the risk, I felt, of infringing on his privacy.

> In the beginning we told lots of people. We were very excited by the pregnancy and by Kara's birth. We were proud of the choice that we'd made and wanted people to know. Then, when Kara was a few years old, I began to have some second thoughts. I began to worry that someone would say something to her that would upset her—and all of us. Ever since then, we've been very private, telling no one new and asking those who do know to maintain our confidence.

People react differently to having a secret. For some who have never been terribly open it is not viewed as stressful; they don't feel a need to tell others about their personal lives. For others, especially those who value openness, the secret is a substantial burden. For them, maintaining a secret can feel like a form of dishonesty. It produces feelings of shame and guilt. Most find that these feelings are in direct conflict with the pride and delight they feel about their child. Those who feel this way and still keep their D.I. a secret do so because they feel they have no choice.

We tell very few people that Brian was conceived by D.I., but we do not like the secrecy. The program we were in stressed to us that this is the way we must be. We disagree with them, but we don't have the strength or the conviction to dismiss their advice.

Isolation and Poor Access to a Peer Group

Those D.I. parents who are troubled by secrecy complain that it isolates them from other D.I. parents. They long to hear how others have dealt with some of the complex issues involved and to compare feelings.

Often I feel stranded. I know that there are other D.I. moms out there, but I don't know who they are and I can't figure out how I can find them. When I see a couple with a child who doesn't look at all like its parents, I wonder. But I know that the child could be adopted or it could be their biological child who simply got Aunt Polly's genes. And even if I did have some way of figuring out who the D.I. families were, I couldn't approach them because they might see me as intruding upon their privacy.

Perhaps the fact that our families and friends know about and accept the fact that our son was conceived by D.I. has decreased our feeling of isolation. I do wish more people would "come out of the closet." It seems archaic and Victorian for it to be such a secretive, hush-hush affair, smacking of shame and guilt, when so many people are born this way! All it would take to eventually change that is for those of us who chose it to stop treating it that way!

The forced isolation of D.I. parents prevents them from talking together about the questions that puzzle and disturb them. How and when should they tell their child? How will they deal with the child telling others outside the family? How can they deal with the lack of information about the donor? How might the news of D.I. interfere with a child's relationship to his father? How will a D.I. father feel once his child knows? Isolation forces couples to deal with these complex questions, and others, on their own.

> We are figuring things out as we go along, and by and large that feels okay. However, as a fairly new mother I am used to consulting other mothers about all sorts of things, from day care to what to give the children for lunch. It is difficult to have this one area of parenting—so central to our experience—separated off. Sometimes I just wish I had a few people, in addition to my husband, to talk with.

When and How
to Talk with a Child about D.I.

The question that D.I. parents struggle with most involves how and when to tell their child about her origins. Having most likely rejected admonitions to hide the truth, they are left with few if any resources to guide them in the telling. They cannot really use the experience of adoptive parents as a guide because adoption is more widely known and accepted than D.I., making the information less loaded. Not only can a child understand the concept of adoption at an earlier age, but she can go public about her origins with fewer social consequences. D.I. parents must not only consider a child's readiness to hear about D.I. but must also consider society's readiness to respond supportively to her.

> I feel that we told our daughter at the right time and in the right way. She was five years old at the time and had a growing curiosity about where babies come from. She was beginning to ask a number of direct questions. We sat down with her and in very simple language explained about egg and sperm. Then we told her that sometimes men don't have sperm or have enough of them and that that was what had happened to her daddy. We explained that when that happens there are nice men who will give people their sperm so that they can have a baby. A good man had gone to the doctor and given the doctor some sperm so that we could have a baby grow inside my tummy. "And guess who that baby was!" we ended the story. Alina smiled in delight and said, "*It was me!*" Then she pointed to my stomach and pointed to herself.

Many D.I. parents express fears that they will either tell too soon or too late. They worry that their child will take the information out of the home, and that others will treat her insensitively. However, they recognize that there are substantial risks in waiting too long. To tell a preadolescent or adolescent about D.I. means running the risk that this confusing information will make a difficult time in the child's life even more turbulent. But waiting until after adolescence is also problematic because by that time a person's identity has been formed and is being consolidated.

> For many reasons, I'd like to wait until my son is a young adult to tell him. I'd like him to grow up with a clear and solid sense of who his father is and not to have any ambiguity to deal with. I know that it would make things easier for my husband, who had a difficult adolescence himself and who already has some fears about what Evan's will be like. But I fear that if we wait until Evan is a young adult, the news will be too jolting. By then he will have a well-developed sense of who he is, where he came from, and where he is going. I'm afraid that to tell him about D.I. then would be to shatter his fundamental assumptions about himself and our family.

The question of how and when to tell is all the more confusing for D.I. parents who have more than one child, especially if the other children were not conceived by D.I. With more than one child, questions arise about telling them separately or together, waiting until both or all are ready—whenever that is—or risking telling one "too soon" so that others are not told "too late."

D.I. parents envy the natural camaraderie that exists among adoptive parents who can easily find and identify each other. D.I. parents seem to resign themselves, albeit reluctantly, to going it alone and figuring things out as they go along.

> The more time passes, the more convinced I am that the secrecy is the hardest part. I have no regrets that we did D.I.; I adore my children, but I feel sad that I have to be so alone. I try to break the isolation by being a RESOLVE contact person and talking with other couples considering D.I. These conversations are very satisfying for me, but I still miss hearing from those who have gone before me.

Donor Anonymity

Although some D.I. parents use a known donor and some participate in programs that provide information about the donor, most
know very little if anything about their donor. They deal with this
lack of information in a variety of ways, both while they are undergoing D.I. and after their child is born. Some dismiss the lack of
information as a given and try not to think about it. Others look
for clues about the donor in their child. They match up all physical and personality characteristics with maternal family members
and learn about the donor by process of elimination. Those who
do know something about the donor may make a positive connection through that information, thereby removing some of the
mystery from the process.

> We were involved with a program that provided very little infor-
> mation about the donors. But since I am a Tay-Sachs carrier and
> wanted a Jewish donor who was not a carrier, I was able to learn
> a little about some of the donors. The donor we picked has red
> hair and is the son of holocaust survivors. We have no red hair in
> either of our families and knew that we were opening ourselves up
> to questions if we had a red-headed child. Still, I chose to go with
> him because his family background in the holocaust gave some
> meaning to all of this. What a wonderful thing he was doing, I
> believed. I felt that he was keeping alive the memory—and the
> blood line—of those who had perished. Our child is due in a few
> weeks and if she has red hair, I will know exactly where it came
> from. I expect I'll feel proud.

Parents through donor insemination talk of their gratitude to
the donor and of their inability to express this to him. Some find
it painful to have a nameless, faceless person out there who has
done so much for them but whom they can never thank. While
some attempt to put these feelings aside, feeling that there is little
that they can do with them, others try to confront them more
actively.

> At the beginning of the inseminations, I was poignantly aware of
> what a great gift the donor was giving us, and it hurt that there

was no way to say thank you. Now that the gift has been given and we have a child, it feels like we do have a way of expressing our appreciation. Our love for our son, unflinching and unbending, is one way that we can say to the donor—though he will probably never really know—that we are grateful to him. I look at our son and often think that someone very wonderful played a big part in giving him life. Our donor may not know this directly, but I will always be rooting for him.

Donor insemination parents have a range of reactions to the child's physical reality. Some feel comfortable assuming that their child resembles the donor. Others take note, with curiosity and delight, that their child bears an uncanny resemblance to his father. These parents are pleased when others unknowingly comment on how much the child looks like Dad. But many D.I. parents seem to be more comfortable connecting the child to his known maternal relatives and seem to be relieved if they can attribute a good many features to family members.

> I have felt almost from the start that Adam is built like my father. That has been a relief to me. As much as I feel gratitude towards the donor, I have a hard time imagining that our son looks like someone whom we've never met. Seeing my father in him is familiar and reassuring.

> When I learned that Jim is sterile, I felt an overwhelming sadness. I had wanted so much to have a child with him—a child who looked like him, who had his wit and sense of humor, a child who even had his funny little cowlick. As we began to talk about D.I. and to accept the infertility, I realized that our child would most likely end up looking somewhat like Jim, and that any child who grew up with him would have to take on his sense of humor. But then there was the cowlick and long after I felt ready to move on to D.I., I cried over that lost clump of hair.
>   Our daughter is a year old now, and after several months of baldness she is getting a full head of hair. To my amazement, and utter delight, she has a little clump of hair that sits at attention atop her head.

Children need to feel a positive identification with both of their parents, and D.I. parents can promote this by noting resemblances between the children and their fathers. In the absence of physical likenesses, they can comment on how a child has her dad's walk or smile or they can note how a particular gesture or expression is just like her father's. These comments can help forge a strong connection between father and child.

D.I. parents, who felt they were able to put their concerns about the donor's anonymity to rest when their children were young, are sometimes surprised to find that these concerns resurface around adolescence. As their children confront questions of identity, parents find that they too are troubled by some of the missing pieces. Although they may have been assured by the programs they worked with that their donor would not father other children in their area, this is something that they cannot be sure of. There are always stories going around of donors who fathered several dozen offspring, and these stories frighten parents whose children are beginning to date. How can they be sure that their children will not somehow happen upon—and fall in love with—a half-sibling or a cousin?

> We all know that it is a "small world." It certainly feels big, but people have a way of finding each other. How can we be sure that our son will not go away to college and become involved with one of our donor's other offspring or with some close relative? We didn't think about it until recently, but what will happen when he marries and has a child, and that child grows up? How will anyone know who is safe for that child to marry? With D.I. someone may appear to be a stranger but really be family.

The Question of an "Unequal" Relationship

Couples comtemplating D.I. frequently worry that the mother and father will have different and unequal relationships with their child. The fear that is often expressed is that mother and child will be close, and that the father will be left out of their exclusive relationship. In actuality, D.I. parents say that they do not find this to be true. Both mothers and fathers refer to close, loving relationships between father and child. In fact, in some families it appears that it is the father who has been more successful at accepting the infertility and moving on to parenting.

My husband has said that he fantasizes that someday our son will, in anger or rebellion, say something like "You can't make me do such-and-such because you're not my real Dad." Bill says that if this does happen, the words will hurt but he feels that he will be well prepared to handle them. His level of caregiving and daily involvement is so high that there will simply be no question whatsoever that he is Paul's real father. In fact, Bill already observes, he and Paul are so close that Paul is likely at some point to actually be looking for some ammunition, such as these taunting words, in order to help him separate.

I am surprised to find that my husband seems to have put infertility behind him more easily than I have. I feel very blessed to have our daughter, but I still feel resentment over what we had to go through in order to have her. My blood starts to boil whenever I hear people complain about their kids—they should only know how easy they had it! My husband, by contrast, doesn't get caught up in old angers and resentments. He is in love with Amy, and that is what he focuses on. Until she was born, I saw him as a reserved kind of guy who didn't show or express many emotions. Now, as a daddy, he is overflowing! He keeps a picture of Amy on his desk and often he phones just to tell me that he was looking at her and smiling.

Ted treats Amy's conception with a sense of humor. Since she looks more like him than she does me, we are constantly encountering comments by strangers who say how much she looks like her dad. Ted of course smiles and says thank you, but afterwards he tells me all the other thoughts that passed through his mind. He thinks of saying such things as "She probably does but who's to know" or "Your guess is as good as mine."

The Wish to Use the Same Donor for a Second Child

D.I. parents often hope their children will have the same donor. Depending on the program that they were in, as well as the donor's continued availability, willingness, and fertility, this is sometimes possible. Those who have succeeded in having the same donor report taking comfort in this. Having had one child by this donor, he is no longer a stranger. Also, they feel that they have offered their child some biological connectedness: she will probably never know many of her ancestors, but she will have one person in this world with whom she has a full genetic connection.

> It is a loss for us that we will not be able to use the same donor next time around. It used to be possible when our program used fresh semen, but it is not available to us now that they are using frozen specimens. This is hard, not only because we feel that it is a loss for Jenny, but also because we feel a connection to the donor. In an odd sort of way he — or at least his genes — have become part of the family. If we take a new donor, we are, in a sense, taking in a stranger.

The Need for Support and Advocacy Groups

In recent years a number of people and organizations have taken steps to reduce the isolation of couples who are considering or have done D.I.

RESOLVE offers a D.I. contact system through its national office in Arlington, Massachusetts. Couples who are interested in talking with D.I. parents can contact them (on a first-name-only basis, if preferred) through the RESOLVE network. On a local level as well, RESOLVE chapters are attempting to ease the isolation of D.I. parents and help them to find each other.

Carol Frost Vercollone, a clinical social worker in Stoneham, Massachusetts, and co-author of the pamphlet, *Understanding Artificial Insemination,* has done some pioneering group work with D.I. couples. Ms. Vercollone offers workshops for those considering D.I. as well as for D.I. parents. She has also served as a consultant to D.I. couples nationwide, advising them to find counselors in their area who can serve as central contact persons as she does, enabling couples to speak with each other and still preserve anonymity.

At the same time others are working actively toward policy change. Elizabeth Noble, a childbirth educator and D.I. mother, wrote *Having Your Baby by Donor Insemination,* in which she speaks out against the secrecy involved in current D.I. practice. Ms. Noble encourages others to take the path that she and her husband chose — that of a known donor — but also argues for major reforms in the practice of D.I. with anonymous donors. She demonstrates through interviews with those involved in D.I. as well as in adoption how damaging secrecy can be to family life and to an individual's sense of a cohesive and positive identity.

Shirley Pratten, another D.I. mother, has spoken publicly about the difficulties that she experienced postpartum, linking many of those difficulties to the secrecy and to the resultant sense of shame. Ms. Pratten has helped found the New Reproductive Alternatives Society in Canada, an organization committed to bringing D.I. into the public eye and to removing the terrible burden of secrecy. The New Reproductive Alternatives Society is involved in legislative efforts in Canada aimed at better protecting the interests of all parties in D.I. Ms. Pratten's organization also functions as a support group for couples contemplating D.I., as well as those undertaking it and those who are already D.I. parents.

> We had a terrible time after our daughter was born. Looking back now I realize that we were inadequately prepared for the experience. We had been trying inseminations with my husband's sperm, and when these were unsuccessful the urologist involved in our case told us to turn to D.I. He presented it to us as if it were really no different than husband insemination. I remember there being extremely powerful emotions around this time—so powerful that I didn't know what to do with them, and there was nobody to talk to. I felt a profound sadness around infertility, and as we continued straight into D.I. I felt emotionally traumatized by the whole experience. To this day seven years later, there are times when that deep-seated grief emerges. I believe that had we acknowledged that what we were going through was a major loss—the loss of our biological children—and had we had time to grieve for that, our whole experience with D.I. might have been different.
>
> When we conceived through D.I., questions arose about how we would tell our child. Our inseminating physician said that most people "didn't say anything," and as we had nobody else to talk to, we tried to do what the doctor advised. It didn't feel right trying to hold it inside; it felt like we had done something very bad, something so bad that it had to be kept hidden.
>
> I hope that the work of our society will spare others our pain, to help them grieve the biological child they did not have together and then to move on to enjoy the real pleasures of having a baby through D.I. Once the secrecy is gone, D.I. should be able to assume its rightful place as an important and accessible reproductive alternative.

Candace Turner, herself an adult D.I. offspring, founded the self-help group Donor's Offspring in 1981. The organization, which publishes a newsletter and other materials, runs self-help meetings and addresses itself primarily to the needs of the offspring, most of whom have very limited access to information about or contact with their biological fathers.

Although many D.I. parents question the secrecy and welcome the possibility of greater openness in D.I., some couples feel caught in the crossfire. Physicians, for the most part, continue to advocate and even insist on secrecy in the practice of D.I. By contrast, activists like Ms. Noble insist on openness. D.I. couples sometimes find themselves confused and unclear about what to think and how to act. The companionship of other couples provides a helpful forum for discussion during these confusing times.

As troubling as the secret is and as isolated as they feel, most D.I. parents say that these burdens are fortunately but a small part of their parenting experience. Much of the time they are too busy changing diapers, running a play group, or coaching little league to focus a great deal on their child's origins. Most of the time they are very busy just being parents.

> Then something happens and I am reminded. Yesterday my daughter Marissa came home from school and announced that one of her friends had a new half sister. Her widowed father had remarried and his new wife had had a baby. Marissa was very curious about this and asked if she might one day have a half-sibling. I felt startled by the question! The truth is that she probably has half-biological siblings out there. Who even knows how many? I felt sad for her and I guess for me this is a question that we will never be able to answer.

Karen and Marty:
Life Restored and Renewed

When Karen and Marty told Karen's parents that they had decided to try to have a baby by donor insemination, they were surprised by the response they got. Not only were her parents supportive, but Karen's father, a physician, revealed that he had been a sperm donor when he was in medical school. Perhaps it was this experience, combined with the fact that his grandson looks a lot like him, that has caused him to take particular delight in Kenny.

> It has meant so much to me to see the relationship between my dad and Kenny. When I was pregnant, I had some fears that I was carrying some unfamiliar and foreign creature. To see a grandpa with his "chip off the old block" has been very reassuring. I am relieved also that we decided to tell some of those closest to us that we were using donor insemination. The program we were in—at a large teaching hospital—counseled us to tell no one. *Counseled* is too mild a word—they insisted. They told us that we would be doing ourselves and our child a real disservice if we let anyone know that he was conceived by D.I.
>
> I think that from the start they set us up to feel really isolated. Not only did they urge us to be secretive with the outside world, but they established—and carefully enforced—a very secretive system within the hospital. The D.I. program had a code name, and elaborate measures were taken to make sure that we could not identify other D.I. couples, let alone donors. It felt like we were part of some bizarre, science-fiction project.

Fortunately, Karen and Marty did not have to be part of the "sci-fi" project for very long. Karen conceived on her fourth cycle and had a healthy term—actually postterm—pregnancy. She remembers how puzzled people were by her patience when Kenny was three weeks late. She recalls wanting to tell them that this was nothing after all their years of suffering.

The three week wait was easy, but the delivery, by caesarean, was difficult. Because there was a drape up preventing her from seeing Kenny being born, Karen remembers having a hard time believing that he was really hers. She was relieved when she saw that he resembled Marty but initially had a hard time connecting this baby to the movement she had felt inside her for several months. Marty's reaction, which was one of pure delight, helped Karen begin to bond with their son.

> Once it clicked in that Kenny was really ours, I began to forge a strong bond. For the first several months of his life I nursed him exclusively, and I only introduced a bottle when he was ten months old. Until then, I did a good job of convincing him that he only wanted to drink from the breast.

As a first-grade teacher, Karen sometimes has children in her class who have been adopted. She has also had parents share with her the fact that they are experiencing secondary infertility. Karen says that moments like these are painful for her, because she wants to share with others the fact that Kenny also was long in coming. Instead, she feels that she must be an imposter — that she is forced to pretend that she is a stranger to infertility. Both she and Marty feel relieved that they have told some people about their infertility and subsequent decision, but wish that D.I. were not so shrouded in secrecy.

> My infertility was a real shock to both of us, but we fully understood how it came about and don't see it as something to be ashamed of. In fact, in an odd sort of way, it represents a victory.
>
> When I was nineteen years old I was diagnosed as having Hodgkin's disease. I was treated with surgery and with radiation and given the optimistic news that the disease was behind me. When I had a recurrence three years later, I underwent chemotherapy. At that time, no one knew — or spoke about — an association between chemotherapy and infertility. Besides, at the time having children was the last thing on my mind. I felt that I was staring death in the face, and I was scared. I was ready to pay any price for my life. Still, I did not know the price I was paying.

It was not until Karen and Marty decided to have children and were concerned that the radiation might have caused genetic abnormalities that they learned chemotherapy had been implicated in infertility. Marty promptly went for a semen analysis. The grim news came abruptly by phone, delivered by a doctor that the couple had never met. "Your count was zero. I'm sorry." was all that he said.

Karen remembers being devastated by the news but also rationalizing her feelings. She'd rather have Marty alive and well than the alternative. The treatment for his disease had robbed them of their chance to bear a child together, but it saved his life. The couple investigated donor insemination, and decided that it was an option for them. They learned that there was a year-and-a-half wait until they could begin inseminations in the program that had been recommended to them. This seemed like an eternity, but later they looked back and were glad that they had been forced to wait. The waiting period offered them an opportunity to really consider what they were undertaking and to grieve the child they would not have together.

> I remember looking at Marty a lot during this time and feeling so sad that our child would not look like him. It was an incredible loss, like someone had died. I felt that something irreplaceable was gone from my life. When Kenny was born it felt like a miracle had occurred. He looked like Marty! The genes had crept through after all!

As time has passed, Karen and Marty have found it increasingly difficult to look ahead and think about how they will tell Kenny about D.I. They see it as something they need to do because they feel that a family cannot live with big secrets. Still, it is painful to think about it because it will involve such a loss of innocence.

> I look at Kenny and wish that I could change the facts of his conception. I worry that the news we tell him will change his relationship with Marty, and that it will never be the same again. At the same time I believe that something positive will come of this. I think that Kenny will understand, more than ever before, how much he was wanted. I think that he will know how much his father really loves him.

Rabbi

To our friends and family—and to the congregation that I serve as a rabbi—we are a fertile couple. We married, waited two years, and had our first child right on schedule. Three years later our second son was born. Now, four years after that, my wife is pregnant once again. The fact that I am a sterile man remains a well-kept secret, hidden in the normalcy of our family.

When people tell me that our older boy looks like me, I smile and say "thank you." When the president of the congregation introduces my family or requests a special blessing in our honor, I beam with pleasure. They are truly mine, I am theirs, and we are a family with countless blessings.

Yet I live with a secret, and at times it haunts me. I can perform naming ceremonies for ten babies without thinking of it, and then the eleventh comes along and I feel a tug, a pull, a quiet longing. Standing there, blessing someone else's baby, I think of my child, the flesh of my flesh, never born. For although I am a father, with all the attendant rights, privileges, and burdens, I have never planted two little feet upon this earth.

Sam goes on to talk about the part of his work that puts him in touch with infertile couples. Some come to him to talk about their infertility, about adoption, pregnancy losses, and occasionally, he even meets with a couple who is considering donor insemination. These meetings are hard for Sam because he is an open person, one who avoids secrecy. He would like to let his congregants know that he understands what they are going through, that he has been there himself. But when they decided to use donor sperm, he and his wife Carole decided they would not be public about their route to parenthood. They have told a few family members and no one else. As difficult as it has been to maintain silence, Sam feels that this is something he wants and needs to do.

Carole and I knew about my infertility before we were married and made decisions accordingly. We learned about it in a strange way. When I was in high school, I liked to fool around with a microscope. On more than one occasion, I tried to look at my sperm. But despite my best efforts, I had never been able to see any swimming around. Naturally, I was too embarrassed to tell anyone what I was doing, so I kept it to myself and remained mildly concerned. Later, when I met Carole, I felt that I owed it to her to tell her about my adolescent experiments. She laughed and told me not to worry. But I did worry because we very much wanted to have a family together, and because I had a terrible feeling that my scientific eye was better than my reproductive system. I went ahead and had a semen analysis, and it confirmed my worst fears: the count was zero.

I had a hard time with the news. Even though I had had some warning, I reacted with disbelief. Why me? Here I was preparing to be a rabbi, devoting myself to a religion that said "be fruitful and multiply," and I was sterile! Could I be angry with God? Should I be angry with myself? What had I done to cause this? What had been done to me? I was filled with questions that had no answers.

Carole had answers. She immediately began talking about donor insemination and quickly found out about it. She was clearly comfortable with the idea from the start, but I was not. I worried that our relationships with the child (children) would be different. I wondered what it would be like to have a son—whether I'd feel envy and competition. I wondered if I could raise a child of unknown paternity. I wondered what Judaism would have to say about all of this.

It took a lot of courage, but I spoke with two of the rabbis who were my most-respected teachers. Each said the same thing. Judaism is a religion that not only supports parenting but also feels that people must create solutions to their problems. D.I. is a solution to childlessness, and therefore it is very much in the spirit of my religion. And as with adoption, the Talmud says that the true parent is not the person who bears the child, but rather the one who raises it.

I felt comforted and reassured by these responses, but troubled by the additional advice that was given to me. Both rabbis advised us to request non-Jewish donors to avoid any possibility of intermarriage. I understood their reasoning, but I had a hard time with it because it felt strange to think that our children would be half-Christian by birth. It had always been very important to me to marry someone Jewish so that we would have children who were Jewish. In addition, I was concerned that children of Christian donors would look different from us, that their Christian features would call attention to this and that it would be harder for both Carole and me to bond with them.

As it has turned out, Sam's two sons are both fair with blue eyes. Their older boy does have a strong resemblance to Sam and fortunately, both boys look like Carole and her family. Sam and Carole feel that they made the right decision when they requested Christian donors, but still feel like it would have been easier for them emotionally had they been able to use Jewish donors. "With Jews we would have felt like we were all part of a larger family."

Most of the time Sam and Carole give little thought to their history. They are proud, involved parents who encourage their children to participate actively in a wide range of activities. On most days they are too busy with soccer or little league, piano lessons, or Hebrew school to give much thought to sperm donors or infertility. Then something happens, and the subject is before them.

Noah, our older son, was found to be near-sighted when he was six years old. I took him to my ophthalmologist who examined him and said, "Well, Noah, you've got your daddy's eyes." I looked at my blue-eyed, near-sighted son (with my dark brown, near-sighted eyes), and at our sweet, keen-eyed doctor and smiled. It's moments like these that remind me, in an ironic sort of way, of the secret.

Sam and Carole have decided to tell their children they were conceived by D.I., but they have not figured out how or when they will tell them. One question they have is whether they should tell them individually or together. If they tell them together, they may have to wait until their eldest is older than they'd like him to be, because they would have to be sure that the youngest was also old enough to understand. For them, as with other D.I. couples, the question sits there on a shelf, waiting to someday be figured out. Occasionally, they take it off the shelf and attempt to answer it, but as yet, with two young children and one on the way, this has not been possible. Most often they return it rapidly to the shelf and wait for the time when the answer will come.

As parents, we face all sorts of questions and challenges raising our children. Many are difficult, but all have answers and solutions of one sort or another. This one feels different. We think about it and answers don't come. Each time we reshelve it, we hope that our problem is simply in timing—that the answer will come to us when the time is right.

14

Surrogacy

I'll never forget the moment that we got the call that Zoe had been born. We had hoped to be there at the delivery, and Caroline, our surrogate, had done her best to give us notice, but Zoe came quickly. Before we could even get to the airport, we had word that we had a daughter. I'll always appreciate the fact that Caroline called us herself, congratulated us, and asked us if we minded if she held our daughter.

I had a hard time in the beginning. Our experience with our surrogate went very smoothly, and we were able to be there for Andrew's birth. We were ecstatic to be parents. But during those first few weeks, I experienced a lot of turmoil. I wondered if I was really his mother. I felt bad every time someone commented on how much he looked like his Dad. I felt worse every time they said he looked like me.

THESE are voices of people who became parents through surrogacy. The practice of one woman carrying a baby for another, known as *surrogate motherhood,* dates back to the biblical story of Abraham and Sarah. When they were unable to have a child together, Abraham turned to a concubine, Hagar, to bear his child. Since then, countless couples have become parents with the help of surrogates. Nonetheless, there are individuals and groups who have been critical of surrogacy, sometimes even condemning it as a radical departure from accepted means of building families.

Couples turn to surrogacy as an avenue to parenthood for a

number of reasons. For some, it feels like an obvious second choice: surrogacy offers them the opportunity to have a child that is biologically connected to at least one of them, and it offers them the opportunity to know something about the prenatal care their child is getting. Surrogacy is often faster than adoption. For these and other reasons, many couples see a surrogate arrangement as preferable to traditional adoption.

For other couples, surrogacy is a third, not a second, choice. These are couples who would prefer to adopt but who have found, for one reason or another, that they are unable to do so. The most common reason for this is age; one or both partners may be too old to qualify for a traditional adoption. Other couples are unable to adopt because they are unmarried (or have not been married long enough), or because one member has had a serious medical problem.

Couples who decide to become parents through surrogacy are in a lonely position. They face a press, media, and often legislatures that seem oblivious to the pain of infertility and to the difficulties involved in adoption. They face women's organizations who tell them they are taking advantage of poor women. They face religious groups that tell them that their path to parenthood is immoral. They face a legal system that threatens to make surrogacy more difficult to arrange. After the disappointment of infertility, and sometimes of failed adoption attempts, they face a new isolation.

Parents through surrogacy face joy as well. Having survived years of infertility and, for some, failed adoptions, they are finally parents. They are well prepared to delight in the children who are finally with them. Moreover, for many parents the experience of working with a surrogate has brought unanticipated satisfaction and pleasure. They have found those circumstances have connected them with another person in a unique and most special way.

This chapter will look at their experience. It will focus on some of the special features of parenting through surrogacy, including:

1. the relationship with the surrogate during pregnancy, labor, and delivery
2. the ongoing relationship with the surrogate and her family

3. talking with the child about surrogacy
4. the lack of societal support
5. the need for a peer group
6. unclaimed losses

The Relationship with the Surrogate During Pregnancy, Labor, and Delivery

There are two kinds of surrogate arrangements commonly used by infertile couples. It is important to distinguish between them before beginning any discussion of the pregnancy, labor, and delivery.

Before the development of IVF and GIFT, couples who turned to surrogacy because of female infertility were looking for a woman who would be artificially inseminated with the husband's sperm. The child she then conceived and carried was his biological child as well as hers. Some women, who might otherwise have been willing to carry a child for an infertile couple, had difficulty with this arrangement because it meant surrendering their biological child.

The new reproductive technologies have given infertile couples and potential surrogates a new option: "gestational" or "host-uterus" surrogacy. With the advances of IVF, GIFT, and zygote intrafallopian transfer (ZIFT), a woman can carry a baby that is not biologically hers. This type of surrogacy is attractive to some women who are willing to carry a baby for another couple but who do not want to face the potential heartache of giving up a child who is their genetic offspring. According to Kathe Linden of the Organization for Parents through Surrogacy (OPTS), it is appealing to infertile couples because there are more surrogates interested in this process than in traditional surrogacy, and also because it offers the couple the opportunity to have a child that is biologically theirs. If the infertile woman does not have viable eggs and the couple still prefers this type of surrogacy, they may be able to obtain donor eggs.

The type of surrogacy arrangement a couple enters into certainly has bearing on their experience, as well as on that of the surrogate. However, for the purposes of this brief and introductory discussion of surrogate pregnancy, traditional surrogacy and gestational surrogacy will be spoken of together.

Couples who have become parents through surrogacy frequently describe the pregnancy as a very intense experience for all involved. Typically, couples and surrogates become very close during this time. There is a bonding that occurs, especially between the two women.

> At first it was a very tentative relationship. The whole experience was new to both of us, and we were not sure how to act. But as Heather's pregnancy progressed, we became very close. We are women from two very different backgrounds, who live in two very different worlds, but there is an incredible bond between us.

Couples who have worked with a surrogate frequently identify the surrogate's husband as a key player in their experience. Many see it as crucial that he be supportive and involved in his wife's experience; not simply someone who passively agrees to a surrogate arrangement. Other members of the surrogate's family are also important. To the extent that they offer support and encouragement, the experience is easier and more positive for all involved.

> We were really touched by Tom's interest and concern for us. He was the one who phoned us when Ryan was born (we live far away and were unable to get there for the delivery) and he was just wonderful on the phone. Like his wife, he made every effort to emphasize that this was our baby.

> When we were looking for a surrogate, one of the things that was most important to us was her relationship with her husband. We knew that some programs accepted divorced or even single women, and that many accepted surrogates whose husbands were not going to be actively involved. We wanted a surrogate who had a very caring and supportive husband, who would be an active participant in this drama. In retrospect, we were very right in making this a priority. I think that things went so well because of who Bill is and because of how he relates to Kathy.

Couples also note that the staff of the agency they work with are key players in establishing and facilitating their relationship with their surrogates. Parents through surrogacy express gratitude toward agencies that demonstrate care and sensitivity in making matches and that offer guidance, combined with flexibility, once a pregnancy has been established.

> We have a lot of faith in our program and especially in the psychologist who matches couples with surrogates. She has great skill in identifying people's priorities and lets you know that she takes your concerns very seriously. Even before meeting our surrogate we felt confident that she would be someone we would like, trust, and come to care deeply about.

Although the entire pregnancy is a powerful experience, many parents through surrogacy identify labor and delivery as the most important time in their bonding with their surrogate. They are often moved by the sensitivity that their surrogates demonstrate toward them. Many are present at the birth, and those who are unable to be there, usually because of geography, are also touched by the way they are included. In addition to the concern and caring the surrogates so often convey, couples appreciate the support that they receive from physicians, nursing staff, and others.

> Annie's arrival was as exhilarating as all our years of infertility were demoralizing. Becky, an experienced mom, was very good at predicting when and how fast the baby would come. She was right on target this time and got us there with lots of time to spare. It was hard to see her in pain but she was really terrific about it. She kept smiling at us and telling us it was worth it. When Annie emerged, Becky told Jim to cut the cord. It was great the way that she did it — no big deal, but a quiet, gentle way she made it clear that this was our baby.

> The hospital staff was great. They had had a few other surrogate births, and they seemed comfortable with the process. They helped us to coach Lisa during her labor, but gave us a lot of room to be with her alone. After she delivered they asked if the three of us wanted some time alone together with our new baby.

The Ongoing Relationship with the Surrogate and Her Family

In entering into a surrogate arrangement, neither the infertile couple nor the surrogate knows what their relationship will be like after the baby is born. That relationship is something that needs to evolve, determined by time, geography, and personalities. However, couples and surrogates often find it helpful to give some thought to their expectations ahead of time and to try to enter into a surrogate arrangement that has some potential for meeting those expectations.

> We know some couples who wanted no contact whatsoever with their surrogates after the baby was born. They wanted to keep things as distant and as anonymous as possible. They needed to find surrogates who felt pretty much the same way. However, for us it was different. We were not hoping to be best friends with our surrogate, but we wanted someone who would want some sort of ongoing contact. It was impossible for us to imagine having someone be so central to our lives and then vanish.

Parents through surrogacy emphasize the need to be open and flexible in their relationship with their surrogate. Some find that the agencies they work with offer them helpful advice in this regard. Because this is all a new experience for them—and one for which they probably have no role models—they welcome guidance about their contacts with their surrogate. At the same time, however, because it is such an intense and intimate relationship, it is also crucial that they be creative and responsive.

> When Susan first conceived, we had a minimum of contact with her. The agency advised us to send letters every few weeks or so but did not encourage us to meet or have more frequent contact. Later in the pregnancy, we felt comfortable departing from this. Susan invited us to come visit her, and we felt that that was something that we wanted to do. Since Karen's birth, we have continued to see the relationship as something that is ever-changing. We all felt we needed a lot of contact during Karen's early weeks, but now that she is nearly two, much of the intensity has diminished.

Parents and their surrogates can choose from a range of ongoing relationships. There are situations in which the surrogate, the couple, or both pull back after birth, perhaps out of a sense of protection for themselves, perhaps in an effort to protect the other.

> We had frequent contact with Nan during Andrew's early months. Then it began to feel like too much. I was struggling with my new identity as his mother and I felt uneasy having her in the background so much of the time. After much soul-searching, I wrote her a letter, explaining that I needed for there to be less contact. I tried to do it sensitively and was very worried about hurting her feelings. She wrote a sweet letter back. She seemed to understand and respect my feelings, but also felt a little hurt at the same time.

Other parents and surrogates find they prefer more active ongoing contact. If geography permits, some have frequent visits. Sometimes these visits include husbands; sometimes it is the women who maintain the close ties. In some situations the children are included in these visits, but often they are not involved. Some couples and/or surrogates find that it is best to leave the children out. They feel that there may be too much ambiguity when children are included.

A big question for parents and their surrogates has to do with contacts with the surrogate's other children. For families who worked with gestational surrogates, this question is not complicated by the issue of biological ties. The surrogate's children have no blood ties with the child born of the surrogacy arrangement and therefore, there is no reason for them to see themselves as siblings. However, for families formed through traditional surrogacy, this can be a thorny issue. The surrogate's children are the half sisters and brothers to the child she bore for the couple. All may have feelings about this, especially if the couple's child remains an only child.

> We feel like we want Nina to know Bonnie's children since they are her half sister and brother. We feel that the best way to do this is for them to see each other from time to time in the early years. We expect that they will relate as long distance first cousins. When

they are old enough to understand, we can explain their relationship to each other.

Another key question between couples and surrogates is
whether she will carry another child for them. Some couples feel
so strongly about their connection to their surrogate that they do
not want to have a child with another surrogate. Some surrogates
feel such a strong allegiance to their couple that they want to bear
their next child for them.

> We are nearly ready for another child and we feel clear that we
> would only have it with Kate. I've thought a lot about this and I
> think I understand why I feel this way. I think that if we used
> another surrogate it would feel like we were somehow minimizing
> the importance of what she did for us. If she decides she doesn't
> want to or can't do it again, we won't have more children.

There are couples who have children with different surrogates
(as well as couples who adopt children or who have biological
children). Some couples feel comfortable having relationships
with two (or more) surrogates and feel that just as their relationships with each of their children is different, so also are their relationships with their surrogates. Conversely, there are surrogates
who bear a child for only one couple, while others elect to bear
a child for a second or third couple. In her book, *Between
Strangers,* Lori Andrews describes the conviction that many
women bring to the experience of surrogacy, as well as the satisfaction they get from undertaking and completing it. It is not surprising, in hearing their stories, that many want to repeat the
experience.

Talking with the Child about Surrogacy

Just as they differ in their feelings about ongoing relationships
with their surrogates, so also do parents through surrogacy take
differing positions about how to deal with their child. There are
some who intend to tell their child nothing, or to pretend that the
child was adopted. However, most parents do believe that they
should tell their child about the surrogate arrangement. For

guidance on how and when to tell the child about her background, some turn to the experience of adoptive parents.

Parents through surrogacy, like adoptive parents, generally believe that they should be open, honest, and direct. However, they also recognize that they should never give their child more information than she needs and can understand. This means listening very carefully to the questions that the child asks and answering them in a simple, age-appropriate way. It means being careful to respond to what seems to be on the child's mind and not to answer out of their own anxiety.

Parents through surrogacy face an additional challenge in talking with their children. While adoptive parents have some concerns about how their child's friends, teachers, and others will respond when she tells them she is adopted, parents through surrogacy have many more concerns about their child being teased or treated with bias. Certainly there is some stigma associated with adoption, but adoption is also increasingly commonplace and accepted. Surrogacy, by contrast, is new to many people. Some are simply curious about it. Others are confused. And still others are openly critical of it. Parents need to balance their child's need for clear, accurate information with their own awareness and concern about the ways in which this information could be intentionally, or inadvertently, misused.

> We feel that it is best to tell Karen that she is adopted. That is something that she will be able to understand and that others will more or less respect. To avoid lying to her, I tell her that she looks like her Dad (which is true). I feel that when she is older, I can explain the truth to her: because of the special circumstances of her birth, she is both adopted and her Dad's biological child.

Parents through surrogacy can take some comfort in the fact that we live in a world in which the concept of family is changing. Divorce, remarriage, foreign adoptions, single parents, homosexual couples, and the new reproductive technologies all contribute to the new landscape. Children born through surrogacy have to deal with differences but so do lots of other children: in school they will encounter a diminishing number of children who come from traditional, intact, two-parent, biologically connected, white-picket-fence families.

> The other day my five-year-old daughter was talking about one of her friends at school. She commented that this friend has "brown skin" and then mentioned that the child's mother is white. She went on to state, in the most matter of fact way, that if the girl's father is also white then she must be adopted but if he is black, she was not. I feel that foreign and interracial adoptions, as well as blended and step-families, are teaching my daughter at an early age to be comfortable with differences.

The Lack of Societal Support

Couples who elect to work with a surrogate are not usually iconoclasts, working toward social change, or are they pursuing surrogacy to make a statement. Most of the time, they do not want to be different. What they want is to be parents.

Although they did not set out to be different, parents through surrogacy form their families in a nonconventional way. While support for surrogacy exists—some individuals and groups oppose this practice. Their opposition is disturbing to some of those who are involved in surrogacy.

> Caroline, our surrogate, was pregnant at a time when there was a lot of negative publicity about surrogacy. We found it very difficult in a number of ways. One was that we were afraid the publicity would make Caroline feel bad, would cause her to feel that she had done the wrong thing. A second was that we weren't sure what we'd tell people when the baby arrived. We had originally intended to say we'd used surrogacy but we changed our minds and decided to say we had adopted.

> When the different women's groups got involved in their antisurrogacy campaigns it felt like they were taking a "let them eat cake" approach to infertility. I felt that they had no understanding of what it meant to be infertile, to long for a baby, to do all you possibly could to have a family. It was easy for them to sit back and say "let them adopt" because they were not adopting. They had no idea that adoption is difficult, that it is not for everyone, and that some of us have very sound reasons for pursuing surrogacy.

One way that parents through surrogacy deal with opposition to surrogacy is to remain circumspect about their decision. While they may not keep it a secret, they may choose to be careful with whom they talk. They feel that they need to be careful because there are children involved, and because information has a way of being misused or abused. For some who feel especially enthusiastic about surrogacy, this can be difficult. Having found that their second- or even third-choice route to parenthood is filled with rewards, they want to share this discovery with others. Like many D.I. parents, they feel that society forces them to be very private about a choice that has brought them great joy. They would like to be able to introduce others to the special satisfactions that come through surrogacy.

> We're very happy about the choice that we made, and we want to tell others about it. But we are also cautious. We know that everybody does not feel as we do about surrogacy, and we also know that it is a subject that people can get very dramatic about. So we are careful to limit our talks to people who are seriously considering using a surrogate or have some other "legitimate" interest in the subject.

The Need for a Peer Group

Up until two years ago, parents through surrogacy dealt with their need for companionship by identifying with adoptive parents, as traditional surrogacy is a form of adoption. This identification was to some extent satisfactory, but in another way, it was frustrating.

> I tried, as much as possible, to be involved with adoptive-parent groups. I am legally Lauren's "adoptive mother" so this seemed like a reasonable thing for me to do. And I was grateful to have the companionship. What I found, however, is that it only went so far toward meeting my needs. The other adoptive mothers wanted to talk about issues that were specific to adoption and not to surrogacy, and once again I felt left out. While I'm glad that we did what we did because we ended up with a terrific child, I sometimes envy the companionship of adoptive parents.

Parents through surrogacy are no longer so isolated. The Organization of Parents through Surrogacy (OPTS) was founded in 1987 by a group of parents whose children were born through surrogacy or other alternate birth methods. According to its newsletter, OPTS "advocates, supports, and protects the birth rights of all children and seeks to keep open the options made available by advances in reproductive technology to those unable to have children in the conventional manner." In addition, OPTS diminishes the isolation of parents through surrogacy by offering them a contact system of "phone phriends" and by organizing social functions, such as an annual picnic. As with other self-help organizations, there are some parents through surrogacy who participate actively in OPTS and others who find that membership and reading the newsletter are enough to let them know that they are not alone.

Unclaimed Losses

According to OPTS, approximately one in ten traditional surrogate pregnancies, and three in ten gestational surrogate pregnancies, ends in miscarriage. The premature and involuntary end of any pregnancy is painful, but the loss of a surrogate pregnancy is especially difficult. Not only was it exceptionally hard to come by, particularly if a new reproductive technology was used, but there probably was not a lot of social support. A miscarriage may prompt feelings that a surrogate pregnancy was tampering with nature and was not meant to be. It may revive old conflicts about surrogacy that had been laid to rest.

This miscarriage of a surrogate pregnancy is also difficult because it is such uncharted territory. Couples and their surrogates have limited guidance on how to conduct themselves during a pregnancy; they have even less guidance when that pregnancy fails. How do they comfort each other, avoid feeling or conveying blame, and sort out if and when to try again?

The other loss experienced by parents through surrogacy—and by their surrogates—is of the experience that they shared together. Hopefully, they have accomplished what they set out to do, but the arrival of the child involves a loss as well as a victory.

The intense, intimate, often loving relationship that develops during a surrogate pregnancy has to change as parents and surrogates go on with their lives.

> There were things that she said and did during the pregnancy that we will take with us and treasure for life.

When they finally have the child or children that they longed for, it is important for couples to look back and acknowledge the losses that they experienced along the way. They need to claim these losses as part of their experience—not a favorite part—but something to be acknowledged nonetheless. By acknowledging these losses, they are able to integrate them into the complex experience that enabled them to become a family.

For all that they have been through, most parents through surrogacy voice few complaints. Not only do they end up with the children they so desperately wanted, but many feel blessed to have had the opportunity to work with a surrogate. The connection they feel to their surrogate is a unique one. There are few, if any, opportunities in life in which strangers come together and give so much to each other and feel that they are getting so much in return.

Ronnie and Steve and Andrea: Three Parents Working Together

> It was a very intense experience. There we were, sitting in an office thousands of miles from home, face to face with someone who would alter the course of our lives. Ahead of time I had no idea how I would feel about her, how I would react to her pregnancy— to our pregnancy. I hadn't anticipated how much I would like her.

Ronnie continues to have very strong and positive feelings toward her surrogate, Andrea, and about the experience that they shared together. After four difficult years of infertility tests and treatments, Andrea enabled Ronnie and her husband Steve to become parents: she gave birth to their daughter, Rebecca.

It was a hectic and exciting summer. As Andrea's due date approached, Steve and I went into a flurry of activity. We bought a crib, a dresser, baby accessories, and anything else that we thought we would need. I remember the thrill that I felt when I saw the room all set up. At long last it felt like there *really* was going to be a baby for us. It was an awesome feeling.

Ronnie enjoys remembering all the excitement and anxiety that she and Steve felt in the weeks before their daughter's arrival. They were in regular contact with Andrea, and when she reached her due date, they both rented beepers. They wanted to be sure that Andrea, or her husband, Nick, could reach them as soon as she went into labor. Ronnie smiles as she remembers wearing her beeper everywhere and waiting eagerly for it to go off. As it turned out, the news came by phone at 3:00 A.M. Nick called to tell them that Andrea was in labor and encouraged them to be on the first flight possible.

We were at the airport at 7 A.M. (Needless to say, we never went back to sleep that night.) We arrived at the hospital in late morning and learned that Andrea had been given medication to lower her skyrocketing blood pressure. She was about to go into the delivery room, and we were directed into the father's waiting room. There we paced, tried to watch the news on T.V., paced some more, and watched down the hall for anyone with news. Two hours later, Nick came out and told us that we had a baby girl.

Ronnie and Steve's delight was slightly tempered by the news that it had been a difficult delivery and that Rebecca's shoulder had been bruised while the doctor was pulling her out of the birth canal. The hospital staff warned them that the baby would look bruised, but told them that any nerve damage would probably correct itself (which it did, within a few weeks). Although Ronnie was worried about the arm, her first reaction to Rebecca was that she was big and beautiful and looked just like her father.

The hospital staff was wonderful. They let us hold and feed Rebecca right away. They let us come and go freely in the nursery, enabling us to spend lots of time with Rebecca. We also spent time with Andrea before she went home. She was exhausted and sore from the labor and delivery but seemed very happy for us after the birth. She told us that she was very glad to have been our surrogate but added, "don't ask me to do it again!"

Ronnie and Steve's experience with surrogacy worked out very well for them, but it was not entirely smooth sailing. Although their friends and families were supportive of their decision to pursue surrogacy, those close to them became concerned when the Mary Beth Whitehead case exploded. At that time, Andrea was four months pregnant; and although Ronnie and Steve felt confident that she would stand by her decision to surrender, it was hard convincing their well-intentioned friends and relatives that they were not in jeopardy. The tension around that case, together with the fact that some relatives were skeptical about the costs involved in surrogacy, caused some stress during the pregnancy.

At the same time, however, there were aspects of the surrogacy experience that were better than anything Ronnie and Steve had imagined. To their suprise and delight, both Andrea and Nick's families were encouraging and helpful. They visited with Andrea, Nick, and their children several times during Andrea's pregnancy and got to know both Andrea's and Nick's parents.

We were really touched by how open and welcoming both of their families were towards us. To our surprise and amazement, Nick's mother held a surprise shower for us. She invited us to her home and when we arrived, we saw balloons and streamers. Fortunately, I was dressed for the occasion in my "Expectant Adoptive Mom" t-shirt. Andrea was wearing the maternity t-shirt that I had given her that said, "#1 Surrogate Mom." It was a great occasion!

Ronnie and Steve describe the first few weeks of parenthood as being both wonderful and tough at the same time. When Rebecca was eight days old they celebrated the Jewish ritual of *Brit Banot*, in which a baby girl is officially presented to the world. After all they had been through, this was a very special occasion. On the other hand, adjusting to round-the-clock baby care was stressful. When Rebecca was only three weeks old, Steve had to go on a ten-day business trip. It turned out that their home town was hit by terrible storms while he was away. Ronnie remembers the flooded streets and recalls her fears that she would run out of baby supplies before the water receded.

Although Ronnie and Steve, like Andrea and Nick, have been very public about their participation in a surrogacy arrangement, they do not make a habit of telling strangers on the street about their daughter's origins, but they've been able to have some fun with the truth. When people ask Ronnie how much weight she gained during the pregnancy she tells them three pounds. When people tell her that Rebecca looks just like her, she is pleased and says thank you. When a woman in a supermarket commented on her ability to push a shopping cart at two weeks post-partum, she responded, "That's nothing. On the night the baby was born, my husband and I went out to dinner!"

Ronnie and Steve are proud and pleased with the way that they became a family. Although Andrea and Nick live very far away from them, the connection between them remains strong. They continue to exchange letters and gifts and to talk by phone. They share pleasure in the fact that things are going well for both their families. They see the relationship between them as one that will evolve and unfold over time.

Bruce and Jenna:
Miracles Do Happen!

This experience has taught me that miracles *do happen!* I can't believe that at age thirty-nine, after nearly nine years of infertility tests and treatments, we are so blessed.

When Bruce and Jenna take their two ten-month-old daughters out in their double stroller, people assume that they are twins. Most often, the proud parents do not correct them, but sometimes, if they become involved in conversation, they will explain the truth: one of their daughters was born to a surrogate; the other was born twenty-two hours later to Jenna.

I want to let people know that people who become parents through surrogacy don't have three heads. We're normal people who have been through the pain of infertility and who desperately want children. I could easily pass them off as twins, but I feel that people need to be educated about surrogacy.

Bruce and Jenna know the pain of infertility all too well. They endured nearly nine years of tests and procedures before concluding that they had best move on to some second-choice route to parenthood. They were familiar with a surrogacy program in their area and decided to apply to it.

Our first attempt at surrogacy was a disappointment. We had a surrogate lined up, and then she changed her mind the day before the insemination was scheduled. That was a real letdown, as I had really gotten my hopes up. Fortunately, we located Mindy soon after. I knew as soon as I met her that she would be the birthmother of our first child. What I didn't know, of course, was that I would be the birthmother of our second child, born only a day later!

Jenna remembers having a strong sense, around the time that Mindy conceived, that she was also about to become pregnant. After so many failures, she was not about to put too much hope into this intuition. Then when she found out that she was pregnant before Mindy knew of her own pregnancy, she was not sure what to do. She was afraid that Mindy would be upset.

As ecstatic as I was to be pregnant, I didn't know what I would say to her. How could I tell this brave woman, who was willing to bear a child for us, that I was already pregnant? On the other hand, there was no way that I could *not* tell her. I chose to wait until my fourth month to tell her. When I did so I could tell that she was upset, but she was also very kind and sensitive about it. I think that we were both tuned into the other's feelings throughout our experience together.

Jenna goes on to say that a particularly difficult time was when she had her amnio. She very much wanted a girl and she knew that Mindy wanted to have a girl for her. When the amnio revealed that she was carrying a daughter, she found it very difficult to tell Mindy. She felt that even if Mindy was also carrying a girl (which she was, but they did not know this until she was born), she would feel bad to hear that Jenna was having a girl. She had been prepared to give a great gift to a childless couple and here they were, able to give themselves the same gift first.

> It was hard. I wanted her to know that she was doing this for a real reason. There had been every indication that I would not get pregnant. We had tried everything including IVF. We had every reason to turn to surrogacy. The fact that I had become pregnant was amazing to our doctors as well as to us.

Jenna and Mindy were able to support each other through Jenna's amnio and later. Even now, ten months after the birth of their daughters, they remain close. Although separated geographically, they stay in touch with each other on a regular basis.

Jenna and Bruce have wonderful memories about the weekend their daughters were born. Although Jenna and Mindy were due two weeks apart, the two little sisters had different plans. They arrived within twenty-two hours of each other.

> We ended up having the most *wonderful* Thanksgiving, but the weekend before it was pretty hectic! Allison was born on Sunday. Leslie was born on Monday. Allison came home on Tuesday. Leslie came home on Wednesday. And Thursday was Thanksgiving. Thank heavens for my mother! She made the four of us a turkey. We set a drumstick in front of each of the girls and Bruce and I just smiled and smiled.

After all the excitement of the births and of this most joyous Thanksgiving, Jenna and Bruce settled into a stressful first month. Allison was a colicky baby, and Leslie was not. Jenna remembers worrying that she would favor Leslie.

> Things were much easier once Allison's colic settled down. I was reassured that I would not love one more than the other simply because she grew within me. I should have known myself well enough not to worry about something like that. Kids are kids, and you love them no matter what.

Jenna expresses confidence about Allison's future feelings as well. She expects to tell Allison, as soon as she is old enough to begin to understand, of Mindy's important role in her life. She wants her to know that there are two mothers who love her and feels that this is something to be proud of. She also wants her to know how much she and Bruce like Mindy. She wants Allison to know Mark, Mindy's husband, and to know that he was supportive to all of them throughout this.

Bruce and Jenna acknowledge that the life they are living is certainly different from anything they ever anticipated for themselves. Their response to their surprise family is to be tickled. They can't quite believe what happened and how it happened but they think it's wonderful.

We are in love. We have two terrific little girls. We have learned to have faith and to trust in miracles.

15

The New Reproductive Technologies

When Evan was born, the nurses on the maternity floor heard that he was conceived by IVF. They were very excited and they came by to see us and to wish us well. I liked the attention and I certainly liked the fact that they knew how much we wanted this baby. But at the same time, I was a little worried by all the hoopla. I wondered if our child would grow up hearing that he was different. I wondered how he would feel about being a "miracle baby"?

Shortly after Megan was born, two elderly volunteers came into our hospital room to arrange for newborn pictures. I told them that I needed an extra 8 × 10 for display at the fertility center where she was conceived. I explained that she was an IVF baby. They looked at each other, and then at Jessica, and said, "Well, she's really pretty—she looks just like a regular baby." I could only laugh and respond, "She is!"

Often I stand outside his room when he is sleeping and think of all that we went through to have him. It was an unbelievably long and difficult process, but when I see him lying there, I have no doubt at all that it was worth it.

Karen is almost a year-and-a-half old now. Since the day of her birth we have been in awe of what a miracle she is. We feel like we must be the happiest couple in the world. This is quite a contrast to the feelings of depression, frustration, and failure we were having during the years we were trying to conceive. We're on an emotional roller coaster. We've been as low as anyone can go, and now we're riding on top of the world. This makes us feel very different from other people.

T HESE are voices of IVF and GIFT parents: couples for whom the new reproductive technologies work. It may be on the first attempt — or the fifth — but for these people, courage and determination have paid off. Although IVF, GIFT, and other new reproductive technologies are improving and becoming more available, a couple still needs to undertake approximately four cycles to have a 50 percent chance of a take-home baby.

What is it like to take home a healthy baby (or babies) after IVF or GIFT? What is it like to be successful, to go from feeling like all luck is against you, to finding that you are now among those who have succeeded? What is it like to raise a child whose conception, at least at this point in time, was unusual, even looked on critically by certain religious and secular groups? What is it like to raise a child whom you and/or others regard as a miracle?

> By and large this has been a terrific experience. After years and years of unsuccessful treatments, I was lucky enough to conceive on my first IVF cycle. I went on to have an easy pregnancy. I even managed to enjoy it and not to worry too much. But there have been times when it has been difficult.
>
> Our IVF clinic invited us to come back and tell a group of prospective patients about our experience. When we got there, we found that we were joined by two other couples: one had IVF twins and the other triplets. I felt a little like we were a side show. "Look, look, come see the miracle parents." I wanted to be sure that no one saw us as smug. I was very much aware, as I looked out upon all the anxious faces, that good fortune had very randomly tapped us on the shoulder.

The following are some of the feelings and experiences reported by IVF parents:

1. disbelief
2. belief
3. feelings that the child is special
4. lingering feelings of loss
5. finances
6. questions about a second child and family planning

Disbelief

Couples would not undertake the physical, emotional, and financial rigors of the new technologies if they did not have some hope of success. Nonetheless, most IVF and GIFT programs take care to inform patients of the limitations of these treatments. Even in the most successful programs, a couple has at best about a 20 percent chance of a successful pregnancy in a given cycle (this can vary greatly according to the couple's age and diagnosis). Therefore, most couples beginning an IVF or GIFT cycle are prepared for it not to work.

Despite the odds that are against them, some couples are successful. Some even conceive on their first attempt with a new reproductive technology. Some, who had become so conditioned to failure they had almost learned to live comfortably with it, now find themselves with a very remarkable success. How do people who have "failed" at something for so long react to this new turn of events?

> I was totally shocked. We had tried for four years, and we went into the GIFT program expecting that it would be more of the same. When I received the call that said that I was pregnant, I simply didn't believe it. I phoned my husband and told him "the test was positive." He said, "You mean you are pregnant?" That was when I discovered that I was unable to use the word *pregnant,* something that did not change for a long time. I even delayed calling an obstetrician because of my fear of the "p word."
>
> As my pregnancy (yes, I eventually learned to use the word) progressed, I found that my disbelief continued. I kept expecting it to go away, or at least diminish, but it remained fairly constant. I kept expecting something to go wrong—a miscarriage, a premature delivery, perhaps the loss of one of the fetuses. I was never able to believe that things would really turn out okay.

> I had fantasized for a long time about what it was going to be like when our doctor would tell us I was pregnant. Of course, when it happened, things didn't turn out like I expected. I was in the hospital suffering from a reaction to the fertility drugs, when the doctor called with the exciting news. I was so stunned that it took me another month before I could begin to celebrate.

Disbelief can prompt a couple to feel alienated from both fertile and infertile friends. Having "beat the odds," couples who succeed with IVF and GIFT often report discomfort with their infertile friends, especially those who are still childless. They know from their own experience that an infertile person finds it especially painful to learn of an infertile pregnancy; the news that someone else succeeded with a high-tech option can be especially difficult. At the same time, however, couples pregnant after IVF and GIFT certainly feel different from their fertile peers.

> When I was pregnant, I felt different from everyone else. My infertile friends knew all about GIFT, but I didn't feel that I could talk with them. My fertile friends had no idea what GIFT was and no conception (no pun intended!) of what I had been through. They seemed to ask dumb questions and to make senseless and insensitive comments.
>
> I found that it was hardest in childbirth class. It was like we were living in a different world. The instructor asked us to go around and talk about what concerned us. One woman was worried that she wouldn't lose the weight she had gained! Others were worried that they would have caesareans. I was worried that my babies would die. Plain and simple. I didn't care about weight. I didn't care how they got them out of me. All I wanted was for my babies to live. I don't think that anyone there could have understood me had I said that.
>
> I was doing fine until I attended an exercise class for pregnant women. I felt so startled to be among them that I became depressed. All that I'd been through and all the losses that I had experienced suddenly came back to me. I actually sought psychotherapy to help me sort out all that I was feeling.

Belief

Belief accompanies disbelief for many "high-tech" parents. Although they express and experience surprise at their IVF and GIFT successes, they are also strong believers. Some put their faith in God or a higher power; others ground their beliefs in medicine or science. Still others believe that it is their own determination that will enable them to succeed. Finally, there are those who believe in magical forces. But wherever it comes from, these people, who have known so much disappointment and defeat, approach the new technologies with some fundamental belief they will work.

> For us it was a lot of money and given our history, it seemed like a crazy thing to do. But something told me that it would work. I had a strong sense that this time our prayers and our efforts would pay off. So we went ahead with it, anticipating disappointment and expecting success.

> I am certainly surprised to find myself the mother of triplets, but in some ways I expected this to happen. Things had been happening to me in threes since our struggle began. I tried different medication regimens for three months at a time, had three cysts on my left ovary, three months of artificial inseminations, even three doctors. By the time that I reached IVF, I had been trying for three years and I had a strong sense that IVF and GIFT (we were going to do a combined procedure) would result in three babies!
>   I was assigned to bed three, and I was the third woman to go down for retrieval. The doctor implanted three eggs for IVF and three for GIFT. I was so determined that this would work that I stayed in bed for three days, not even venturing up for a shower. I really was quite extreme but I felt I could and would do everything in my power to make this work.

Feelings That the Child Is Special

Parents view their children as special, and children thrive on knowing that they are, indeed, the "gleam" in someone's eyes. For IVF and GIFT parents, the feeling that their child is special is reinforced by the circumstances of the child's conception and birth. Because IVF and GIFT pregnancies are still fairly unusual, the birth of an IVF or GIFT baby remains cause for special celebration. But how do IVF and GIFT parents raise their "miracle" babies so they can feel both special and normal? IVG and GIFT parents also feel a sense of loss around the normal birth story. They wonder how they will tell their child of his "high-tech" conception, and worry about how the child will react to this news. Some parents fear that their miracle offspring will experience a kind of identity confusion not entirely unlike that of adoptees.

We think that he is absolutely spectacular, and of course we want him to know this. However, it does make me feel uncomfortable when I hear other people refer to him as a "test tube" baby or even when I hear relatives call him "a miracle." He is very precious to us but I don't want him hearing that he is the miracle kid. I think that kind of labeling could be confusing and damaging.

The question of how special the baby is may be related to the familiar dilemma among infertile parents: privacy versus secrecy. Once they entered into high-tech treatment, these couples became accustomed to having their private lives made public. After all, in undergoing IVF or GIFT they allowed the most private parts of themselves—their eggs and their sperm—to be scientifically scrutinized and possibly subjected to new forms of treatment. Now grateful that the new technologies actually worked for them, IVF or GIFT parents may want to talk with others about their experiences.

As delighted as they are with their experience and its outcome, some high-tech parents have reservations about being outspoken regarding their child's origins. They recognize that not everyone understands or supports the new reproductive technologies and know that they may be opening themselves—and later, their children—to negative comments. They also recognize that, although infertility forces people to relinquish privacy, the act of creation is still a very personal matter. Some may need to actively instruct themselves to reclaim privacy.

> I am in conflict. I love to talk about my experience with IVF, both because I have such happy memories and also because I like to offer some hope to people going through it. However, I am afraid to be very public about it because I don't want Eric to become a sideshow freak, "the test tube" baby.

> When I was trying to become pregnant, I became so accustomed to the procedures and the terminology that I forgot that they remain foreign to most people. Now, as a parent, I have to familiarize myself with their unfamiliarity. Most people don't understand what IVF is and some still have an old notion of test-tube babies. I find that I am more comfortable simply telling people that I was treated for infertility and leaving out the details about IVF.

> If the moment presents itself and is appropriate, I tell people how

my children were conceived. Otherwise, it's no one's business. It's like telling them they were conceived in the back seat of a car.

While IVF and GIFT parents express some reservations about the fact that their children are miracle babies, hopefully, they are also able to enjoy having had such a special experience. Most went through a great deal to have their children. The fact that their efforts not only paid off but are also being acknowledged is satisfying.

Our daughter was the first GIFT baby in our city. We had been interviewed on T.V. when we were undergoing the procedure and when she was born, the T.V. station announced her arrival. Many people were excited by the news, and we found that a real momentum developed. Presents and cards arrived from all over, many from people we barely knew. My feeling was that she represented love to people and that prompted them to respond with their love. I enjoyed it all and felt that she started off life with a bang.

IVF parents sometimes comment that their experience has convinced them the birth of every child is a miracle.

Before my grandmother died, I took my first IVF child to visit her. I asked her how it felt to have a "miracle grandchild" and she told me that *every* child is a miracle. Since then, I haven't considered my children miracles because they are IVF children but because they are the wonderful little people that they are!

Lingering Feelings of Loss

Those who are able to have babies through IVF and GIFT feel very lucky indeed. They have succeeded at something that many do not have the opportunity to try and that many others attempt and fail. They feel grateful it worked for them. But feeling so blessed, it can make it hard to acknowledge accompanying feelings of loss.

The losses are multiple. Most IVF and GIFT parents have lost their dream child: the child they were going to conceive romantically, spontaneously, or right on schedule. Couples have different dreams of conception, but none set out to begin a family fantasizing about Pergonal amps and egg retrieval. The process of IVF (and GIFT, perhaps to a slightly lesser extent) feels unnatural. Some IVF patients say that they feel like "passive participants," "guinea pigs," "freaks."

> I am very grateful to have had an uneventful, vaginal delivery. When I was trying to conceive, I got angry at women who complained about caesarean births. I knew that I'd be delighted to have a baby any which way that I could. But the GIFT procedure, miraculous as it was, made me feel that I'd been separated from nature. Instead of being the result of a natural and rhythmic process, my pregnancy felt like a bizarre scientific experiment. For me, delivering vaginally—and naturally, without any medication—proved to be very reassuring. I finally felt like I was part of nature and not separated from it.

There is also time lost. Chances are that it took years of treatment to get to IVF/GIFT, and possibly a good deal more time to succeed at it. Gratitude for eventual success does not erase the sadness that results from time lost.

> We spent so many years pursuing pregnancy, that now we are geriatric parents. Our friends have teenagers, some even have kids in college, and we have a toddler. We laugh a lot and say that Ericka keeps us young, which she does; but we didn't choose to have it this way. Unlike some people, who electively chose to delay parenting, we have no positive account for the years. It's not like we had much satisfaction or success in the years that we spent waiting!

Unfortunately, for some IVF and GIFT parents, the birth of one (or more) babies brings back the sad memory of the loss of others. Some pregnancies prior to IVF or GIFT and some that were a result of IVF or GIFT ended in miscarriage, ectopic pregnancy, or stillbirth. The success of a later pregnancy, especially one established with the help of IVF or GIFT, brings great joy; but it does not remove the immense loss that parents feel in the aftermath of pregnancy loss.

> My first GIFT pregnancy was like a fairy tale. We had tried to conceive for several years with no known cause of infertility. Even-

tually, we traveled to a program that had a good reputation for work with GIFT. To our amazement and great joy, I conceived on the very first cycle. What followed was a relaxed and happy eight-and-one-half months of pregnancy.

At thirty-eight weeks I noticed that I no longer felt movement. I reacted first with disbelief and then with acute grief. After all that we'd been through, it seemed impossible that our baby would die.

She had strangled on the cord. It was a freak accident they said, "Nothing related to GIFT," they reassured me. I had an "excellent chance of going on to a successful pregnancy." Yes, but my loss is boundless. My firstborn daughter lies in a cemetery, and I will always, always miss her.

Another loss that IVF and GIFT parents are sometimes forced to deal with is elective abortion. Like many other infertile women (and fertile women as well), women undergoing IVF and GIFT often have histories of elective abortion. Although they may have made a decision that was right for them at the time, there is a sad irony now: they are undergoing heroic efforts to become pregnant when once they suffered with an unplanned pregnancy. This irony can activate feelings of loss and guilt and magical thoughts of punishment and retribution.

However they may have felt about abortion in the past, most infertile women have a great deal of difficulty thinking about abortion. Many are pro-choice and actively support women's right to abortion, but they have a hard time thinking about ever aborting a future pregnancy. Nonetheless, there are some infertile couples who find themselves in the painful predicament of having to consider abortion.

There are two ways in which infertile couples are confronted with decisions about abortion. One comes as a result of amniocentesis. Because they are older parents, many elect to have this pre-natal diagnostic test, aware that a "bad" report will force them to consider ending their much longed for pregnancy.

A second abortion dilemma arises as a direct result of IVF and GIFT and involves what is known as "selective reduction." When a woman is carrying four or more fetuses, she may be advised to undergo a process in which a doctor attempts to abort two or more of the fetuses so that two of the others will survive. This rela-

tively new procedure has met with some success and has enabled
some women to successfully carry multiples who might otherwise
have been in jeopardy. However, for couples expecting triplets,
selective reduction poses a real dilemma: a triplet pregnancy is
difficult and involves risks, but it often has a successful outcome.
On the other hand, a twin pregnancy is a good deal easier for
everyone. Can a couple decide to abort one of their fetuses so that
the other two will have a better start in life?

> Having had a twin pregnancy which was scary at times, I am glad
> that I was never in the position of having to think about aborting
> a fetus. I can remember feeling concern for each of my babies and
> hoping that they were existing in harmony within me. I worried at
> times that one would get all the nutrients and that the other would
> be in distress. I think that it would be very confusing to be carrying
> three or more, fearing that because of sheer numbers they might
> be jeopardizing each other.

Finally, IVF/GIFT parents often have strong feelings about
being survivors. In this way, high-tech successes promote feelings
somewhat akin to a posttraumatic stress disorder. Having beaten
the odds, they feel some grief and guilt as well as gratitude. They
are left puzzled at why it worked for them and not for others
whose infertility seemed no more hopeless.

> One of the hardest things about IVF is that you have no idea how
> it works. The doctors seem to have a handle on what is a good egg,
> what is a good embryo, and how many embryos it should take to
> establish a pregnancy. But what happens in utero? No one seems
> to have any idea why some embryos "take," and go on to become
> healthy little babies and others mysteriously vanish. I've seen peo-
> ple devastated when they are canceled along the way, and certainly
> devastated when they become pregnant and miscarry, but the
> cruelest punishment seems to come to those who have two or three
> good embryos put back, only to be followed by a negative preg-
> nancy test.

> My "survivor's guilt" relates to access to treatment. I feel fortunate
> that we live near a major medical center and can afford to partic-
> ipate in their program. I feel sad that there are couples who, for
> one reason or another, don't even have the opportunity to try IVF.

Finances

The new reproductive technologies are very costly, financially as well as emotionally. Although some couples are fortunate to have insurance coverage (RESOLVE has been successful in shepherding insurance bills through some state legislatures, mandating coverage for infertility treatment including IVF and GIFT), many are forced to pay out of pocket for their high-tech treatments. Because the current cost per cycle is anywhere from $6,000 to $8,000, and because there is often good reason to try four or five cycles, IVF and GIFT attempts can run into many thousands of dollars. Although some couples are fortunate to have great financial resources, most IVF and GIFT candidates find the costs overwhelming, if not prohibitive. If they result in a successful pregnancy and birth, their impact diminishes; but for some high-tech parents, the financial burden continues after birth.

> Soon after we were married, we began saving for our children's future. We expected that our savings would go toward college and other major expenses. Now we have a wonderful daughter, but we spent all the money we had saved on her conception. It seems so unfair that we must now start saving all over again.

Those who are able to afford IVF and GIFT express sadness and guilt for those who cannot. Infertility is unfair enough; it seems even more unjust that people should have or lose the opportunity to parent based on their ability to pay.

Questions about a Second Child and Family Planning

As with nearly all parents after infertility, couples who become parents with the help of IVF or GIFT face a number of questions about family planning. They have had success with the new reproductive technologies, but they know they cannot assume that IVF or GIFT will work for them again.

I remember so well the women I would meet in the lab as we waited for blood tests and ultrasounds. In the beginning, everyone was anxious and hopeful. We had all traveled a rough road to get there, and just being in the program demonstrated enormous emotional and financial commitment. I recall looking around and thinking that everyone there really deserved to have a baby. Then I reminded myself that deserving had nothing to do with any of this; a few of us would probably be successful and we had no idea who it would be.

Some of the women in my program were canceled along the way. That's the horrible experience that occurs when you ripen too many follicles too fast or too few too slow or some such combination of misfortunes. Those women were devastated. However, it was hard to be of much help to them because I knew that they envied me for not being canceled.

When I made it through the cycle and then had a positive pregnancy test I was jubilant, but I also felt very sad for the other women in the program. I knew that as happy and excited as I was, there were women who felt horrible. And it all was very random. Why had it worked for me and not for them?

Couples for whom IVF/GIFT works once know that it may not work again. They are good candidates, but they are well aware that other good candidates did not make it through the cycle. Or if they did, they did not necessarily get fertilization or carry to term. They are afraid the chances are substantial that their efforts to have a second child by IVF or GIFT would be met with failure.

Even if they could be sure that returning to IVF/GIFT would result in another baby, there are other things to consider. One is the cost: some have exhausted their financial resources with their first baby.

So many people have asked me, "When are you going to have another baby?" as if we have some control over it like other people. I wish that I could say to them, "Well, this one cost $40,000. Would you like to donate to the cause?" Instead, I just give them a vague answer and change the subject.

A second dilemma for many IVF/GIFT parents is timing. Well versed in the statistics regarding IVF and GIFT, they know what a critical factor age can be. Having had success, they are reluctant to wait and let their advanced age present a serious problem. Even the most successful programs report very limited success in women over forty, so limited that some programs refuse to treat couples in which the woman is over the age of forty-one.

> I feel vulnerable again. Kim is only a few months old, but we are thinking that perhaps we should try again soon. I am thirty-eight and have heard of only a few women my age or older who have had success with IVF. But then again, we are really enjoying Kim — and the first break that we have had in over six years from thinking about or attempting pregnancy!

IVF/GIFT parents who have had multiple births find themselves in a different situation. They are not likely to think immediately about another pregnancy; they are too busy adjusting to the instant family that they have. Still, the matter of family planning does sit in the background. Some of these couples, those who planned to have large families, anticipate that they will eventually want to take steps to enlarge their families (and having had one multiple birth, they may be wary of having another).

> We have always wanted a large family. Now we've been blessed with twins. Our daughters take up twenty-five hours a day, and it is hard to imagine how we could ever have time for more. Nonetheless, I know that someday we would like to have at least one more child. Since it took so long to have the twins, I don't know that we can afford to wait. But since we've had a multiple birth, we know that it really does happen, especially with IVF and GIFT. Even if we're lucky enough to have another pregnancy, who is to say that it won't be triplets this time? Yes, I wanted a large family; but three at once is not what I had in mind!

Couples who have embryos frozen during an IVF procedure have additional concerns regarding the future of those embryos. Some worry they might someday find themselves in the ironic position of having to think about discarding their embryos or possibly donating them to a childless couple.

> We chose to freeze some of our embryos to lower the risk of multiple birth. Having those embryos is an awesome responsibility. I

worry about what I am going to do if we are successful conceiving a second child and we still have embryos left over.

As IVF/GIFT become more available and more successful, the experience for all those involved in the new reproductive technologies will undoubtedly change. The time may not be too far away when parents will regard an IVF conception as commonplace, not markedly different from an ultrasound or amniocentesis. When this happens, feelings of being special, of being different, of bearing miracle children will diminish greatly, if not vanish. But for now, IVF/GIFT successes remain unusual, exciting causes for celebration. Couples who become parents through these techniques feel a mixture of relief, surprise, sadness, gratitude, and great delight.

Susan, Nick, and Jonathan: When Luck Turned Around

When Jonathan was two months old, the IVF clinic we had gone to asked us to come back and speak before a group of incoming couples. We were asked to bring Jonathan along and to plan to tell the audience our story.

What a strange experience it turned out to be. There we were, suddenly on the other side of things after having spent years and years feeling like we were the most hopeless case. There we were, now the success story, with our miracle baby in tow. The strangest part of all was when the audience applauded us. I felt embarrassed to be there.

Nick and Susan both have had a hard time believing that she actually became pregnant on their first IVF attempt, and that this miracle pregnancy resulted in the birth of their son, Jonathan. Theirs was a long, arduous bout with infertility: ten years of tests, surgery, long trials of Pergonal, as well as samplings of other medications and treatments. If any couple ever looked hopeless, it was them. If any couple was ever determined to find something that would work, it was also them.

When it became clear that none of the "conventional" treatments were working, we decided to do IVF. At that time it was still pretty new, and also insurance coverage was rare. So for many reasons we had to choose a program carefully. We were not sure we'd be able to afford a second try.

In one way, our story has a very happy ending. IVF worked. Susan had a great pregnancy, and we are blessed with Jonathan. We're among the very lucky few. Still, I feel like we've had to deal with a lot of losses, and those are usually hard to talk about given our outcome.

The big loss that I feel is of time. Susan and I both put our lives on hold during the years that we were pursuing pregnancy. We put everything aside to have our baby. Maybe that is what we had to do. Perhaps we would not be parents today had we not put so much energy into pursuing treatment. Nonetheless, it is difficult to look back and wonder where the time went.

Another loss that we feel is one of companionship. Before we were infertile, we had lots of friends. Some of those friendships survived our infertility, and some did not. All were challenged. During our infertility, we sought and found wonderful companionship among other infertile couples. Similarly, when we were going through IVF we welcomed contacts with other couples in our program. Now we are isolated. We don't quite fit in with our fertile friends, but having a baby, especially by IVF, has separated us from the infertile community.

The losses are there but the overwhelming feeling Susan and Nick share is of joy. They are thrilled to finally be parents, to be Jonathan's parents, to have had the fortitude and the good fortune to be able to try IVF. They have a strong sense that their luck, so bad for so long, has turned around.

When I think back about what it was like two or three years ago, I never could have imagined this outcome. I remember feeling that it would never be over, that we would never have a child together. I feel very lucky that we somehow knew that we had to keep trying.

Janet and Ray:
Where We Never Expected to Be

Our infertility took us places that we never, ever expected to be. Who would have thought that one friend would read about Jeanna's birth in Paris and another in Alaska. There we were, on the front page of *USA TODAY!* Who would have ever thought that we would be holding a press conference in the postpartum unit?

As parents of the first IVF baby conceived in the state of Georgia, Janet and Ray received a good deal of media attention and public acclaim. Janet acknowledges that some of this was exciting and fun but that it went far beyond what they anticipated when they agreed to go public with their IVF pregnancy.

> We had given a lot of thought to the question of publicity. We are generally fairly private people and we don't seek out public attention. But when I conceived during our infertility clinic's first treatment cycle (to say nothing of it being *my* first attempt) there was a lot of excitement. The doctors in our clinic wanted public recognition and we, as a physician and a nurse, could understand this.

Janet and Ray go on to say that they felt their going public might offer hope to others who, like themselves, were battling long-term infertility. They had gone through five years of tests and procedures and had turned to IVF as a last resort. Suffering from multiple problems including low sperm count, low motility, sperm antibody, luteal phase defect, and tubal problems, they had little hope that anything could help them.

> Our hope for a pregnancy was growing dim. Then we heard that they were starting an IVF program in Atlanta, and our doctor thought it might be worth a try. We were very hesitant both because of the cost and because nothing else had worked. However, our greatest reluctance had to do with something else: our religion. We are practicing Catholics, and while the Vatican had not yet spoken on IVF, we had some inklings of what it would say.

> We grappled with the ethical questions for a long time and finally arrived at a decision that we felt we could live with. We decided that our desire for a child was very much within the tenets of our faith. We thought that if we agreed to replace every egg, whether or not it fertilized, we would not be doing anything immoral.

To Janet and Ray's great surprise, IVF worked. Their first attempt resulted in the birth of a healthy baby girl, Jeanna. Ten months later, they revisited their original questions about IVF and decided to go ahead with it a second time. Once again, a first attempt resulted in pregnancy and the birth of another baby girl, Christina.

> We felt incredibly blessed. Having been infertile for so long, we knew lots of people struggling with the problem. We had friends who had tried IVF five and six times without success. From our long years of infertility, we had some idea of what that felt like. And there we were, by contrast, twice blessed. It was a new and odd position to be in.

Although they were delighted to have two children, Janet and Ray had wanted a larger family. Not long after Christina's birth, the Vatican did come out with a strong statement in opposition to IVF. Now Ray and Janet faced a much greater moral dilemma: should they actually go ahead with a process their religion condemned? After much struggle, they concluded that they had been blessed with two children and that they had best not tamper with the natural order of things.

> We were very lucky to be rewarded for our struggle. I call it divine intervention. When Christina was two years old, Janet discovered that she was pregnant.

> I couldn't believe it! To succeed at IVF was one thing, but to just do it on our own was quite another! I was astounded. I couldn't believe that I could get pregnant, just like that!

Janet and Ray feel very fortunate. They see each of their children's arrival as very special. Jeanna was the miracle baby, the child born when all else had failed. Christina was a second miracle; it happened once but they had been doubtful that it could happen again, especially on the first try. And then Christopher came along—a different kind of little miracle.

> We do wonder what they will think of this when they are older. We wonder how Christopher will react to the fact that his sisters were IVF babies and he was not. We wonder how Jeanna will react to all the publicity that surrounded her birth. We have, of course, saved all the clippings. She's in kindergarten now, and so far she has been treated like all the other kids. But we wonder if people will say

things to her. We're so grateful that there are so many other IVF babies. We know that she and her sister will grow up with lots of company.

The publicity around Jeanna's origins has created some stresses for Janet and Ray, but they see the legacy of infertility as a bigger challenge. Janet says that there are times when she feels that she holds herself to standards that are too high. She remembers making promises when she was infertile and now feels obliged to hold to them. Having been rewarded with what she wanted for so long — having succeeded where so many others have failed — she feels bound to be an exceptionally patient mother.

> There are lots of times when I ask myself if I am doing it right. I feel like I should be a whiz at this. Having beaten the odds, I now find that I sometimes beat myself against the wall.

Janet also admits that it sometimes feels lonely to be the one who beat the odds. She remains involved with RESOLVE and sometimes has a hard time telling fellow RESOLVE members that she has three children. Although she and Ray went through a lot to have them, she knows that others went through as much or more without success.

> Our infertility taught us long ago that life is not fair. In a different sort of way, our successes have brought that home to us. We feel very grateful for our children, but our infertility has changed us. It has left us with a real appreciation for the miracles of conception and of life.

Lisa and Peter:
Our Favorite Gift

Our infertility was especially difficult because we went for so long without a diagnosis. I suppose that if this were years ago, or if we did not have such good medical care, we would still not know what was wrong with us. But we were fortunate to eventually learn that I have leutenized unruptured follicle syndrome (LVF). It is a rare

form of infertility in which the follicles develop normally but fail
to release the eggs.

Once we had a diagnosis, our doctor recommended GIFT. It
didn't have a high success rate, but he felt that ours was a condition
that it could help. Although I didn't hold out much hope for it, I
loved my doctor and his staff and wanted to go with his recommendation. So after much thought, and many long discussions, we
decided to go for it.

Lisa goes on to describe the anxiety she felt as she approached
GIFT. She was not afraid of the procedure itself but reports being
afraid of her own emotions. She knew there was a good chance
it would not work, and she was concerned that this was something
she would not be able to handle. Although she had always felt like
a stable person, infertility had seriously challenged her well-
being. There were times when it got so bad that she even had
thoughts of suicide.

One of the reasons that I went ahead with GIFT was Peter's enthusiasm and support. We had recently learned that he had a low-
normal sperm count, another condition that GIFT was likely to
help. Also, Peter is a physician, and he had considerable faith in
the new technologies.

On the night before the GIFT surgery, Peter ate oysters, hoping
(although we both knew better!) that it would help his count. The
next morning I went to surgery and was initially pleased that it
went well. They got nine eggs and put four back, holding five out
for IVF. I felt hopeful for a day and then received some crushing
news: the five IVF eggs had disintegrated. My doctor said that there
was little hope that I had conceived with GIFT.

Here comes the good part! A week later I went in for the stan-
dard blood-serum pregnancy test. Then I went out for lunch with
a friend who was supporting and consoling me. We were in the
middle of our meal when Peter came in with tears in his eyes. My
first thought was that someone had died. Then he hugged me and
asked if it was too late for me to buy him a Father's Day card (it
was mid-June)! Then the three of us started crying and screaming.
We made quite a scene in the restaurant!

Lisa goes on to describe her pregnancy. It was a very stressful time for her. She had difficulty believing that it had really

happened and had lots of worries that it would end in failure. She remembers doing things to try to protect herself from disappointment. For example, when she and Peter were relocating, she insisted on a house in the city rather than the suburbs; she worried that she would feel too lonely in the suburbs without children.

> It is sad that I worried so much, because my pregnancy was actually an easy one. It went smoothly, and I had a wonderful, happy delivery.

Lisa adds that her anxiety did not end with pregnancy. She says that she feels very vulnerable as a mother. She worries that Jenny will be her only child and fears that she might be overprotective. She is sad that the pressure she feels to have a second child is interfering with her time with Jenny. For example, she would have liked to nurse for a longer time but stopped early so that nursing would not interfere with her fertility.

Lisa looks forward to telling Jenny about her exciting conception. When she feels that Jenny is old enough to understand, she and Peter will show her the GIFT surgery on videotape, along with an ultrasound at twenty-eight weeks. She feels that these pictures and the stories that will accompany them will show Jenny how much she was wanted.

> The neatest realization that has come from all of our struggles was the answer to "Why me, God?" Now we can see why we needed to wait. It was so that we would end up with Jenny. She was definitely the one for us, and we are forever thankful!

Ken, Laurie, Elissa, and Jacob: IVF Works!

Had it been up to me, we would have quit after our fourth IVF attempt. At that time we had had two unsuccessful cycles and two failed pregnancies. I was burnt out, and I felt like we were playing a numbers game. Each time Laurie went under general anesthesia

I was more frightened than the time before. It was starting to feel like Russian roulette.

Ken looks back now and feels very grateful that Laurie was more willing to play the odds than he was. Even after two failed pregnancies she was determined to keep going.

She told me that she had to try it one last time. I reluctantly agreed, saying that this would be the last time. Fortunately, we were both right. That was the cycle we conceived Jacob.

At two and one-half, Jacob is an active and energetic little boy. As he zooms through the house on his tricycle, he has no idea of how long and how hard his parents worked to have him. Their efforts began many years before his birth and included a long, difficult tubal surgery as well as all the IVF attempts.

When we embarked upon IVF we were real pioneers. In those days—the early 1980s—it was still a new procedure, available at only a few medical centers. We had to travel several hours to get there. Our ordeal was all the more difficult because our daughter, Elissa, whom we adopted as a newborn, was still very young.

Ken seems a bit amused when he looks back at the early IVF attempts. He describes how seriously he and Laurie approached things, how they stayed in a motel for an extended period of time and how they were extremely cautious during and after the procedure. He contrasts these early attempts with the cycle in which Jacob was conceived, noting that by that time, they were almost easygoing about the process. They traveled back and forth to the program, continued work, and pursued most of their normal activities.

If Laurie and Ken learned from experience to treat IVF attempts casually, they also learned to treat all pregnancies with the utmost of seriousness. They had lost one pregnancy at seven weeks and another at twenty, so they knew that you can never be sure of the outcome of a pregnancy. Even when things seem to be going well, something can suddenly go wrong.

With Jacob, we were prepared for the worst. Every step along the way we watched and waited, afraid something was about to go wrong. In a sense, it is lucky that we were so cautious. When Laurie was twenty-eight weeks pregnant, we were out shopping one evening. She complained of feeling sick and the next thing we knew, she was bleeding heavily. I was terrified that it was all over then and rushed her to the hospital. She was admitted that evening and remained there for the duration of her pregnancy. We were told that our goal was to prevent premature labor and that each week Jacob could remain in utero went far toward ensuring his survival and his health.

The next eight weeks seemed eternal. For Laurie they were both suspenseful and boring. For Elissa and me, it meant not having Mommy at home and having to commute back and forth to the hospital. Had I known there would be a happy outcome, I think that it would have been a whole lot easier. But it was hard to go through this having learned that even heroic efforts often meet with disappointment.

Both Ken and Laurie give her obstetrician a great deal of credit for helping them through this dreadful time. They found him compassionate and committed, always there for them. When they lost their earlier IVF pregnancies, he shared in their sadness. When it looked like Jacob was also in trouble, he declared that "he would kill himself if the baby did not survive." Ken and Laurie did not feel like they'd had much luck on their side, but they always knew that their doctor was with them.

The end of Laurie's pregnancy was long and tedious, but it had a great outcome. Jacob was delivered by a caesarean section just three weeks early. He was a healthy baby, and his vigor helped both of his parents to forget all that they'd been through.

Needless to say, we'll never forget it all, but the great thing about IVF is that you really can end up with a baby. Sometimes I stand in his doorway at night and think about the journey that brought us together. He was conceived on one of the more than one-hundred cycles that we attempted to have a baby. He grew from one of the eighteen eggs that were fertilized. He is truly a miracle. His very existence has broadened my appreciation for all human life.

Jacob's parents are awed by him, but they are also tickled. They see him as a miracle, but at the same time they do not take him too seriously. It's important to them that they all have fun together. They enjoy it when strangers comment on how much Jacob looks like his sister and have fun telling curious people that he is an IVF baby.

We haven't shied away from being public about Jacob's being an IVF baby. We're proud of him and we're proud of IVF. We think that it's a great thing, and we'd like to help others to do it. We think that Jacob is a terrific advertisement for the procedure.

Ken and Laurie have not closed the door on another IVF attempt nor are they rapidly returning to treatment. Given how hard it was for them to build the family they have, they cannot minimize what might be involved in expanding it.

The amazing thing about IVF is that in the end you can end up with a child. Admittedly, I was the one who was ready to quit along the way. I was the one who was frightened by the procedure. And I was never the one whose body was going through all of this. So perhaps it's easy for me to say—after the fact and as the bystander—that it was all worth it. But when the end result is a Jacob, it's hard to imagine not going through it. We have real live proof that IVF works.

16

Multiple Births

While I was going through Pergonal treatment, I didn't give much thought to what it would really be like to have more than one. For one thing, I didn't believe that it could happen. I was someone who couldn't even manage to get pregnant with one; how could I possibly have twins?

Multiple births? Not me! Multiple births meant heightened fertility, not subfertility, which was how I saw myself. I felt I'd be very lucky to manage to get one baby out. More than one? Impossible!

People used to say, "Twins? Why you are so brave, dear." Brave? Did they think I volunteered for this, or that if I had felt cowardly I could have given the twins back?

T HESE are voices of parents of twins and triplets. For them, all the joys and frustrations of parenthood—all the diapers and bottles, the car seats and Snuglis—arrive in multiples. They are individuals who often wish they had more than two hands, more than twenty-four hours in the day, more than a few hours of restful sleep for weeks on end. They are couples who need to be organized, calm, and energetic as they barrel into parenthood.

In the midst of infertility treatment, few people really picture themselves with a multiple birth. Even when they are well informed of the possibility, most approach this information with a kind of denial. They regard multiple births as something that happens to other people.

One reason that infertile couples deny or minimize their chance of multiples is that most people associate multiple births with heightened fertility (and they see themselves as having diminished fertility). Those who have never been pregnant feel that it would take nothing short of a miracle for them to produce one baby.

Couples undergoing fertility treatment often adopt a "more-the-merrier" approach to parenthood. It has been so difficult for them to conceive or carry a pregnancy that they feel they would be very fortunate if they could have more than one baby at a time. "Instant family" some call it, usually conveying a sense of curiosity, daring, and disbelief. Others who are older see multiple births as a practical solution to their race against time.

All in all, few infertile couples ever picture themselves wheeling a double or triple stroller. Few women imagine themselves with babies sucking at both breasts. Few are in any way prepared for the multiple challenges and joys that come from having more than one.

> I thought that we were prepared. We were experienced parents of a five-year-old daughter, and we had spent three years trying to conceive again. We were very excited when we heard that I was having twins. But when they arrived, I was overwhelmed. I would lie there in bed totally exhausted, and pray for an hour's uninterrupted sleep. But no sooner had I dozed off than I'd hear that familiar whimpering, soon to become a piercing shriek if I didn't go running.
>
> I felt like a handicapped person. I'd see my friends buzzing about with one child, and I felt like I could not begin to do half of what they did. I'd hear them complaining about being tired and frustrated, and I'd feel that they had no idea how easy they had it.

The following are some of the special features of parenting multiples:

1. multiple gestation
2. double — or triple — delivery
3. privacy and public reaction
4. adopting multiples
5. feelings about the formation and configuration of the family

6. raising separate individuals versus "packaging"
7. the absence of a one-to-one relationship with a child
8. feeling special

Multiple Gestation

The challenges of multiple births usually begin early in pregnancy. Women who used Pergonal to conceive, with or without IVF, GIFT, or ZIFT, are monitored for multiple gestation. Other infertility patients often have an early ultrasound in an attempt to locate a sac and a fetal heart beat. Hence, for one reason or another, infertility patients know early on in their pregnancies if they are carrying more than one.

> I was huge by about thirteen weeks. I had not taken fertility drugs, nor was there any family history of multiple births, so I didn't take anybody seriously when they guessed I was carrying twins. I had had extensive tubal surgery and felt that I'd be very lucky if one embryo found its way into my uterus. I went for an ultrasound, fearful that there might be something terribly wrong with me. To my relief and total amazement, I learned that I was carrying twins! I remember when the technician looked at the screen and said, "Here's one and here's another sac." At that moment I said to myself, "Please, please let her stop there!"

When they are in their more-the-merrier mode, few infertile couples think about the fact that any multiple gestation is, by definition, a high-risk pregnancy. While infertility prepares people well for the stresses and strains of high-risk obstetrics, there is still the loss of the experience of a normal, uneventful pregnancy.

> I was stunned when my doctor told me that I would have to go to bed at twenty-five weeks. At first I didn't think that I had heard him correctly—I thought that he meant that I'd have to take it easy if I was having problems. But that was not what he was saying at all. He was not saying "take it easy," he was saying "get into bed." And he was not waiting for problems to develop—he was attempting to avoid them.

The second half of any multiple pregnancy is very stressful. Even those women who are not on strict bedrest have a hard time because there is always the threat of premature delivery. Their size alone often makes things difficult for them.

> I came to see myself as an incubator. I felt that if I could just stay pregnant a little longer, I'd be giving my children some advantages. Every day that passed was an accomplishment, but none of it was fun.

> I was one of the lucky ones. My twin pregnancy went very well, and I carried relatively comfortably. But just to be safe, my doctor kept a watchful eye on things. After thirty weeks, there were frequent tests to make sure that both babies were doing okay. When it seemed like our son was interfering with our daughter's growth, the doctors decided to induce me. Even then, I considered myself lucky. I had made it to thirty-five weeks and was able to have a vaginal delivery. What a surprise it was moments after I delivered my daughter vaginally to learn that I required an emergency section to deliver my son.

Double – or Triple – Delivery

The arrival of twins or triplets undoubtedly meets with a good deal of fanfare. Everyone is excited by the relative novelty of the multiple births, and everyone is eager to greet the babies. What the well-wishers may not fully appreciate is the degree to which the new parents are exhausted and overwhelmed.

> I remember feeling trapped that whole first year. Whenever I wanted to go someplace I had to figure out if it could possibly be done with two babies. It was always an unbelievable ordeal figuring out how I'd carry the two of them up a staircase or through the supermarket where the carts seat only one. More often than not I'd end up staying home because it was easier than trying to figure out how I'd maneuver.

In recent years, improvements in the function and design of baby equipment have helped ease the adjustment of parents of multiples. Double strollers are available, car seats are easier to use, and there are new and easier baby carriers. These changes all make it somewhat less complicated to maneuver with more than one infant. Nonetheless, the arrival of multiples remains a juggling act.

> I think that several months went by before I was able to go to the bathroom alone. When the twins were little, one or the other needed me at all times. If I needed to make a run to the toilet, I always had at least one baby with me. When I started leaving them with a baby-sitter, one of my great luxuries was a trip to a public restroom!

Privacy and Public Reaction

The issue of privacy, which runs through all infertility diagnoses and treatments, is especially applicable to parents of multiples. If every stranger on the street notices one baby, people manage to come out of the woodwork when there are twins. And triplets prompt even more attention.

> I'm a very friendly person, and before I had the triplets I enjoyed it when strangers smiled and said hello. All that changed when I found out what it was like to venture out with my three babies. People can be awful! They bothered me constantly, asked a million questions that were none of their business, offered advice that I did not want or need, and generally made me feel that I had given up my rights as a private citizen.

Parents of twins fare only slightly better when it comes to maintaining their right to privacy. Most find that it gets easier as their children get older and their "twinness" is less evident. But when they are babies, it is very difficult.

> My daughters do not look alike so their twinness did not attract much attention once they were out of their stroller. However, when they were babies, people stopped us *everyplace* we went. And everyone had a comment. We heard about people's third cousins twice removed who were twins, and about someone's sister who had one set of twins and then had another (just what I needed to

hear!) We never knew there were so many grandmothers of twins in this world!

People who didn't have twin stories to tell had twin questions to ask. "How do you tell them apart?" (That was obvious!) "What do you do when they're both crying at once?" (Cry myself!) "Do they weigh the same?" "Which one is older?" Total strangers had no trouble talking with us in the most intimate and personal way.

> I was really, really surprised by the way people acted. The first time we took the twins to a shopping mall, we had dozens of people coming up to us and asking us all sorts of questions. Since I'm a private sort of person, I was totally unprepared for this. It took a long time for me to realize that I didn't have to answer questions just because people asked them.

An added challenge for parents of multiples is dealing with negative reactions to multiple births. There are some people who think that having twins, or more, would be a terrible burden, and they do not hesitate to comment on this to the parents of multiples. When parents have struggled long and hard to have their children, it can be difficult to listen to someone's "sympathy."

> We considered the twins to be the great miracle of our lives. They came after many years of infertility, and although it was hard at times, we were thrilled. When we took them out, however, we often encountered comments that diminished or misunderstood our experience. People were often quick to say how terrible it must be, how awful my pregnancy had to have been, how exhausted we must feel. I briefly joined a mothers of twins group but found that I encountered much of the same sentiment there. I left after just a few meetings, feeling that the last thing I wanted to hear—there or elsewhere—was how terrible it was to have twins!

At the same time that they appreciate and enjoy their children, parents of multiples do feel overwhelmed. The comments of others can activate conflicts between expressing frustration and camouflaging it. After all, infertility has taught them to be grateful for their bounty and not to complain. It is important that infertile parents of multiples somehow free themselves from this burden of gratitude and accept the fact that there are moments when they may need to collapse.

Adopting Multiples

Most adoption applications ask couples if they are willing to adopt twins. Again, prospective parents can easily take a more-the-merrier approach, assuming it will not happen to them; and that even if it does, it will be wonderful. After all the years of infertility, they welcome the idea of an instant family.

For adoptive parents there are some advantages to adopting twins. One is that people find the adoption process, including the homestudy and the costs, to be quite stressful. The idea that their efforts will result in two babies at once feels to some like ample reward for all that they have been through. They like the idea that a twin placement will save them time, energy, emotions, and probably money.

A second, and for many a more compelling, reason to adopt multiples is that parents like the idea of their children growing up with a full-blood relative. Aware of how much some adoptees suffer with genealogical bewilderment, they feel that the presence of a sibling will go a long way in helping a person feel grounded and connected.

Couples who adopt twins usually do not have much time to prepare for the fact that they will be getting two babies instead of one. Unlike expectant parents, who usually learn in the first trimester that they are having multiples, adoptive parents of twins are likely to get a surprise phone call.

> It was culture shock. We had checked off twins as something we would accept when we were filling out the adoption application. It never dawned on us that one day we'd really get a call informing us that we had *both* a son and a daughter!

Couples who adopt twins face multiple challenges to their privacy. Inevitably, strangers will stop them and ask when they found out that they were having twins, whether twins run in their families, whether they took fertility pills, and more. Although they may intend to maintain some privacy about the adoption, adoptive parents of multiples may find that some earnest inquisitors make this nearly impossible.

We were asked everything. How much weight did I gain? How did
I lose it so quickly? Were there twins in either of our families?
Were we surprised? I decided that it was a lot easier to announce
at the start that our children were adopted than to make my way
through a minefield of questions.

Feelings about the Formation and Configuration of the Family

Like other parents after infertility, parents of multiples feel that
they have lost the ability to plan their families. While they may
have adopted a cavalier more-the-merrier or "let's-catch-up-with-
our-friends-all-at-once" attitude when faced with the prospect of
twins or triplets, the fact is that multiple births do dramatically
alter the way in which they will build their family.

> I always wanted three children, but for several reasons we never
> tried for more after the twins. I might never have conceived again,
> but I would like to have tried.
>
> When the boys were very young, I was too busy and too over-
> whelmed to imagine adding another baby to the chaos. Then when
> they were in grade school and it seemed more doable, I wondered
> if there would be too many years between them. More than that,
> I wondered how it would be for a single child to follow "The
> Twins." I felt that this child, especially if it was another boy, would
> always be overshadowed by his brothers. I felt that I would owe it
> to our third child to have a fourth soon after. And of course, I
> didn't know if that could happen.
>
> So I never had more children, and I feel sad about that. The
> twins are terrific, but there are two other children missing in our
> family. Having twins was a unique and wonderful experience, but
> it meant giving up a lot.

One of the losses that parents of multiples feel is of a pregnancy experience. Not only is a multiple gestation stressful, without some of the pleasures of a normal pregnancy, but it may also
mean that a mother misses out on another opportunity to be pregnant. Similarly, a multiple birth is inevitably more complicated
than a single delivery, detracting from a woman's experience of

labor and delivery. Should she and her husband decide not to have more children or if they are unable to do so, she misses out on another opportunity to experience the miracle of birth.

> I was never someone who wanted to be pregnant. However, I did want to have our biological children so I prepared myself for what I expected to be the inconvenience and discomfort of pregnancy. Then when I went through years of infertility my feelings about pregnancy changed. When I finally did conceive, I was thrilled to be pregnant. I feel very grateful for that experience and especially for my children. Still, I wish that I could feel the wonder of life inside me one more time.

Many parents of multiples do have the opportunity to have another pregnancy and to enjoy the relative ease of carrying just one baby. Some speak of feeling "more normal" this time around, especially if the pregnancy came without heroic efforts. At the same time, however, some subsequent pregnancies are not welcomed, or they are met with mixed emotions.

> After the twins were born, we were advised to use birth control. My reaction to this was that our doctor had forgotten who we are. There was no way that after nine years of trying to conceive and one Clomid pregnancy I needed to use birth control!
>
> I discovered that I was pregnant when the boys were two years old. While it was hard to imagine three in diapers, I was essentially delighted to be pregnant. I now felt like a real woman; I no longer felt defective.
>
> After our third child was born, we did heed medical advice and used contraception. Nonetheless, nature fooled us again and I conceived when our baby was just a year old. This time I was not so happy about the pregnancy and even had thoughts of ending it. That was a very painful time for me; I realized that even though I support abortion for others, infertility had eliminated it as an option for me. I could never, ever end a pregnancy when I know how hard they are to come by.
>
> Now we have four children. There are many times when I feel guilt at the largesse. Having longed for many years to celebrate Mother's Day, I now feel uncomfortable when it rolls around. I know of couples who still struggle for one child and we have ended up with more than we planned for.

Raising Separate Individuals
versus "Packaging"

An ongoing challenge for all parents of multiples involves to what degree they and others respond to their children as separate individuals versus seeing them as a unit. It used to be fashionable to dress twins in the same clothes and often to give them similar or rhyming names. In recent years, parents have deliberately moved away from these practices and worked to do what they can to promote and nurture separate identities.

> I remember always feeling it was essential that they have two birthday cakes, even when they were very young and there were only a few kids coming to their party. I felt that to make one cake was to imply that they were one person. I tried to convey to them and others that they were two people who just happened to have the same birthday.

> We felt that it was very important that our boys not be regarded as one. From an early age we have done what we could to make sure that they have the opportunity to grow up as separate individuals. We sent them to different nursery schools and requested that they be placed in separate classrooms in public school. The fact that they do not look alike has made this easier for us; people often do not know they are twins, and we don't tell them.

All parents know that life is not fair and that neither they nor the world will treat their children equally. Nonetheless, when there are twins or triplets, more questions arise about equality. These questions come from the children as well as the parents.

> I felt very torn when one of the twins was invited to a birthday party and the other was not. I knew that the other mother had not known that the invited son was a twin (they were in separate classes) and that I could easily call up and get my other son an invitation. But I felt that there was an important lesson to be learned in this, and that I should use it to help them begin to understand that life would not be fair. Nonetheless, I still felt very sad for my son who was not invited. It must be hard to be excluded from something that your brother is excited about.

As multiples get older, issues of separateness and equality become much more complex. The issues at hand are no longer whether they should have twin party dresses, but rather what happens when one is a better student than the other, or when one is more socially advanced or skilled than the other. Parents can feel torn, not wanting one child to miss out on an opportunity because it is not available to his twin but also feeling concern for what the event will mean to the other twin's self-esteem.

It was hard when the boys began looking at colleges. Rick is a much better student and really does deserve to get into a better school than Steven. But Steven liked some of the same schools that Rick liked and wanted to apply to them as well. I worried about what would happen. Would any school dare to accept one brother and reject another? And if so, what would the repercussions be in our family? What if a school decided to reject Rick simply because it felt that it could not accept his brother?

Sometimes I worry that Dana holds herself back so that she will not hurt Alexis's feelings. Dana seemed to feel enormous relief when Alexis was elected class secretary. For once she did not have to worry about being better than her sister.

Although parents make an effort to avoid packaging, some find that their children do some packaging on their own. They see that their children are very close, that they prefer to be together, and that they sometimes resist separations. Hence, an added challenge for parents of multiples involves respecting and supporting the closeness of their children's relationship while at the same time doing all that they can to help each child develop as a separate and whole individual.

The Absence of a One-to-One Relationship with a Child

One of the things that parents of twins or triplets miss out on is the opportunity to have a one-to-one relationship with each child. Certainly, most try to carve out individual time with their children; but this involves a deliberate effort, very different from the natural one-to-one relationship that begins with a single birth.

> When they were babies, I remember feeling that each was being held only half as much as she should have been. I don't think that I ever relaxed and enjoyed holding one without feeling that it was time to move on to the other. I ended up feeling like all of us were being shortchanged.

> With three there was never any time to just be with one. I was able to bathe and diaper one at a time, but feeding always felt like a juggling act. And there was never the luxury of just sitting and holding one of them, quietly enjoying being together.

Some parents after infertility regard the absence of a one-to-one relationship with a child as beneficial. Aware that they might have been overly focused on a single, long-awaited child, they see multiples as providing a healthy distraction.

> I am really glad that we have twins, because I am afraid that I would have smothered our baby had we had only one. With the twins, I am so busy that I don't have any time to be overly involved with or overly protective of one. And with twins, we each have a baby to hold!

Feeling Special

Everyone sees multiples as special, and that of course includes their parents. While parents of multiples feel overwhelmed when their children are young, and sometimes resent all the questions and comments about their offspring, hopefully they are not too tired to also enjoy what they do have. They have gone from the agony of childlessness to a bounty of children.

Parents whose first children are multiples can never say that they were eased into parenthood. They will never look back on quiet, easy times with one very portable baby. For them, parenthood was a crash landing. But having yearned for so long to be parents, the commotion of two or more babies can be exhilarating as well as exhausting.

I felt that having twins was very special. I imagined that having one baby would feel very ordinary, uneventful, boring. As hard as some days were, I would not have traded places with anyone.

Karen, Andy, and the Boys

I'm always amused—and a bit relieved—when Alex and Jeremy envy Peter. "Why does he get to go to special gym?" They ask. "How come he gets to go to his new school by cab?" "Why does he get so much attention?" It's harder for me to see the look on his face when his brothers begin a new activity or come upon an opportunity that is unavailable to him because of his limitations.

Peter's limitations have been a focus of Karen's energy and concern from the time that she was thirty-two weeks pregnant. At that point, a routine ultrasound revealed that one of the triplets had a problem, of unclear severity, with the ventricles of his heart. It seemed that the flow of fluid to his brain was being compromised, and that there was the possibility that he would be hydrocephalic. It was also clear from the ultrasound that the other boys were doing fine.

> The news that we got that day changed everything. No one knew for sure what it meant, but we knew that life would not be the same from that time on. It had been wild enough adjusting to the idea that we'd have three at once, but it was a cosmic leap to accept that one of them would be sick. Andy was an intern at the time, so we had access to all sorts of medical consultation, but no one could really tell us much of anything.

The news that Peter was in trouble was especially jarring to Karen because her pregnancy had been going so well. Energetic and fit, she had completed a marathon weeks before conceiving. Even when she was well into her triplet pregnancy, she maintained an active life-style.

> I was very big in front, but I had lots of energy and I felt good. My doctor felt that because I was doing so well, there was no reason to put me on bedrest or to provide any special treatment. The boys weren't even premature.

The boys were delivered at thirty-eight weeks by caesarean section. Jeremy and Alex were strong and healthy; Peter was very sick. Karen and Andy took two babies home and left their third in neonatal intensive care, unclear whether he would ever join his brothers at home.

Those first few weeks were an incredibly difficult time. With two at home and one in the hospital, we were constantly shuttling back and forth between home and the hospital. To make matters worse, Andy was still in training. In those days he was unable to make his own hours. His senior resident was sympathetic to our situation, but he had his own staffing needs. Unfortunately, a lot landed on my shoulders.

Karen and Andy both feel that they were very fortunate to have help at home. Not only were they able to afford baby-sitters and household help, but they also had a lot of family support. Their parents were eager to help out in any way they could.

Things changed for us at eighteen months. Up until that point I had not felt clear that Peter would survive. He'd had some good periods in there, but he was also a very sick little boy. At eighteen months, and the very same week that Alex began having febrile seizures, Peter went into cardiac arrest. That moment will forever be imprinted on my mind.

As horrible as that week was, it served a purpose. From that time on I felt clear that I had three sons and that they would all survive. Finally, we knew who was in our family. I was prepared now to fight for Peter's survival.

Karen recalls that the struggle in those days was not only for Peter's health, but it was also for her own well-being. She realized that as a mother of triplets, one of whom had problems, she would have to figure out how to get some time for herself.

I realized that one of the things that I'd have to give up was private time with Alex and Jeremy. Peter and I were alone together when we went to one of his many specialists, and Andy and I carved out time because we knew that we had to tend to our relationship. But if I was going to have any time at all to myself, I didn't have much opportunity to be alone with either Alex or Jeremy. That's been a loss for me and I know it's been so for them, but there are trade-offs. It's been crucial to me that I find a few minutes every day to run or swim or take a quiet walk.

Karen and Andy have resisted what Karen calls the packaging of triplets. She has felt that it is important not to do this, important to maintain their separateness and individuality. This has happened naturally with Peter, who has had individual needs, but it was initially more difficult with Alex and Jeremy.

It was so tempting to package them as twins. When they were babies, I always needed one adult to tend to Peter and one for the others. If I went out with them I took a helper along, and if we were all home I always had someone on hand to help with Peter. Alex and Jeremy very quickly became a twosome. But fortunately they helped us avoid packaging. Very early on, each emerged with a clear and individual presence.

Another challenge that Karen and Andy have faced, and which they see as a universal experience in parenting multiples, has been dealing with a curious and intrusive outside world. It's easier now that the boys are older, but when they were babies in a triple stroller they were the constant focus of attention. Karen, who is by nature warm and friendly, poignantly describes her efforts to maintain some privacy each time that she ventured out of her home.

I remember doing all that I could to avoid eye contact. I'd keep my head down, eyes focused on the stroller, and I'd march forward. Despite my best efforts to remain anonymous, everyone had something to say. I discovered then that people have no judgment and no boundaries. I had some people ask me if I took fertility drugs, and others asked if my husband made enough money to support all three. Some people would look at Alex and Jeremy and then at Peter and say, "Is there something wrong with anybody?" Yes, there was something wrong with these nosy, intrusive, senseless people. I felt like cursing at some of them, but usually I responded with a cold reserve.

When I am out now, alone, I like to look at parents with their twins and triplets. I watch the attention that they inevitably attract, and I see how they try to avoid it—and deal with it. Sometimes

I go up to them and quietly say, "I understand how difficult it is for you: I have triplets." They usually seem appreciative, pleased to have an ally among the busybodies.

Four years ago, when the boys had just turned six, the un-expected happened; Karen found herself pregnant. Neither she nor Andy knew how to react to this spontaneous pregnancy. Having one sick child had made them very wary: they were frightened that it could happen again. They also felt a strong preference for a girl, and worried about how they would feel if they had a fourth son.

> I had an amnio, and decided that I wouldn't find out the sex of the baby. I feared that I'd be too disappointed if we had another boy and felt that I'd had enough experience with bad news in utero. However, when I phoned for the results of the test, my curiosity got the best of me. As I had feared, the triplets were soon to have a baby brother.
>
> I found that I had a very mixed reaction to learning that I would be the mother of boys. I had wanted a girl for so long, and felt that with triplets I should have had a good shot at it. It felt terribly unfair. On the other hand, infertility had taught me that life is any-thing but fair, and it reminded me how very lucky I was to be able to have four children. That reminder went a long way in helping me through my disappointment. I was surprised to find that I began looking forward to having another son.

As it turned out, Ricky was a full-term, healthy baby who delights his parents and his big brothers. For Karen, it was wonder-ful to have the chance to hold and cuddle and play with one baby without always looking around and tending the other two. For Andy, it was a great relief to have a healthy baby, because Peter's tough times had somehow prepared him for more difficulties. For Alex and Jeremy and Peter, it has been great fun to have a little brother to play with and teach things to and pick on. This has been especially nice for Peter who is glad that, for once, he is not trailing up the rear.

> This isn't the life that I planned for myself when I was in business school preparing for a high-powered career in marketing, nor is

it what I imagined when I thought of replicating the close and tender relationship that I have with my mother. It's a much harder life, but I am glad that I am leading it. I have risen to the occasion, and that is something that I am proud of. When it was clear that Peter would live and would be okay I said to myself, "This is the life that is yours; go for it."

17

Only Children after Infertility

"An only child is a lonely child" was the message that I was raised with. I believed it (and perhaps still do) and would never have set out to have one child. But we were not able to have a child together, and adoption was not easy for us, financially or emotionally. We feel blessed to have successfully adopted one terrific child, but we are unable, for many reasons, to try again. This feels like the only decision that we can make, but it also represents a loss for us.

We had planned to have three, maybe even four children, but it has not worked out that way. We began trying to have a second child when Eric was a little over one year old; he is now six. Since neither of us feels comfortable with adoption, and since nothing seems to be happening biologically, it looks like he will be our only one.

THESE are voices of parents who have only one child; not because it fit their careers or suited their life-style, or because it was economical or expedient. Rather, these are parents who wanted two or more children but were unable to have or adopt more than one. For them, having only one child represents a major loss: someone is missing from their family.

I find it very difficult when people ask us why we have just one. They always phrase it in an accusatory way, suggesting that we are selfish, that we are ignoring the best interests of the child, that we have never adequately considered this serious subject. They should only know what we have been through and the incredible anguish that we feel.

Infertile parents become parents of only one child for a number of reasons. Some adopt one and are then unable to adopt a second, either due to costs or agency policy. Others may be able to adopt another but feel unwilling. They say that they were lucky once but fear that a second adoption would not turn out as well. Some parents through D.I. or surrogacy seem to have similar sentiments. They feel that they tried something that was risky once, and it worked. Given their luck, they believe that they had best not try again.

Many couples have one successful pregnancy and birth, and then find that they are unable to have a second. For some this comes as a surprise, because they had no difficulty conceiving or carrying the first time. For others, those who experienced primary infertility or who suffered some illness or injury to their reproductive systems during delivery or since their child's birth, there is a warning. In either situation, these parents eventually reach a point at which they must turn to adoption or some other alternative route to parenthood or remain one-child families. Many conclude that they are blessed with the child they have and do not pursue a parenting alternative.

How do parents who originally set out to have two, three, four, or more children accept and adjust to the fact that they have one? Can they protect an only child from feeling lonely, especially when they themselves feel lonely? Can they close the ranks of their family so that there is not always the sense that someone is missing? How do they stop waiting for a second child so that they can appreciate some of the special pleasures of having one?

The following are some of the challenges facing parents who have one child but who had wanted more:

1. dealing with their child's wish for a sibling
2. coping with the grief they feel at not having another child
3. coping with the absence of external support
4. closing the boundaries of their family and moving on
5. vulnerability to loss

Dealing with Their Child's Wish
for a Sibling

As the saying goes, when parents tell a child that he is soon to be a big brother it is like a husband saying to his wife, "I love you so much that I'm bringing home another wife." Many a child wonders why his parents would want another child if he is so wonderful. The prospect of a sibling makes some children question whether they are really good enough.

With second child infertility, the issue is not dealing with how the prospect of another child affects the child, but rather with how the absence of a sibling burdens him. For all the difficulties they have around the anticipated and real arrival of another child, most children do want to have siblings. Beginning in nursery school, when they see their friends becoming big brothers and sisters, children begin asking for a new baby.

> It was very hard for us when Allison began to come home from nursery school asking for a baby sister. It seems that she was in a class of first children, and the year that she was three everyone's mother was pregnant. We didn't know what we could and should tell her. She was asking questions, but we felt that there was little of this that she could understand.

Parents sometimes confuse their child's interest in having a sibling with their own longings for another child. Children ask for siblings without knowing what it means to their parents — nor having any idea how the arrival of a brother or sister would change their lives. Their parents, in pain over their inability to bring another child into the family, project their feelings onto the child and feel an additional loss.

Children adjust to all sorts of family situations, the absence of siblings among them. They have friends, they have pets; many have cousins. If their parents can feel some closure on the subject, children can accept the fact that this is one way in which they may differ from their friends. If their parents are able to enjoy some of the advantages of having a one-child family, children also can begin to appreciate these advantages.

I do think that Sara would have liked to have a sister or a brother, but I also feel that she accepts the fact that this will not happen. She gets to see and be with her friends' siblings, and she also gets a chance to see how they tease each other and fight. We try not to spoil her, but the fact is that, as an only child, she does get more than she would if there were others. I hope that she can enjoy this and not feel burdened or guilty over it. All the only children I have known have been really fine people who have done well in life.

Coping with the Grief They Feel at Not Having Another Child

For many parents, the inability to have or adopt a second child is an enormous loss. It leaves them with a family that feels incomplete. Some who had very much wanted a son or a daughter experience the loss in a gender-related way, fantasizing that, if they had been able to have another child, they would have had the son or daughter they dreamed of. Others feel the loss more in numbers, having always pictured themselves with a certain number of children and now feeling like they have come up short.

Nine. Nine was how many children I wanted and expected we would have. I was always a jock and Alex was, too. We were going to have our baseball team. We were going to have a gang. We were going to enjoy a crowded, happy, usually messy household. Instead, we have one lovely little boy, whom we love dearly, but who is not enough.

Parents who planned to have two or more children and discover or decide they can only have one need to close the boundaries of their families and then move on. Just as some infertile couples decide to live child-free rather than remaining childless, couples with one child need, at some point, to accept that this is their family.

I very much wanted a second child and would have been happy to adopt. When it became clear to me that Richard could not accept adoption, I was really upset. We went through a very difficult period, and for a time it felt like we would never resolve things.

Eventually, I realized that I had to give something up. We would not have another child, and I owed it to all of us to begin to believe this. I took more active steps to get on with my career, which had been on hold since Amanda's birth. We began doing things as a family of three that would not have been possible had a new baby come along.

Coping with the Absence of External Support

Remaining a one-child family is a lonely position in our society. The infertile community has little empathy for the couple with one child; many look on with envy and feel that these people should be very grateful to be parents. Families with two or more children say there are real advantages to having just one and often fail to understand why their friends with one child feel so troubled. To make matters worse, people who do not know the couple wants another child may misjudge them. They are perceived as selfish, overly involved in their child, and unaware of the pleasures and rewards of a larger family. Questions are asked and comments are made that only add to the pain of the one-child parents.

> When Seth was younger, we were always getting comments. "When are you going to have another?" People would ask this as if we could pop children out as easily as we could sign up for cable TV or buy a new toaster oven. They had no idea how hard this was for us, how much we wanted to be able to add to our family just like everyone else.
>
> Now that Seth is older, we're not expected to be enlarging our family. His age alone defines us as a one-child family. Let others assume what they will about our motives for having one child, as long as they are not constantly asking us about it.

People do make assumptions, including infertile parents with one child who see other one-child families. Some of the very same people who feel that no one understands their predicament look at others with one child and decide that this is their choice. The fact is that because of delayed parenting, many couples find themselves in the position of being unable to have or adopt a second child. Whether or not they had difficulty the first time around, their age is now a major factor in preventing pregnancy or prohibiting adoption. Because these couples often have exciting, high-powered careers, they may appear from the outside to prefer the simplicity of a one-child family.

> I have a good career as a psychologist with a teaching appointment at one of the medical schools, and an interesting private practice. We have a seven year old, Caroline, who was born "right on schedule," when I turned thirty. I'm sure that everyone looks at us and assumes that Caroline is an only child by design. How wrong they are! We would have loved to have more children, and we spent a good part of the last four years trying to make that happen. When I got pregnant with IVF and then miscarried, we decided that it was time to give up.

Just as childless couples who are going through infertility treatment frequently decide to acknowledge their infertility in order to protect themselves from hurtful comments, some infertile parents of one child also find that they feel less isolated if they are direct in telling people that they had hoped to have more children.

> I've learned how to talk with people so as to find out if they really preferred to have one child or if they, too, would have liked a larger family. If I meet someone with just one child over the age of four, my antennas go up. I don't come right out and ask them if they plan to have more children (because I know what that feels like!), but I do make some comment that lets them know about my situation. I'm always amazed and comforted by how many people then come forth and tell me how hard they are trying for another or what they went through before giving up.

Closing the Boundaries of Their Family and Moving On

Couples who decide to give up on further efforts to have more children grieve the loss of their dream family and then, hopefully, move on. That is not to say that a lingering sadness does not remain and that feelings of loss do not resurface periodically. When friends and family announce pregnancies, when there are family occasions and religious celebrations, and at major milestones such as a child's graduation from high school or her marriage, old feelings regarding the incompleteness of their family are likely to return. What parents of one child can hope for, however, is a sense of closure, a feeling, on a day-to-day basis, of satisfaction with the family that they have.

> Yes, we originally wanted more, but life is very full with Laura. Bill travels a lot, so Laura and I spend a lot of time together. These times as a twosome have caused us to grow very close. I suppose that if we had been able to have other children, things would be more difficult and less relaxed. I wouldn't have the same opportunity for one-to-one time that I have come to treasure.

Vulnerability to Loss

Although they know that no parent, no matter how many children they have, is protected from loss, parents of one child feel that they are somehow more vulnerable to loss. The possibility that something could happen to their child is too horrible to think about, yet it sits there at the back of their minds.

There are neither easy answers nor antidotes to the vulnerability experienced by parents of one child. They struggle with it and try to balance out their need to protect the child with his need to separate and have some independence.

> When Jim was younger, I was surely an overprotective mother. I kept a watchful eye on him as much as I could. Now he is fourteen and active in sports. I worry that he will get hurt, but I also recognize that what he is doing is good for him. I know that if I intervene in his activities, I will only spoil things for him.

Parents of one child do find ways to avoid having a lonely only. For one thing, these parents usually have more time and energy to put into promoting their child's friendships. Some make a point of encouraging their child to always bring a friend along when they are doing something as a family.

Whenever we are going someplace—whether it is to MacDonald's or to Europe—Brent knows that he can bring a friend. He doesn't even have to ask us: at ten we let him make most of the plans. Usually it works out well for all of us. We enjoy his friends; he likes having someone to be with and play with, and his friends are thrilled to get to do things that they would never have a chance to do in their own families.

Parents of one child can take some comfort from the fact that there has been a trend toward smaller families. Although many couples are electing to have three children, it is unusual to find a family with more than three. Many couples are choosing, for some of the reasons mentioned earlier, to have just one child. With these and other changes in the structure of families, children who have no siblings are less likely to feel alone.

There are times, when we see families together at a school picnic or a church fair, that I feel a pang and wish that we had been able to have more children. It's especially hard to see little girls, because I had wanted a daughter. Seth, wonderful as he is, does not fill that need. But most of the time I feel happy. After years of waiting we have a child. After years of longing, we are a family.

Allison, Robert, and Robby: Three Is Family

When Robert and I married, we planned to have three or more children. We're both child-oriented people, and we knew we would enjoy parenting together. We used birth control for about a year and then left nature to take its course. To our surprise and dismay, nothing happened. We were young at the time, and relatively unsophisticated about medical care. Hence, we tried for over three years before going to see a fertility specialist.

I conceived on our third Clomid cycle, and we were jubilant. My pregnancy went well, and I gave birth to a full-term, healthy baby boy. We named him Robert, Jr., and agreed to call him Robby. We expected that our infertility was behind us and that we would go on to have other children—most likely with the help of Clomid—when we wanted them.

Things did not work out for Allison and Robert as they had hoped and planned. Efforts to have a second child, which began when Robby was a year and a half, proved more disappointing and confusing than their original attempts to start a family. They watched Robby get older as one treatment regimen after another failed them.

> Then it happened—or seemed to. I was pregnant! Again we were jubilant, but this time our joy was short-lived. Soon after we got the news of the positive pregnancy test, I developed acute pain. It was an ectopic. I was rushed to the hospital for emergency surgery. The operation saved my life, but it cost me a tube and an ovary. I recovered fully, but the recuperation was slow. It was during that time that I decided that I did not want to try for another pregnancy. I knew that Robert was not willing to adopt, so that meant that our family would be complete with Robby.

It was one thing for Allison and Robert to make the decision to remain a one-child family and another to come to grips with what that meant for them. For one thing, it meant giving up any hopes of having a daughter. That was a real loss for Allison, who had imagined herself as the mother of girls. She described it as a double loss: she had to simultaneously accept the fact that she would have only one child and that she would never have a daughter. Robert, who had wanted sons, felt a different kind of loss.

> I pictured myself with a baseball team. Realistically, I had known that I would never have more than three or four children, but when I pictured myself as a father, I saw myself with a whole team of boys. I have two brothers, and although we fought a lot, I have some very good memories of the times we spent together with our father. When I realized we would only have Robby, I felt a loss for myself and also for him. He would never have the companionship of brothers.

Allison and Robert say that they went through a period of grieving, she for her daughters and he for his boys. It was a tough time, but they found that somewhere along the way, a healing process began.

> We began to talk more about feeling happy about the child that we had and thought less about those that we never had.

We began to realize, also, that there were some advantages to having one child. We both work, and we'd been anxious about how we would juggle our careers and childrearing. We realized that with one child, mixing career and parenthood would be a lot smoother.

Once they had accustomed themselves to the fact that they would remain a one-child family, Allison and Robert began to think about some of the special challenges of one-child parenting. They both felt strongly that they wanted Robby to have a childhood and not to become a little adult. They had seen other only children who seemed unusually comfortable with adults and rather awkward with children. They saw Robby as a "rough and tumble" little boy and didn't want that to happen to him.

We tried to make sure that he always had friends to play with, and that we didn't just drag him along to adult activities. Nonetheless, we see that despite our efforts, he is a kid who feels especially at ease around adults and who does feel somewhat different from other kids. We have no idea, of course, whether he might have been that way even if he had siblings.

Whatever the reason, at ten Robby is a very interesting and original little boy. He plays with the other boys, but he is a kid who really enjoys being alone. He uses his time alone to investigate and develop his interests; finance and meteorology.

We never have to worry about Robby oversleeping. He is up every morning at 5:30 A.M. to listen to the full weather report, the full stock market report, and the news. We never have to tell him how to dress for school, because he has up-to-date information on every cold front and knows whether there is any chance of rain. We had no difficulty finding him a birthday present, because he let us know months in advance that he had his heart set on a subscription to the *Wall Street Journal*.

Besides being interesting, Allison and Robert find that Robby is adaptable. He can be comfortable in most any situation, and he brings a certain maturity to new experiences. On the other hand, there are times when he can be very immature. Allison feels this is a consequence of his always being at the center of things.

We try not to spoil him with toys nor to shower him with too much attention. Nonetheless, he does receive a great deal of affection. I think that in some ways that keeps him a little less mature. But in a world of hurried children, I'm not sure that that is a bad thing.

Allison and Robert express some continued disappointment at not being able to have more children, but they also express acceptance. They derive enormous pleasure from Robby and feel fortunate to have the time to spend with him. Life has not turned out as they had planned, but they do have many satisfactions and much joy.

18

Special-Needs Children

When we found out that Richard was multiply handicapped, friends and relatives asked us if we were going to send him back to the adoption agency. They seemed to think that because he was not perfect, he was less ours.

I have to admit that there are moments when I have the fantasy that his birthmother will come back and relieve me of him. I love him, but he is a very difficult child.

T HESE are voices of parents of special-needs children. They are people who face challenges on a daily basis, challenges that parents of "normal" children never have to think about. They are people who have very different families from those that they pictured when they first set out to become parents.

Infertile couples become the parents of special-needs children in a variety of ways. Some become pregnant, and because of some problem in the pregnancy, such as prematurity, they give birth to children who have special needs. Others may be older by the time they conceive but decide against amniocentesis (either because they are concerned about the risks involved or because they would not have an abortion anyway) and give birth to a child with genetic abnormalities. Finally, there are couples who suffer through infertility, and then, by sad coincidence, they give birth to a child who has—or develops—special needs.

Some infertile parents decide to adopt children with special needs. These couples often feel that infertility has presented them with an opportunity to do something for someone else.

They prefer to offer a home to a child in need rather than join childless couples in pursuit of a healthy newborn. Other infertile parents adopt a child who appears to be normal at birth, but who later develops special needs.

A comprehensive discussion of special-needs parenting is beyond the scope of this book. "Special needs" can mean many different things, each of which has a very different impact on the child and on the family. This chapter identifies some of the feelings and experiences that apply to a number of special-needs parents, including:

1. Why Me? Why Us?
2. adjusting expectations
3. becoming an advocate for your child
4. dealing with your child's feelings about the special need
5. dealing with public reactions

Why Me? Why Us?

Although some couples elect to adopt a child with special needs, most infertile parents do not anticipate it. Many feel that they "did their time" with infertility and expect that once they have a child, things will go smoothly. They are not prepared for the challenges that await them as special-needs parents.

> I worried when I was pregnant but kept telling myself that there was nothing to be concerned about. The pregnancy was going well, and there was every indication that I would deliver a healthy baby. As time went on, I convinced myself that my worrying was simply conditioning from infertility; it had taught me to expect disappointment. Unfortunately, disappointment did come, and it was devastating. I felt sad and cheated. My husband reacted with anger. We both wondered how, after all we had been through, this could happen to us?

> When I was pregnant, I worried about pregnancy loss but somehow assumed that if I made it to a live birth, the baby would be perfect. Richard was born with a heart problem—one that can be managed medically and surgically—and I was stunned. I think that my experience with infertility made it more difficult for me

to accept Richard's problems because they seemed all the more unfair.

Couples who go to great efforts to become parents and then find themselves with a special-needs child often feel guilt as well as sadness and anger. They wonder if God, or some higher power, was telling them that they were not meant to be parents, and that they are being punished for ignoring this message. Some who had misgivings about an infertility treatment, especially one of the new high-tech options, may feel that this is what happens to you when you go against the natural order of things.

> Guilt is one of the hardest parts of this. I worry that I should not have taken all of those drugs. I don't really believe (although I do sometimes wonder about it) that the drugs could have caused my son's problems, but I do feel that perhaps I should not have taken them.

> When I begin to feel really bad about myself, I remind myself of all the teenage mothers that I see hanging around shopping malls, smoking cigarettes, and grumbling at their children. I look at them and say to myself, "How could they have been meant to be mothers, and I was not?" That helps me to feel less guilty, but then I end up feeling angry. I guess that there is no justice in any of this.

Other feelings arise when a couple adopts a child and then learns that he has special needs. Here, anger and confusion are more common reactions than guilt. Often, a couple has gone to tremendous effort and expense to adopt a "healthy" baby, and expected that adoption would offer some guarantees that are not available with biological parenting. They may know intellectually that anything can happen, but they assume their bad luck is behind them.

> We turned to adoption because we figured it would work. Pregnancy wasn't working, and adoption had worked for lots of people we knew. We figured that there would be problems associated with raising an adopted child but that our child would be healthy. We cried a lot when we found out, once again, that life is never fair.

When we applied to adopt and were asked what sorts of problems we were prepared to handle, I thought carefully and said, "anything but retardation." As it's turned out, Robin, our youngest, is retarded. I know that there are no more guarantees with adoption than there are with pregnancy, but I do feel angry. I feel that the agency knew more than they told us.

Adjusting Expectations

Parents have dreams for their children. They have fantasies about what they will do with a child and ideas about what the child will be able to do on her own. Infertility causes people to alter their dreams and to accept the fact that they probably will not have the family they had hoped for.

The arrival of a special-needs child forces parents to do much more than modify their dreams: they are forced to rework them. One of the first things they realize as special-needs parents is that they have to change their expectations. A mother who had imagined that she would run a marathon with her child may have a daughter who will never walk. A father who had looked forward to coaching competitive soccer may have a deaf child who has to play in a special league. Parents of special-needs children realize early on that the things that matter to them now are not the things they thought about when they looked forward to becoming parents.

> I worry a lot about whether he will have friends. I see the groups of retarded people, and hope that he will not always have to be with them. I want him to have some normal friends. We had a lot of dreams for him before he was born, but now I just want him to function as well as he can.

Parents of special-needs children report that they experience some rewards in lowering their expectations. They report taking great delight in everything their children are able to do. Nothing is assumed; everything is an accomplishment.

> You learn to focus on what they *can* do and not to think about what they cannot do. That has been really wonderful for me. I get very

excited each time he does something new. Even seemingly small things are cause for celebration.

Special-needs parents point out that it is easier to be comfortable with their new expectations when they are at home with their child or when they are together with other special-needs families. What is difficult is when they are around other children and their parents; then the differences stand out. At those times it becomes more difficult to celebrate what their children are doing and easier to sink back into sadness for all that is lost.

> I find that I have real highs and real lows. When I am alone with him, I am happy and proud of all that he is learning to do. But when we are with other families, it can be very difficult. It's at those times that I can't help but think of how different he is, and I can't help but feel that we're all missing out on some good things.

Becoming an Advocate for Your Child

Special-needs children need special help. Although state and charitable organizations do offer an array of services, a large part of special-needs parenting involves advocacy. Parents need to identify the services their children need and then work to be sure they get them.

> I have learned that I have to fight for my children, especially in the schools. I've found that our school system will always take the easiest way out, and in my son's case that meant parking him in a class for disabled children. It was really important to us that that not happen. It took a lot of fighting but he is now in a regular class, working at grade level, with an aide to help with his physical needs.

Not all parents take to advocacy easily. For one thing, it is not something that they expected to have to do when they decided to become parents. Some find it stressful dealing with bureaucracy, and many become very confused when they are trying to maneuver their way through the system. Because they care so much about their children, people learn to do things that they would otherwise avoid.

I never thought of myself as an activist. When I was in college, I was in the library while others were out protesting. But that was something that I had a choice about. Now, with a daughter who has a number of special needs, I have no choice. If I'm not down at the school seeking services for her, no one else will.

Couples going through infertility learn a lot about advocacy. They realize they need to stay on top of their medical situation and to inform themselves about their particular problem and the available treatments. They learn how to advocate for themselves with doctors, with insurance agencies, and with adoption agencies. However, most assume that this advocacy role will end when they become parents.

After infertility, I really didn't think this could happen to us. I feel like we've gone from one minority group to another without a breather. I am grateful for all the services that are offered to us, but I wish that I did not have to be sorting them out, scheduling appointments, participating in new programs and projects. What I've wanted all along is to be a "normal" parent, busy with the things that normal parents do.

Dealing with Your Child's Feelings about the Special Need

From a very early age, children are keenly aware of how they are like and different from other children. Most want to avoid differences and fear that they will not be accepted because of them. Often, their fears are well-founded, as other children can be remarkably harsh and cruel.

Special-needs parents must not only deal with their own disappointment at having a child that is different, but they must also deal with their child's feelings about these differences. Depending on the nature of the special need or disability, this task will vary. A child with a learning disability certainly has a different set of obstacles than one who is blind. A child who is retarded will inevitably experience his handicap differently from one who cannot walk. However, what all special-needs parents share is the challenge of helping their child understand, accept, and manage with a disability or handicap.

> I had known that Eric felt uncomfortable about going to a special school, but I had no idea of the degree of that embarrassment until an incident occurred at the zoo. We were there on a beautiful spring day, and a reporter and photographer were doing a feature for the city paper. They took a photo of Eric and his two younger sisters and then asked each of them what school they went to. It was so hard to watch Eric become visibly uncomfortable and then refuse to say the name of his school.

> It was very important to me that Debby be "mainstreamed." I felt that she would feel less different being the only child in a wheelchair in a regular class than she would being placed in a special class with all the other children with disabilities. I think that the decision we made was a good one. She seems to feel that she is different from the other kids in one way—one very important way— but like them in so many others.

For some couples, the hardest part of special-needs parenting is anticipating their child's reaction to the news that she has a special need. Recognizing the impact of the disability, parents want to protect their child. Some report worrying about how and when they will explain the problem to their child. Most recall feeling great relief once they had spoken with their child.

> One of the hardest things about learning that Adam has cystic fibrosis was figuring out how we would explain it to him. He knew that something was different because he took an enzyme with meals, and because we made frequent visits to the hospital. However, until it had a name for him—and some explanation—we worried terribly. When and how should we tell him? How would he understand the news? Were there ways that we could make it easier for him to bear?

Dealing with Public Reactions

People who have not had personal experience with handicaps may not understand them. They probably don't have a clear idea how a handicap limits a person's life (as well as how it does not); nor do they have a sense about how it affects family members.

People lack understanding of handicaps, but they do not lack curiosity. Many have no problem going up to strangers, asking questions and making comments. Young children are particularly vocal in this regard; they seldom hesitate to express their curiosity about people who look and seem different. At times their comments can be cruel, but most often they are simply curious.

Others shy away from people with handicaps. Perhaps embarrassed by their curiosity or fearful that they will say the wrong thing, they avoid the person with the handicap. Their behavior can be more troubling to a handicapped person or his family than that of someone who is outwardly curious and intrusive. Avoidance behavior can be isolating.

> I have had a range of experiences when I go out with Alex. There are the little children who come right up to us and ask us about his wheelchair. "Why is he in it?" "Can he walk?" "Will his legs get better?" Then there are their parents who look mortified and try to run the other way. I can take either of those reactions but I have a hard time with the sympathy-givers. Neither Adam nor I want anyone's pity, and some of the sympathetic looks and comments that I get really put me off.

There are many children whose special need is invisible. They and their families do not have to deal with an assortment of reactions each time that they go out in public, but they have to adjust to people's reactions in other ways. Parents of children who are hyperactive, for example, have to deal with the fact that people often see their children as rambunctious or misbehaved when the children are acting in a way that is, for the most part, beyond their control.

> Evin was six when he was diagnosed as having Attention Deficit Disorder and was started on medications that have helped him immensely. Before we understood his problem and had a way of treating it, it was often difficult to be with him. When we were around other people, I had the sense that they found his constant activity objectionable. Some would make comments indicating that they felt I should do a better job disciplining him.

Couples who become the parents of special-needs children, whether it be by birth or adoption, value a positive outlook. Many remember feeling angry or disbelieving when they learned their child had a special need, but report they rapidly moved on to the challenges of parenting.

> We left no time for feeling depressed, plunging instead into physical and occupational therapies, fitting him with hearing aids and other communication systems, and learning sign language. He intently watched us as our hands flew, and watched our mouths as they moved.

Some parents of special-needs children say that, although they would not have chosen to have a child with problems, they have discovered that there are unexpected satisfactions that come from special-needs parenting. They speak of simpler pleasures, of seeing a child do something that no one thought was possible, of witnessing the power of determination and love.

> Although we hadn't planned to become the parents of a child with disabilities, we found in it numerous challenges, and an incredible love for our son. His determination and his affection encouraged us to push ahead, and we decided to adopt another special-needs child. Occasionally we meet people who can't believe we'd knowingly adopt a handicapped child, let alone keep a child we didn't know had handicaps to begin with. They ask us why we do it. Sometimes we ask ourselves. Our answer is that it has brought love and joy to our lives.

Judi and Peter: Different Dreams

> I have always loved music and wanted to share that love with my children. I also love to hike and had looked forward to backpacking with my child. Peter and I had hoped to move closer to the mountains that are not far from our home. Two of our four children have hearing losses. Our son is a quadraplegic, and we are tied to our school system because of the array of special services that our children need; services we have fought long and hard for. We have had to give up many of our dreams, but we have a wonderful family. For us, this has overall been a positive experience.

Judi and Peter were married twelve years ago. At that time, Judi was pregnant and miscarried. It was her third miscarriage, and although she very much wanted a baby, she decided not to let the miscarriage spoil her wedding. She knew, from her earlier pregnancy losses that there was nothing she could do, and so she resolved to have a good time. That approach — that you make the best of a situation once you are in it — is one that Judi applies to much, if not all, of her life.

Judi and Peter have, indeed, made the best of some tough situations. Following their marriage, Judi had two more pregnancies that ended in miscarriage. Judi initially sought medical treatment after her third and fourth pregnancy losses, but it was not until she had lost her fifth pregnancy that she and Peter underwent a new and promising treatment. This new approach to multiple miscarriage is based on the premise that the woman is rejecting the fetus as a foreign body, and attempts to reverse this pattern by inoculating the woman with her husband's white blood cells.

Although Judi and Peter had some hope that the treatment would work, they had applied to adopt a baby from India and wanted to go ahead with their plans. Their son Dana, who is now seven, joined their family when he was eight weeks old. They were delighted to be parents, but Judi recalls having concerns almost from the start that her son was not progressing in his physical development.

> I didn't want it to be true, but I was worried that Dana had a hearing loss, so worried that I traveled from our home in Oregon to Boston, where we consulted with a specialist. He was a kind and sensitive man, but his assessment confirmed my fears: Dana not only had a hearing loss, but due to his premature birth he also has cerebral palsy. The doctor told us that he would be quadraplegic and would most likely be mentally retarded. We cried a lot that night.

Fortunately, one important piece of the doctor's dire prognosis was incorrect: Dana is not retarded. He is a bright and alert seven year old who is engaging and eager to learn. As his mother describes him, "he's a terrific kid who just can't use his arms and legs." Judi is proud of him and of the fact that he is in a regular public-school classroom. She is proud of his determination and his enthusiasm.

> We had never anticipated being a special-needs family. When we adopted, the agency tried to prepare us by telling us that we could end up with a child with a disability. We somehow assumed that it could happen to someone else, but not to us. When it happened to us, we not only adjusted to it but discovered that a special-needs child can also be a very special person. When it came time to expand our family, we decided to apply for another child with a disability. Our son, Chandan, who is now about twelve, was placed with us when he was about seven.

It has not been easy with Chandan. Judi says that she becomes physically exhausted dealing with Dana but that is easier for her than the mental exhaustion that she feels with her older son. Chandan lived in a prison for several years before joining Judi and Peter's family. He has many emotional scars from his years of suffering as well as a severe hearing deficit. In addition to his hearing loss, Chandan has a communication disorder (aphasia) and severe learning disabilities. Consequently, he functions as though he is mentally retarded. Judi openly acknowledges that it has been difficult with Chandan, though she says they have not considered disruption.

Two years ago Judi traveled to India to help escort some other children home to America. While she was there, she met a nine-year-old girl whom she and Peter decided to adopt.

> I fully expected that Rehema would have some sort of disability. She did come with TB but when that was treated, we found for the first time that we were the parents of a healthy child. At that point I realized how full our family was and remembered that it was still possible that I could become pregnant. Having struggled for so many years to have a family, Peter and I made the amazing decision that he would have a vasectomy.

Shortly before Peter was to undergo his vasectomy, his surgeon ran over Peter and Judi's cat and did not stop to tell them. They were so shaken by the incident that they decided to cancel the surgery. Shortly thereafter, they learned that Judi was pregnant.

The pregnancy was a difficult experience for Judi in a number of ways. For one thing, it was very hard to be pregnant and to parent a severely handicapped child. For another, Judi had a lot of bleeding in the beginning. Expecting to miscarry, she did not feel that she could bond with the fetus. Finally, Judi did not feel that she had the option of amniocentesis. How could they consider aborting a fetus when they had two children with severe handicaps? They felt that a decision to abort would be a statement to their handicapped children that they could not accept children who were not perfect. So Judi went ahead with the pregnancy, worried that there would be a problem with the baby.

When Judi was five-months pregnant, she began to have signs of premature labor. Her doctor instructed her to spend the remainder of the pregnancy on bedrest, not an easy prescription for any woman and a particularly difficult one for a mother of two special-needs boys and an active, growing daughter, to say nothing of her full-time job! Judi describes this time as especially stressful emotionally; she worried that the baby would not be well, and she worried that she might not feel as intensely toward her birthchild as she did her other three children. She recalls lying in bed and feeling very frightened.

Thirteen months ago, Judi delivered a healthy baby boy, Jacob. She says that it has been quite an adjustment; she is accustomed to disabilities and she is also accustomed to brown-skinned children. It has been a new and different experience to have a healthy, white baby.

Life is hectic these days for Judi and Peter. They both work full-time and their four children require a lot of attention and care. Good child care is hard to come by, especially with two special-needs children, and access to special services in the schools is never easy. Judi and Peter have found that their goals for themselves and their children have changed.

> This isn't the family we imagined we'd have, but it is a wonderful family. I suppose that people look at us and feel sorry for us, having a child in a wheelchair and having obviously adopted. But we feel fortunate. Each of our children entered our family in a very special way. Each of our children enriches our lives. We have learned that we can be flexible, that we can adjust, and that we can have lots of fun in the process.

Resources and Readings

Resources

ORGANIZATIONS, SUPPORT GROUPS, AND COUNSELING SERVICES

Any list of services to infertile couples must begin with RESOLVE, Inc., the national support group that provides a range of services to infertile couples. RESOLVE offers information in the form of telephone counseling and referral, and it publishes fact sheets and pamphlets on a wide range of topics of interest and concern to infertile couples. RESOLVE offers support groups for individuals and couples in all stages of infertility, adoption, donor insemination, and parenting after infertility. RESOLVE offers medical information and referral to reproductive endocrinologists and related specialists. RESOLVE advocates for infertile people and helps them to advocate for themselves. Its local chapters have played a major role in obtaining and maintaining better insurance coverage for infertility treatment. RESOLVE may be contacted at the following address:

> 5 Water St.
> Arlington, Massachusetts 02174
> (617) 643-2424

ADOPTION

Adoptive Families of America (formerly **OURS, Inc.**)
3317 Highway 100 North, Suite 203
Minneapolis, Minnesota 55422
(umbrella organization for local adoption support groups—offers publications and information)

Adoptive Parents for Open Records
9 Marjorie Drive
Hackettstown, New Jersey 07840

Families Adopting Children Everywhere (FACE)
P.O. Box 102
Bel Air, Maryland 21014
(an adoptive parents support organization)

Friends of Adoption
Box 7270
Buxton Ave.
Middletown Springs, Vermont 05757
(assists couples interested in private adoption)

International Soundex Reunion Registry
P.O. Box 2312
Carson City, Nevada 89702
(for those involved in adoption or D.I. who are searching for offspring or for birthparents)

Latin American Adoptive Families
40 Upland Road
Duxbury, Massachusetts 02332
(support and social group for families who have adopted from Latin America)

North American Council on Adoptable Children
P.O. Box 14808
Minneapolis, Minnesota 55414

Open Door Society
600 Washington St.
Boston, Massachusetts 02111
(support and information organization for adoptive families)

Post Adoption Center for Education and Research (PACER)
477 Fifteenth St., Room 200
Oakland, California 94612

Parenting Resources
250 Camino Real, Suite 111
Tustin, California 92680
(education and counseling services for adoptive and birth
families)

Stars of David
Temple Shalom Emeth
14–16 Lexington St.
Burlington, Massachusetts 01803
(national support group for Jewish adoptive families)

Sibling Group Adoption

Sibling Group Group
Gail Scott
51 Homeward Lane
Walpole, Massachusetts 02081
(support group for families who adopted sibling groups)

Donor Insemination

American Society for Law and Medicine
765 Commonwealth Ave.
Boston, Massachusetts 02215

Carol Frost Vercollone
29 Cedar Avenue
Stoneham, Massachusetts 12180
(counseling for families involved with D.I.)

Donors Offspring
P.O. Box 33
Sarcoxie, Missouri 64862

New Reproductive Alternatives Society
641 Cadogan St.
Nanaimo, B.C., Canada V9S 1T6
(support and advocacy group for families involved with D.I.)

SURROGACY

Organization for Parents through Surrogacy
P.O. Box 2268
Redondo Beach, California 90278

SPECIAL NEEDS

Depending on the nature of the special need, there are a range of organizations and support services available to families.

Readings

Please note that the books and articles listed here are but a small sampling of the many useful publications on these subjects.

GENERAL ADOPTION

Adopted Child Newsletter
Lois Melina, Editor and Publisher
P.O. Box 9362
Moscow, Idaho 83843

Ours Magazine
3307 Highway 100 North, Suite 203
Minneapolis, Minnesota 55422

Suzanne Arms. (1984). *To Love and Let Go.* (New York: Knopf).

Maria Berger and Jill Hodges. (1982). Some Thoughts on the Question of When to Tell the Child That He Is Adopted. *Journal of Child Psychotherapy* 8, 67–87.

David Brodzinsky, L.M. Singer, and A.M. Braff. (1984). Children's Understanding of Adoption. *Child Development,* 55, 869–78.

Claudia Jewett. (1982). *Helping Children Cope with Separation and Loss.* (Boston: Harvard Common Press).

H. David Kirk. (1984). *Shared Fate: A Theory and Method of Adoptive Relationships.* (Ben-Simon Publications P.O. Box 318 Brentwood Bay, B.C. Canada V0S 1A0).

H. David Kirk. (1985). *Adoptive Kinship: A Modern Institution in Need of Reform.* (Ben-Simon Publications P.O. Box 318 Brentwood Bay, B.C. Canada V0S 1A0).

Katherine Kowal and Karen Shilling. (1985, July). Adoption through the Eyes of Adult Adoptees. *American Journal of Orthopsychiatry,* 55(3), 354–62.

Betty Jean Lifton. (1979). *Lost and Found.* (New York: Harper & Row).

Katrina Maxtone-Graham. (1983). *An Adopted Woman.* (New York: Remi Books).

Lois Melina. (1986). *Raising Adopted Children: A Manual for Adoptive Parents.* (New York: Harper & Row).

Lois Melina. (1989). *Making Sense of Adoption: A Parent's Guide.* (New York: Harper & Row).

Sandra Kay Musser. (1979). *I Would Have Searched Forever.* (Plainfield, N.J.: Haven Books of Logos International).

Jacqueline Plumez. (1987). *Successful Adoption.* (New York: Crown).

Lois Raynor. (1980). *The Adopted Child Comes of Age.* (Winchester, Mass.: Allen and Unwin).

Marshall D. Schechter. (1960, July). Observations on Adopted Children. *Archives of General Psychiatry,* 3, 45–56.

Arthur D. Sorosky, Annette Baran, and Reuban Pannor. (1984). *The Adoption Triangle: Sealed or Open Records: How They Affect Adoptees, Birth Parents and Adoptive Parents.* (Garden City, N.Y.: Anchor Press/Doubleday).

ADOPTION BOOKS FOR CHILDREN

Susan and Gordon Adopt a Baby. (1986). Based on the Sesame Street television scripts written by Judy Freudbery and Tony Geiss. (New York: Random House/Children's Television Workshop).

Ann Angel. (1988). *Real For Sure Sister.* (Indianapolis: Perspectives Press).

Anne Braff Brodzinsky. (1986). *The Mulberry Bird.* (Indianapolis: Perspectives Press).

Julia First. (1982). *I, Rebekah, Take You, The Lawrences.* (New York: Franklin Watts).

Linda Walvoord Girard. (1986). *Adoption Is for Always.* (Niles, Ill.: Albert Whitman).

Jill Krementz. (1982). *How It Feels to Be Adopted.* (New York: Knopf).

Betty Jean Lifton. (1986). *I'm Still Me.* (New York: Bantam Books).

Carole Livingston. (1978). *Why Was I Adopted?* (Secaucus, N.J.: Lyle Stuart).

Barbara Parrish-Benson. (1973). *Families Grow in Different Ways.* (Waterloo, Ont.: Before We Are Six).

Fred Powledge. (1982). *So You're Adopted.* (New York: Charles Scribner's Sons).

Maxine Rosenberg. (1984). *Being Adopted.* (New York: Lothrop Lee and Shepard Books).

Patricia Schaffer. (1988) *How Babies and Families are Made (There Is More Than One Way!).* (Berkeley, Calif.: Tabor Sarah Books).

Harriet L. Sobol. (1984). *We Don't Look Like Our Mom and Dad.* (New York: Coward-McCann).

TRANSRACIAL and INTERNATIONAL ADOPTION

Owen Gil and Barbara Jackson. (1983). *Adoption and Race: Black, Asian, and Mixed Race Children in White Families.* (New York: St. Martin's Press/London: Batsford Academic and Educational Ltd.).

Frances Koh. (1981). *Oriental Children in American Homes: How Do They Adjust?* (Minneapolis, Minn.: East-West Press).

Ruth McRoy and Louis Zurcher, Jr. (1983). *Transracial and Inracial Adoptees: The Adolescent Years.* (Springfield, Ill.: Charles Thomas).

Rita Simon and Howard Alstein. (1977). *Transracial Adoption.* (New York: John Wiley and Son).

Hei Sook Park Wilkinson. (1985). *Birth Is More Than Once: The Inner World of Adopted Korean Children.* (Bloomfield Hills, Mich.: Sunrise Ventures).

INTERNATIONAL AND TRANSRACIAL
ADOPTION BOOKS FOR CHILDREN

Catherine Bunin and Sherry Bunin. (1976). *Is That Your Sister?* (New York: Pantheon Books).

Iris Fisher. (1988). *Katie-Bo: An Adoption Story.* (New York: Adama Books).

Jane Claypool Miner. (1982). *Miracle of Time: Adopting a Sister.* (Mankato, Minn.: Crestwood House).

Harriet L. Sobol. (1984). *We Don't Look Like Our Mom and Dad.* (New York: Coward–McCann).

SPECIAL NEEDS

Joan McNamara and Bernard McNamara. (1977). *The Special Child Handbook*. (New York: Hawthorn Books).

DONOR INSEMINATION

Rona Achilles. (1986). *The Social Meaning of Biological Ties: A Study of Participants in Artificial Insemination by Donor.* Dept. of Ed., University of Toronto.

Annette Baran and Reuben Pannor. (1989). *Lethal Secrets: The Shocking Consequences and Unsolved Problems of Artificial Insemination.* (New York: Warner Books).

Elizabeth Noble. (1987). *Having Your Baby by Donor Insemination: A Complete Resource Guide.* (Boston: Houghton Mifflin).

William Schlaff and Carol Frost Vercollone. *Understanding Artificial Insemination: A Guide for Patients.*
(a pamphlet published by ZETEK, Inc. 794 Ventura St. Aurora, Colo. 80011 or RESOLVE 5 Water St. Arlington, Mass. 02174)

R. Snowden and G.D. Mitchell. (1981). *The Artificial Family.* (London: Unwin Paperbacks).

DONOR INSEMINATION BOOKS FOR CHILDREN

Julia Paul, ed. (1988). *How I Began: The Story of Donor Insemination.* (Fertility Society of Australia, Care Reproductive Biology Unit, The Royal Women's Hospital, 132 Grattan St. Carlton, Victoria, 3053, Australia).

Patricia Schaffer. (1988). *How Babies and Families Are Made (There Is More Than One Way!).* (Berkeley, Calif.: Tabor Sarah Books).

SURROGACY

Lori Andrews. (1985). *New Conceptions.* (New York: Ballantine Books).

Lori Andrews. (1989). *Between Strangers.* (New York: Harper & Row).

Diana Frank and Marta Vogel. (1988). *The Baby Makers.* (New York: Carroll and Graf Publishers).

Amy Zuckerman Overvold. (1988). *Surrogate Parenting.* (New York: Pharos Books).

NEW REPRODUCTIVE TECHNOLOGIES

Lori Andrews. (1985). *New Conceptions.* (New York: Ballantine Books).

Lesley Brown and John Brown with Sue Freeman. (1979). *Our Miracle Called Louise: A Parent's Story.* (New York and London: Paddington Press).

Judith Lasker and Susan Borg. (1987). *In Search of Parenthood.* (Boston: Beacon Press).

NEW REPRODUCTIVE TECHNOLOGIES
BOOKS FOR CHILDREN

Patricia Schaffer. (1988). *How Babies and Families are Made (There Is More Than One Way!).* (Berkeley, Calif.: Tabor Sarah Books).

Gerald S. Snyder. (1982). *Test-Tube Life.* (Julian Messner Prentice Hall Bldg. Route 9W Englewood Cliffs, N.J. 07632).

About the Author

Ellen Sarasohn Glazer is a clinical social worker specializing in the areas of infertility, pregnancy loss, adoption, and parenting after infertility. She is on the staff of the psychiatry department of Mt. Auburn Hospital, Cambridge, Mass., and is co-author (with Susan Lewis Cooper) of *Without Child: Experiencing and Resolving Infertility.* She is a former member of the national board of directors of RESOLVE, Inc.